How to Better Hate Your Job

hating what we do is
what we love to do the most

by
Egbert Sukop

Unkraut Publishing

How To Better Hate Your Job. Copyright © 2008 by Egbert Sukop. All rights reserved. Printed in the USA. No part of this book may be used or reproduced in any manner whatsoever without written permission except in the case of brief quotations embodied in critical articles and reviews.

The author and the publisher assume no responsibility for any injuries suffered or damages or losses incurred during or as a result of following this information. All information should be carefully studied and clearly understood before taking any action based on the information or advice in this book. You assume full responsibility for the consequences of your own actions. If you can't agree to these terms, do not turn the page.

Editing by Cheryl Ambrose

Cover Design inspired by Renata Chanrai
Cover Image based on 'Hell' by Hieronymus Bosch

Unkraut Publishing
P.O. Box 14331
Scottsdale, AZ 85267-4331
U.S.A.

For further information visit moneybymistake.com

Library of Congress Control Number: 2008909821
ISBN: 978-0-578-00314-6

First Edition

Dedicated to my ex-wives and ex-girlfriends. On second thought, slightly more to the ex-girlfriends.
I still love them all.

"True," said Candide, "but still there must certainly be a pleasure in criticizing everything, and in perceiving faults where others think they see beauties."

"That is," replied Martin, "there is a pleasure in having no pleasure."

Francois Marie Arouet "Voltaire" in Candide

Contents

Introduction			
Chapter I	Employed and Unhappy	....	7
Chapter II	Something for Nothing	....	17
Chapter III	Before and After	....	27
Chapter IV	Poverty and Prosperity	....	35
Chapter V	Fairness and Freedom	....	49
Chapter VI	Strength and Weakness	....	59
Chapter VII	Individual and Independent	....	67
Chapter VIII	Slave and Master	....	77
Chapter IX	Sex and Substance	....	87
Chapter X	Money and Problems	....	95
Chapter XI	Pain and Passion	....	107
Chapter XII	Losing and Confidence	....	127
Chapter XIII	Reward and Punishment	....	135
Chapter XIV	Excellence and Performance	....	147
Chapter XV	Regrets and Motivation	....	157
Chapter XVI	Money and Meaning	....	167
Chapter XVII	Common Nonsense	....	177
Chapter XVIII	Love and Hate	....	187
Chapter XIX	To Do or Not To Do	....	197
Chapter XX	Getting and Giving	....	209
Appendix			

Introduction

"Hate has a lot in common with love, chiefly with that self-transcending aspect of love, the fixation on others, the dependence on them and in fact the delegation of a piece of one's own identity to them. The hater longs for the object of his hatred."

Vaclav Havel

'Today I am worse than I will be tomorrow.' The unwritten tenet of self-improvement. We don't like our reality too much. We want the world to be a better place. We want our children to be better than we are--within reason, naturally. We want a better job or an early retirement, something better than what we have to deal with every day. And we want to better ourselves. Nothing wrong with that, except our stern determination to improve the quality of our future butchers today's happiness. Self-improvement guarantees a depressing status quo.

Today you will never be as good as you could be tomorrow. Tomorrow--jocular advertisements of *Free Beer Tomorrow* should have taught you this lesson long ago--will never please you. You only have today, and if you are addicted to improving yourself, today--and *today* means YOU--will never be good enough. Self-improvement is overrated. The job to build a better you is frustrating. You, trying to improve your current job or trying to find a better one, will experience continued frustration also. You can be happy with a job you hate, but you can't be happy with a job you're trying to improve. Say what? Yeah I know, we'll have to address this paradox at some point I'm afraid, but not now.

I have bad news for you: world peace is not in the cards during your lifetime. Sorry! We are living in a solution driven society. We believe problems we are facing today have a solution and we're adamant about finding the damned thing whatever it takes. That's nice, but then we realize many solutions become new problems. Hydra's heads--Hercules cut one off and two more grew back in its place--may have first been described in Greek mythology, but each of us has experienced the same phenomenon in the 21st century. I don't intend to discourage your quest to solve your problems. On the contrary. But the expectation that the solution to your most urgent problem will make you feel better and will put you in a tremendously improved position in life is--with all due disrespect—childish.

Solution or no solution, we learn to live in our messes and with ongoing tension, or life will pass us by with a bunch of drunk, happy hours but only a few happy days. Your chance to be happy is today, not when there is peace in the Middle East, the war on terror is won, or when your daughter comes home with better grades in math. Status quo ecstasy. Thrill of the mess. Joy of chaos. A rather bitter-sweet outlook? I agree, but I'm afraid there won't be any other. Life and order have little in common.

Are you happy? Let me spell that out for you: are you making yourself happy? If you are not, I am not attempting to change your miserable attitude. $20 million more in your bank account won't do the trick--despite people's idiotic hopes and expectations--and neither can I perform magic to exalt your spirit. Maybe you will have a slight chance to enjoy your misery a little better. Do you hate what you do? Perfect. This book is for you. No, I won't talk you into wearing rose-colored glasses helping you to hate your job less. I'll spare you the snake oil treatment. I am trying to help you hate your job *better*. Seriously. Generations of employees--your parents, overpaid and under-worked schoolteachers, underpaid and over-worked mismanagers--have pulled the wool over your eyes. Sad result was, you began craving better jobs and you have had one after another.

Most likely you never really wanted a job but you believed you had to have one. Perhaps you left the job scene behind and you became finally and proudly self-employed. Same thing: if it didn't work out financially you began hating it, and yourself, for leaving job, benefits, and seniority behind. If your entrepreneurial adventure did indeed work out well financially, you may hate it because you are now the slave of your own business. In any case, you hate what you do--or parts of it--for good reasons. The environment you're working in is despicable, your co-workers are professional backstabbers, or your employees steal the last three hairs off your head. It doesn't matter. The world of work is no paradise and if you try hard enough you'll dig up something you can hate.

With my gentle help you will be able to increase the sophistication of your hatred. I am confident you will surpass the lukewarm water cooler hatred of your colleagues. Go beyond the irksome gossiping with your sorry peers. Admit it, conversations about your job are just as repugnant as the job itself. It costs you precious minutes of your life and you will never get them back. Neither will you ever get compensated for the time you have wasted listening to your own and other people's prattle.

You will hate your job passionately. You may come to like the way you hate. You won't be a victim of the job monster much longer. You will be able to live, apply, and exploit your finest side; your individuality. Jobs are not created to expand one's freedom. *How To Better Hate Your Job* is. Freedom to live as you please is not an important subject of the brood of self-improvers. The self-help industry has tried desperately to change you to make you fit into a world that demands a better you.

True individuals never fit. Don't change! Forget self-improvement rubbish. It doesn't work and you have every reason to be happy for it. You're fine as you are today, not perfect but perfectly fine. You may evolve in the future or you may not. I don't care, but your happiness should not depend on your ability to adapt to an insane environment. Jobs suppress individuality and so does self-employment if you don't watch out. The world needs your individual footprint. Human beings are fiercely unique, but we try our entire lives to become the most boring professionals, employees, entrepreneurs. Still, we will never be good enough. No wonder our lives suck and we count the days to retirement.

This book will offer you a couple of choices. You may rediscover options you have known and buried years ago. Freedom of choice is usually accompanied by confusion. Don't let confusion intimidate you. Death, taxes, and slavery come with certainties. Being a slave of your own convictions is not an exception. Freedom is neither clear nor certain: it's marred and messy, clouded in confusion. Welcome confusion and then make up your mind quickly. The future holds no freedom for you: your freedom always begins this minute.

What lies underneath? A secret of course. Are you worthy? Thanksgiving Day, I happened to be listening to a radio show when a lady called in, telling a story about her father. Year after year, her alcoholic dad had managed to ruin Thanksgiving dinners with loud offensive attacks on family members. After joining AA meetings, the now sober father continued being a pest. Irritating and abrasive, he brought randomly chosen loved ones to tears of pain, every year. Since he has passed on, the memories of his cruel and tactless behavior have become the most cherished part of annual Thanksgiving get-togethers. Duh.

In case you haven't noticed, all of our families are dysfunctional, and all of us are weird in other people's perspective. According to the *Diagnostic and Statistical Manual of Mental Disorders* (DSM IV), we are all nuts anyway. Aunt Betsy, Hitler, the Pope, Mom, you, me--everybody. You may not have realized so far, the same things we disapprove of in other individuals--even behavior we hate in our parents, siblings, or children--are the very things we love in these people.

Perhaps a bit difficult for you to admit, the most irritating habits of your son are more endearing in your eyes than his fabulous grades in school. You don't love your kids more when they bring home better grades. You love them for the strange individuals they are. Have you been able to change your children? No? I thought so. We won't change our stubborn siblings nor our parents, even if it takes 50 years to get that through our thick skulls. See, I really don't care about your family members (they haven't bought my book yet, have they?).

Shamelessly I used them to demonstrate that if you haven't changed your kids and parents yet, you won't improve the messed-up individuals you see at work any time soon. You will hate them for a long time.

We are not how everybody likes us to be, and--being our own worst enemy and critic--<u>we</u> don't even like how we turned out. Nagging won't lead you to better approval ratings in the future. Stop it. Enjoy yourself and your environment as it presents itself today. There's no Option B. Happy individuals turn the world into a better place, instantly. People, trying to make the world a better place, aren't happy. That's why they want a better world first, in order to be happy THEN. Unhappy people make the world worse, also instantly, and it hardly matters how successful their desperate attempts are to improve this or that.

So, what is the damn secret? Hatred has a bad reputation these days, yet hatred may have untouched properties we can exploit emotionally and even financially. Perverted as you may find my theory, hatred is not always what it appears to be on first sight. Most employees hate their jobs. Have you witnessed their excitement when they express their disdain? What if they love to hate their jobs? What if hating your job with an elevated sophistication beats the futile attempt to land a better job--which you will also hate in the not-so-distant future?

What if hate is not public enemy No. 1 and it needs to be scrutinized with a cool head? For instance, it's rather ignorant to believe hatred killed six million Holocaust victims and was at the root of other Third Reich atrocities. A few hundred or even thousands of hateful Nazis did not commit the actual murder; it took millions of loving German family daddies to engage in something that left more than 100 million people dead worldwide. However, that subject will fill a different book. For now, hating may be the sweetest thing we can do ... well, I don't know about that. At least, give hate a chance and, who knows, you may fall in love with it.

Digging through this book you may look up often with the

questions, "Where does this lead?" "What's the conclusion of this mess?" "I am confused. What is the answer?" See, I may be a condescending jerk in the way I present this material to you, but I am in no position to have answers for you and how you should live your life. This book is meant to promote freedom and individuality: Yours! If my stuff leads to anything, it must lead to <u>your</u> answers. If there are conclusions, they need to be yours. Confusion is a crucial prerequisite to freedom. You don't know? You are confused? Perfect mindset to make unbiased decisions. Your life is up to you. All I can say is Good Luck!

You may find some of my ideas strange, controversial, and provocative. I'd be surprised if you didn't. You did not buy this book to see again what's been pounded into your fragile little mind repeatedly by scores of numbnuts. You wanted something else. So there! You asked for it. Now live with it.

Egbert Sukop, December 2008

Chapter One
Employed and Unhappy

"Every day millions of people trudge to the wrong job in the wrong place to produce the wrong goods."

The Economist, September 1991

Jobs suck. Job opportunities are oxymorons. Opportunities for what? You hate your job now and even more after an advanced career, because an exalted position makes you so much more vulnerable. Successful careers increase your dependency, and a potential fall into the abyss threatens in direct proportion to your rising star.

Employees hate their jobs by definition. Gallup research finds 74% of employees are either not engaged in what they are doing or actively disengaged. I am afraid the situation is worse. Everyone looking forward to retirement obviously can't wait to end what they're doing. Whether you are insulted by puny wages or compensated with a hefty salary doesn't matter. If you want to retire you know your life sucks. Of course you hate your job when you contemplate ending it.

Sorry, I forgot to mention the 5% of happy employees who love to hide for 40 years in the gray shadows of their cubicle walls, the ones who could go on until a heart attack or a banana peel has mercy on their mediocre souls. The habitually happy employee discovers how much she hates her job on the day her rotten employer forces her into retirement, to make room for a younger slacker who wears less obtrusive perfume. Yeah, yeah, I know; the Jack Welch's and Lee Iacocca's are employees too, and Google makes its slaves so happy. Right, but you aren't one of them.

87% of Americans don't like their jobs, according to Forbes Magazine. How high do you think is the percentage of employers who dislike what they do? Close to the same number, I'm afraid.

That's why this book applies to the self-employed just as much as to the employed work hater. No entrepreneur loves everything she is doing but she, unlike most employees, works with the awareness that her job--challenges and discomfort included--is subject to her choices. Anyway, my wild guess is that only 1 - 3% of all people are happily enjoying what they do. Nevertheless, society begs politicians to create a gazillion new jobs. Why? We love to hate our jobs! We simply love to hate.

Isn't it love that we aim for? We want to love what we do eventually. For now, most of us hate our daily grind. We despise it. We look for a better job and, once we have a more promising position, we hate it just as much as we did our previous assignment. We hate what we do. The average employee hates her job with a passion. Passion? There it is. We are so passionate about our subject of hatred that I suspect hatred may not be the only feeling we harbor toward our jobs.

Hate is not a pretty word. Families forbid their children to use it. What's so wrong with hate? Do we hate to hate? We do it all day anyway. We hate when our children pick their noses. We hate when our spouses speak of us in a condescending tone in public. We hate responsibilities just as we hate not having any. We love to hate. Period. Unbelievable? We hate our jobs on Tuesdays, and we hate to be without the jobs we hate so much. When we get fired from our hated position, we don't feel relief and certainly we aren't grateful and happy. No, we sue our ex-employers to get our repulsive jobs back. We hate the job, we hate losing it, and we hate when we have it back. It's the least we deserve, isn't it? No doubt, we are insane. We can't stomach the idea of losing that nasty job. Obviously, we love hating what we do. As far as jobs are concerned we are anything but rational.

Do we really hate our jobs? Rich or poor--nobody has a proper definition what that means and who the rich or the poor may be--the majority of people either dreams of or plans for retirement. State lotteries live off that dream. Ask around. At the drop of a hat, many of us would stop doing what we're doing from one day to the next, if we hit the $20 million jackpot. We are whores. We are willing to do plenty of stuff for money, and minimum wage measures how cheap we really are. Yep, we are cheap whores. For 5 bucks we can be coaxed into screwing up our lives. Corruption doesn't begin with millions. Corruption has nothing to do with the amount of money that changes hands. A couple of bucks helps you line up people around the block for any questionable cause. For the change in your pocket, you get 90% of the world's population to do what they don't want to do.

Disgusted by crooked politicians--eager to please for cash and votes--we easily forget how corrupt we are ourselves. Integrity? How much integrity does one have who sells her life's aspirations for $20, $50, or even $1,000 per hour? If you don't do what you truly want to do--at least parallel to the job you despise--you are cheap, inconsistent, and ultimately not trustworthy.

Duty calls? Sure, but who calls it duty? We were the ones who chose the line of work we seem to be nailed to like Jesus to the cross. I don't intend to offend you. Not at all, but I do believe our society's craving for a difficult life is rooted in our Judeo-Christian background that glorifies suffering.

It's too hard to pass up the benefits that come with your job? No one besides us came up with that fateful idea. We felt compelled to do something responsible. Glum emotional weight may have accompanied our choice. It is unlikely that playfulness was source and background of our decision-making. We needed to discover what to do with our lives and we had our first bills to pay. Maybe we intended to provide for a family. We engaged in activities we thought we had to do to make money, to pay rent, and to be responsible members of society. As if that was a virtue in itself.

We made up our mushy teenage minds and picked some stupid thing we felt a connection with, or our choice expressed rebellion against our stubborn parents. What we ended up doing is quite bizarre and shockingly random. Nobody forced us into the pain we may be experiencing today. It was our job to land this job. Nobody is to blame. It was an inside job. We were the makers of our own bad luck. Hallelujah. What could be more valuable than this discovery?! The problem with our decision to become a serious member of society is its weight. It doesn't have to be on our shoulders for the rest of our lives; we can decide to hate our work more playfully.

Pain is the measure of our work. Money does not measure our performance at all. Pain does. We want to work hard for our income or we won't respect the results. Who taught us this nonsense? We aren't happy unless we are sacrificing our lives. It's not that we stumble across self-sabotage unintentionally. Self-sabotage is our mission. Our sacred purpose is to destroy our individuality. We aren't happy until our freedom is annihilated. We crave suffering. We love to see our options shrinking. Facing our limitations all day makes us feel right at home. Giving goods and services in exchange for money is not what we have in mind: we are peddling pain. No pain, no gain. Cash is not compensation for work. Employees demand money as indemnification for self-inflicted injury.

Goodness. Freedom and individuality can expand only if you would do for free what you are willing to do for money. Can you see yourself doing what you're doing without the exchange of money? Without looking at the clock? Without constantly thinking what you're getting out of it? I am not asking you to work for free. I'm not suggesting you should decline payment for your work. On the contrary, I wish for you to get paid royally.

However, trying to get blood money in exchange for pain is pretty dumb and limited. People's tolerance for pain is limited and so is the money they can get for it. Hence, hard work will never pay enough. I am not trying to talk you out of your hatred for your daily grind. Go on despising what you do with one slight variation: hate playfully. Do what you do for its own sake, for no purpose, just because you decided to do it. You are doing it for yourself, selfishly, and for no other reason. If you can't be selfish, you will never be a truly generous individual.

Work because you WANT to work, and not because some mysterious demon is riding you into the ground. Take a minimum of responsibility for messing up your life day by day. Why? If you really didn't want to be there, you would have left long ago. You chose doing it and in fact you are choosing it again every morning you pull up your pants. Responsibility talk may cause you to yawn but more importantly, it gives you your own power back. And you need that power to have some control over what you're doing with your day and with your life.

Feeling trapped on a repulsive job because you must do it to pay bills and to feed your family turns you into a victim. No, not a victim of your messed-up job but a victim of your damned family. You're holding them responsible for your miserable life, and hating a job may very well be diverted hatred for your damned brats without whom you wouldn't have to wait for 35 years until your retirement or 'til you go postal--whichever comes first. Seeing yourself as the cause for what you do--no matter how hard that may be for you currently--increases your options. As a bonus you're regaining your most valuable asset right away; self-confidence.

Groundhog Day. The sameness of our jobs is perhaps more despicable than anything else in our work life. Zero variation. Same place, the same faces. The same smells and noises for years if not for decades. Horrifying! Jobs are fine. What we really hate is ourselves. We can't stand not to have the guts to get up and leave. We condemn ourselves for getting us into this dependency. Daily we punish ourselves for our lack of confidence. To us, it's beyond comprehension we haven't come up with something better, with more creative ideas to spend our lives and to earn a living. Boss, job, and co-workers are lucky bastards compared with us. The job-hating employee hates herself much more than her job or the world around her, because she does not do what she wants to do. The ultimate failure! The most successful employee can feel like the lowest loser.

Anger flares up when someone dares to take away what we so hate: fire a person who detests her job and as I said before, she will not thank you for it. Open hostility is what you'll get from her. Don't deprive anyone of their enemies. It is a person's birthright to hate, and they will do anything and everything to keep it that way. Did I say we love to hate? It's worse. We are addicted to feeling revulsion. We can't live without aversion. Abomination is what we thrive on. There is hardly a difference between loving or hating what we do. Either way, we are mourning its loss. We are a bit messed up in the head, aren't we?

Now, it's a common idea among employees that they would enjoy their jobs a lot better if they were paid sufficiently. They seriously believe there is an amount of money powerful enough to transform current hatred into passionate love. That is nonsense, of course. Yet again, it shows how corrupt our thinking is: for the right amount I may be willing to feel fabulous. Oh, really? It's not money that makes people do what they loathe, and it is not money that makes people do what they love. There is no correlation between someone's love for his work and his salary. People *choose* what they want to do, especially those who swear it isn't so. And then they point out puny or exorbitant amounts of money as reasons for their droll choices. Nothing could be further from the truth. You can't be bribed to love what you've hated so far, just as you were not corrupted into what you may despise doing today.

Freedom can't be had in a group. Job hating is dumbass group behavior. Our hatred is not based on freedom. We hate like sheep. We are doing it because everybody else does it. Freedom to do what we want can be gained only by claiming our individuality. You are making bunches of mistakes when you act as an individual, sure, but it can't be as devastating as throwing your life away in the mass hysteria of getting a job like everybody else. Destruction of the individual is the most painful process on every job. People are looking for the best available job for themselves, but chances are close to none of finding it. The probability of an employer finding the best available employee for a vacant job is much greater.

As an employee, you must give up important parts of your individuality to fit in. Well, that may even be a positive learning experience, as not all our quirks are helpful or appropriate.

However, jobs are not meant to support anybody in expressing or unfolding her individuality. It's more like school, exceptional characters get their wings clipped. Jobs mutilate people's individuality. Your true area of genius will be burned and buried. Remarkable virtues are forced to vegetate in the dark, suffocating under dull and daily chores. Suppressing your individuality murders your confidence, and without confidence you will never leave the pseudo-safe and benefit-lined lap of a hated job.

Freedom can only be discovered and claimed by individuals, by confident individuals. Not everything you do will turn out to be enjoyable or profitable. More often than not your individual decisions may turn up duds. Especially for successful people, losers are more common than winning ideas, and mistakes are made more often than not. I am not talking about your impulse purchases, weird choices of life partners, etc. I am referring to business oriented activities you decide to engage in. They have a chance to be profitable, but only if you are willing to deal with emotions that accompany frequent mistakes and constant tension. Guess what? There will be plenty to hate, and if you don't love it you're doomed.

Intensify your hatred for your job! Refuse to go soft. I mean it literally when I promise to show you *how to better hate your job*. Make worse what's bad. You can't sweet talk your way out of hatred into a nice relationship with your wretched job. If it's bad it's bad. Hate it some more. Parallel to your utmost repulsion, realize how much you enjoy the feeling. Can you see how engaged you are, how alert your senses become, and how quickly you respond to something or someone triggering your red lights to flash? We feel alive when we hate. Blind hatred allows us to exude pure passion. Automatically a transformation occurs and hating our jobs is not what it used to be.

Bad is good. We are fascinated with bad things. The negative sells more newspaper copy than the positive. Bad boys are more attractive than boring and predictable nice guys. Our dislikes elicit emotional reactions that the things we like cannot compete with. We aren't talking all day about the great and fabulous in our lives. We love the bad. Bad has a mysterious side to it, an unpredictable and dark nature. It's like real life. As we love the threatening formation of thunderclouds over the horizon, our infatuation with bad jobs doesn't come as a surprise.

Control is the most important part of our fascination with the bad. Do you have it in your hands to control how good the bad things in your life are? If not, bad is bad. Awareness of the fun you are having with dark and gloomy areas of your life can transform the awful into something awfully enjoyable. Over time, the most terrible experiences will provide entertaining stories to tell. Once you have established an emotional distance, you can laugh about every horrendous thing that has happened to you. Our experiences beg for our direction. You have an option to label your experiences at will and all of a sudden the bad develops unexpected and unlimited positive qualities.

Guilt turns hatred into something bad. Feelings of guilt appear when we believe we shouldn't have chosen this job or we should not hate it. That's no fun and you better talk yourself out of it quickly. See, there's absolutely nothing wrong with having or hating your job. Hate with pleasure and you may enjoy it for a long time. I have watched a father instilling guilt feelings into his children whenever they mentioned the word 'hate'. What a dangerous idiot! Hatred does not hurt people, only ACTING on your hatred can be hazardous for your and other people's health. One more time, baby, hatred did not murder 6 million Jews during the Holocaust: indifference killed them. Nice and quiet people, who lacked the balls to say what they really hated, committed heinous crimes and mass murder. Hell, feel free to hate. There are moments in life when red-hot hatred is the right thing to do, and it may even save lives. Yeah I know, there are hate crimes. Trust me, love crimes are equally perilous.

Pain is not necessarily what everybody thinks it is. Monks figured out in medieval times that flagellation can be used as a source of intense sexual pleasure. Under the pretense of penance, while displaying obvious pain, the hard-core faithful have always known how to have a little fun. As outlandish and absurd as it may seem to you, lust is the flip side of pain, and fortunately this experience is not at all limited to monks. The existence of the S/M world may scare the bejeezus out of our prudish and religious friends but it's based entirely on findings of monks, just like beer.

Who would have thought? Adults get all giggly and inhibited considering S/M in their bedrooms, but cubicle S/M is as normal as pizza and beer for roughly 90% of the population. Our dark sides are not as dark as their reputation suggests. Pain can be sweet and nothing can be taken at face value. From that perspective, your hideous day job has the potential to be transformed into a source of wild and wicked fun. Eh?

Hitmen take money for their bloody craft, yet they don't necessarily hate the subject of their interest. They don't feel much of an emotional connection with their task at hand--well, ideally. Employees take blood money also. An employee who hates what she's doing butchers her work and assassinates her individuality. And she is emotionally attached to her work. Very much so. Employees must believe they are paid to hate. You may want to learn from the average hitman: it's nothing personal, just business. Do your job and take the money. Getting all worked up over it doesn't help anybody. Unless you know by now how to extract pleasure out of pain, you have the least to gain from suffering in exchange for money.

Income, depending on pain and suffering, is limited. Any half-wit will tolerate abuse only to a certain extent. Why wait until that moment? Once we know what we're doing is painful for the most part, we may as well stop playing the game of testing our tolerance. Oh no, I did not tell you to quit your job. In fact, I am not telling you at all what you should or should not do. You are 100% responsible for the things you do, before and after reading my material. Dull hatred for your job puts a cap on your income potential and on your ability to enjoy yourself. Go on hating like everybody else and your development as an individual has practically come to a grinding halt. Continuing a hated career is absolutely, positively nuts ... unless you love hating it, of course.

Confused? Confusion is the prerequisite for total freedom.

If you like one option better than another, you are biased and not free at all. When you have no clue what to do, when you are utterly confused, you are completely free to choose. Whatever you do, DON'T QUIT YOUR JOB just yet. You may want to start something else parallel to your job. Two conditions though: it must be fun and interesting enough so that you would do it for its own sake, without ever getting paid for it. AND, you must take money for it.

Chapter Two
Something for Nothing

"If a man could have half his wishes, he would double his troubles."

Benjamin Franklin

Exchange is the sacred cow in our relationship with money. We are eager to get something in exchange for our hard-earned cash, and we feel terrible unless we give something in exchange for the money we accept from others. 'You can't have something for nothing,' is in the domain of common nonsense.

    Yes, you can indeed get something for nothing, except it's almost impossible to give nothing--unless you are a complete dud, that is. You are so much more valuable than anything you could do or give. You are not nothing. Your presence is something you'd better treasure and acknowledge as high value *before* you think of exchanging money for goods and services. Dullards evoking 'There is no such thing as a free lunch,' display subzero self-confidence. No one asks these people for their opinion and when they volunteer their worn out no-free-lunch claptrap, you know they must think of themselves and you as human garbage.

    Without offering anything in exchange we are worth more than hatefully bungled jobs, our products. You have to decide that for yourself, of course. I don't know anything about your self-worth. As long as you are part of the deal, there is no such thing as nothing. Others may think differently about you, but you ought to puff up your ego a little bit, shouldn't you?

    Self-esteem isn't worth much if you don't consider yourself worthy of money without providing goods or services in exchange. The person who doesn't believe in a free lunch thinks she is worth less than money and less than the crap she usually exchanges for cash. You owe it to yourself to raise the perception of your value and self-esteem. You are worth money. Goods and services are your products. You were here first. Human beings were here before we invented money for the sake of convenience. The purpose of all that stuff is to serve you. It's not the other way around like the no-free-lunch perverts want to make you believe. What idiocy to shrink and shrivel up in awe of this phenomenon money.

If you aren't capable of seeing your value as the highest in the ridiculous hierarchy of terms like work, money, products, etc., money will put you in your place. It's going to be a low position, I'm afraid. Money and your shabby job will define you and your miserable value. Don't expect much money there, and you won't get a leading role in your life either. There'll always be somebody or something leading you by the nose to the wrong places. You know what? Screw other people's values! Your real job is to invent and define your life and your own value.

Cost of living is a term that makes me cringe: is living a liability? Since costs are considered negative by many, living is perhaps negative also. Or is it? Does being alive disturb you? How awful is it for you to live? Well, I see there are a bunch of benefits to having a life and besides for a few financial obligations here and there, life can produce more than it costs. What are the benefits of being alive? In monetary terms, what is it worth to you to be able to run around and do stuff? Numbers anybody, in dollars and cents?

Maintaining a life is expensive. You know the cost. You are paying the bills. Yep, life sucks. Does it, now? How about changing your perspective and developing a view that your life is rather of profitable nature? Obviously, you are making money and if you are not showing a profit, you may have spent more money in the past than what you have made. I have. That, of course, is not life's fault. Life is not by nature this or that. Your minute by minute choice of perspective makes it what it is. What you spend is to a large extent under your control, and so is your option to turn your life into something wildly profitable. Have it your way: expensive or profitable?

Incompetence makes more money than competence. Weird? Most people are utterly incompetent. How do I know? They hate what they are doing. When you compare the output of someone who is in *his element* to the product of a person who ails along hour after creeping hour, possibly being disturbed in this misery by a customer, you know the happy employee outperforms the wretch. Alas, incompetent sleepers shuffling along through the day are in the majority.

Hence the incompetent masses in our society win. As little as it may be for each individual, as a collective glob of the inept they're making more money than any other group of people on Earth. You disagree with my definition of incompetence? I don't care how much one knows or how experienced a person may be. She can be a Mensa member with an IQ five times my waistline: if she doesn't conduct her business with a minimum of grace, she lacks competence.

Now, if the armada of the incompetent would quit their jobs and do something they can excel and thrive in, they would have a chance to make more money as individuals than their self-loathing colleagues. But that would require greater trust in one's ability than in the power of self-chosen incompetence and slavery.

To deserve is some sort of a developmental illness. Nobody deserves anything. Reality does not support mental fabrications like fairness or deserving. Both work to a limited degree in the world of children, but once you emerge from the sandlot deserving has no place in your life. Simply put, we don't get what we deserve—ever.

Some deserve to live in peace, happiness, and relaxation, but they get cancer for no reason. Someone else deserves to get slapped all day every day with a bag of clothespins, but he gets to live in paradise on Earth. You will never get what you deserve. Forget it. You may not get what you want, either. Get over it. You will get what you'll get--no more, no less.

Results are difficult and in most cases impossible to control. The result of your actions depends on the influence of myriads of factors. You don't control the outcome of any damned thing you do, and results of our actions are less predictable than weather in April--they are quite random. What can you control? Everything you DO! You can go to the bathroom successfully. There may be delays when you're stuck in traffic, but you have managed to overcome most obstacles in the past.

Have lunch. Take a walk with your pooch. Go bicycling. Learn scuba diving. Start a business. Pick up a new language. You may have to train in new activities, but nothing stops you from DOING. It took me several months to keep my balance on a unicycle, for instance, but we can indeed control what we do. People may call you a dork or laugh at you, but you can still do thousands of things you choose to do. Control over what you want to *be* or *have* is extremely limited.

Strangely enough, we are magically attracted to areas of life we have little or no control over. Obsessed with what we want to be once we grow up, with money and toys we crave, and with results--success--we're often too paralyzed to concentrate on the possible. I am not talking you out of your goals, your dreams of grandeur and millions of chips.

Knock yourself out with the newest or oldest secret to crack the code of prosperity, tap the *law of attraction*, think positive, feel positive, imagine whatever the crap your little heart desires. Plan, prepare, and pursue success. It's all perfectly fine entertainment, but be aware you are not in control and you are looking as silly as a huge bug desperately trying to fly through a glass window. Instead you could *do* something, anything, and you'd be in charge. What do you think promises more fun?

Hatred is something you gain from doing your job, lifelong. But what does your job cost you? Expansion of your income, most likely, and unfolding of your personality. No, there was no misunderstanding: jobs prevent your income from increasing, and as if that wasn't enough to mourn, jobs transform individuals to *induhviduals* as Scott Adams pointed out in *Dilbert*.

Jobs don't inspire and promote development of any abilities and skills that are not absolutely necessary to perform the task at hand. Jobs are the coffins of individuality. You earn the questionable privilege of hobbling about in a narrow world in exchange for a check. People pay with their lives for the benefits of having a job. It's time-released suicide of whatever potential you started with.

Loser is something nobody likes to be called. In fact we hate it. We are groomed to be winners and yet, the difference between the two may be a 1,000th of a second. Truth is, both types depend on outside validation. Proud winners and ashamed losers alike are stuck at the emotional stage of a three-year-old. Approval seeking adults usually look pathetic. If your emotional make-up is largely affected by other people's judgment, you are a puppet, easily manipulated and in turn prone to be manipulative yourself. Beware of the teenager syndrome. It's obnoxious enough when kids do it but unbearable when grownups hold on to it for dear life.

A real loser has to muster the confidence to be who she is in order to live through the next day. Somehow she must come up with a minimum of self-respect. Without at least a sliver of confidence, she'd take a handful of sleeping pills. Losers rely on themselves to stay alive and to move on. They don't *get fed* like winners. Winning is just an image, you know? If and when it happens it is extremely temporary.

Somebody is celebrated for his performance, or maybe for someone else's performance he took credit for (not that uncommon in job environments, is it?). Results are random, remember, and the average winner is merely a lucky someone connected to positive results by his actions. Praised for traits or pseudo traits, a winner's happiness is short-lived. We are winners for moments, minutes, maybe for hours if we get drunk quick enough, but it won't last for a lifetime.

Unfortunately for the average success junkie, there is a life after winning. Your environment may still admire you as a winner for a couple of days, but you are already back in loserland, up to your ears in the morass of domestic problems, not feeling too much the winner at all. None of us are winning all the time. The idea of being a winner for good is horse shit.

You really want to win? Get comfortable living most of your life as a loser who enjoys losing *and* winning, or whatever comes next. The content loser does not need to win. Not being emotionally attached to the outcome of his endeavors makes him more powerful, less vulnerable, and increases his chance to win.

Strengths are valuable to your employer. For you, your strengths are no more valuable than your weaknesses. Duty calls for strength, but a bunch of our pleasures come from our weaknesses. Reason enough to hold them in high regard. No? Jobs are acquired by peddling your strengths, the ones you have and strengths you think you should have, but on the market--the real market, I mean, not the job market--they may not be worth as much as your finest weakness.

Employees are limited to making money with their strengths. When you are working for yourself, you can cash in on anything you choose, and some of your weaknesses could provide stronger motivation than anything else. Do you need incentives and motivational drivel to pursue your weaknesses? Exactly. Motivation is necessary only when you do what you don't want to do. Impressive as your strengths may look, you could be bored out of your mind, stressed, or both if that's all you are permitted to work with throughout your day. Weakness has intrinsic motivators. You don't need to concern yourself with the modus operandi of your favorite weakness.

The first step to a promising business: your greatest weakness! Trust me, you are not the only one who gets a kick out of that one. Plenty of people are willing to pay plenty of money to anyone who offers ideas to indulge in it more intensely and in new ways. You are proof of it.

Solutions for our monetary problems aren't necessarily to be found where we are searching. It's an old myth that money solves money problems. It doesn't. Cash injections may delay the impact of a pressing issue but in most cases money cannot solve financial problems at all. On the contrary, money can increase and intensify unsatisfactory financial situations exponentially. Something for nothing? Trying to eliminate money problems with cash usually proves you got nothing in exchange for a very expensive something. Money used for problem solving is wasted most of the time. Spare yourself the embarrassment and dig deeper to unearth the real problem. As outlandish as it may appear to you, money is never the cause of, or solution to, your problems.

Still thinking about your strengths? Danger can emanate from your strengths. Identify yourself with your greatest strength and you're making a bad move. Stinky hubris is in the air. People who do this often try to save the damned world with their strengths. Soon they feel needed and have a hard time comprehending that everybody is expendable, especially everybody's stupid strengths. Lamenting about too many childbirths elsewhere looks pretty dumb while you are busy convincing yourself how important you are and that you should make another couple of babies.

In their strength people feel superior. An air of arrogance comes with strength and sooner or later the strength junkie hits a point when her strength turns into her most dangerous weakness. People are too attached to what they're good at. They have something to lose. Perfection drives them, and their so-called strength proves to be their most hard-assed addiction. Geezus, not even smoking and drinking can be that bad.

Individuals operating predominantly on strength have no sense of humor: these guys are dead serious and it's no fun to get in their way. Hey, there is nothing wrong with your strengths. Just make sure you apply that stuff playfully and with caution.

Weakness is to be celebrated. Too many of us feel bad and guilty about our soft spots. We believe we have to work on our less impressive character traits, get rid of them, or hone them sufficiently to elevate them to a status of semi-strengths. Drop it: I did not suggest you should hate yourself. That's self-improvement territory. Changing yourself or several of your selves doesn't work anyway and you're just messing yourself up. You may be losing what makes you so endearing in the first place. Embrace your weaknesses.

You are a mess. You are a strange human being. You are one of a kind, and we'll be just as thankful that there aren't more of your type as you can be grateful that you are exactly the way you are. You are doing fine, weaknesses and all. Cultivate them. Don't let your weaknesses weaken or kill you, but stop the guilt trip. There are numerous reasons to be proud of your quirks and inclinations, and that may be a foundation solid enough to exploit them as strengths. And that means for profit.

Performance is not measured by money. You are definitely not paid according to your performance. A secret: no one is. Performance related pay is a corporate myth. It has never happened and it never will, but it appeared to be an inspiring and motivating idea at the time. Uh, it's wonderful to dangle incentives before employees' eyes, like luring donkeys with carrots. It's especially effective and cheap when we use incentives nobody can reach. Pay based on your performance is an urban legend.

$15.75 or forty bucks may look as if they were a realistic compensation for your time and effort, but they are not related to your output. You don't have to search long to find somebody who works harder and earns less than you do, and your cubicle neighbor may work a lot less, producing nothing perhaps, and he takes home twice as much as you do. Relatively large chunks of money are not the equivalent of an individual's performance by any measure. The hours your lawyer bills you have painfully little to do with the real hours she has spent on your behalf, and the salary she gets from her firm are hardly directly related to her toil. The boat load of dough her firm shakes out of the next class-action lawsuit have certainly nothing to do with performance. Give me a break.

The truth about your performance: nobody cares about it besides you. Be proud, gloat, enjoy your arrogance but don't expect anybody else in the world to reward you for it. The last person who wants to pay you for your performance is your boss. He'll make sure not to throw good money after bad, feeding your ego.

Differences between the so-called rich and poor hardly exist. Rich people often behave like poor people with a lot of money. Poor people can turn into multi-millionaires and they continue pointing their fingers at the *rich* as the evil force in the world. You won't find two individuals who could give you an identical definition of the dividing line between rich and poor. There is none. Granted, half of our planet's population lives off $2 a day, with about a billion people who have less than a buck a day to spend. Compared with them, everybody living in the U.S., Japan, Europe, Scandinavia, New Zealand, etc. is filthy rich--you and me included.

I know, that's not what people like to hear. They don't want to be called rich. Most people on Earth have no money. True. You and I do, yet it does not improve anyone's desperate plight in sub-Saharan Africa when you crank the wheels of the rich/poor smoke machine to obscure the fact that you have more than you want others to believe. I'm not making friends here, I'm afraid: terms of poverty and wealth, rich and poor are pure idiocy. They help certain individuals to get political mileage and recognition from suckers who hate the rich--who hate themselves, that is, besides hating you and me--but they don't help a few billion people to get clean water and food.

People who don't have enough to eat today also lack the luxury of hating anybody, especially the rich. Those who decry the *evil rich*--who want them to be punished with more taxes for instance, who push to limit their income--are never really poor themselves. Rather, they look like Warren Buffet, Ted Kennedy, or George Soros. And regardless of their real age, the self-proclaimed poor in our society have plateaued in their emotional development at a stage of rebellion against mom and dad.

The difference between people who don't have food or shelter and those who display a belligerent attitude toward the rich is that the haters of the rich *choose* to be on the poor side of that imaginary line. The truly hungry and starving aren't dumb enough to insist on their status quo. The professionally poor refuse to cross the line even when their bank balances prove them to be liars. Drawing a line between poor and rich is foolish, and I am amazed nobody has condemned it yet as segregation. The fake poor are still too happy pretending to be poor, I guess. It must be a romantic thing.

Rich or *wealthy* sounds good, doesn't it? Or bad of course, depending on your warped perspective. Either way, you can't get there. You just cannot get rich, whatever complicated methods you may employ. A hypothetical line that does not exist in reality can't be crossed. If there is no rich and poor, you can't get to *the other side*. Where or what should that be? It is impossible for you to get rich. The idea or image of getting rich is a chimera. The ones you call rich would never see themselves as rich. They'd bite their tongue before they would say such a foolish thing. Ask them.

No one is rich. With a hundred or a thousand times more moolah than you have right now in assets, you will still be the same person. Particularly disappointing, you will perceive yourself as the same. You will have the same problems, the same flaws, you will be the same droll individual. Rich? Don't be ridiculous! Some people waste their time trying to get rich, quickly or slowly, while others work away trying hard to never become one of the rich. Childish, all of it. Getting rich is the idiotic idea of folks with drooping IQs. Hey, why don't you pile up a decent heap of money instead?

Chapter Three
Before and After

"Nothing is so good as it seems beforehand."

George Eliot

Solutions are overrated. Eagerly we believe life will be better after we find solutions for our pressing problems. Not so. We don't change, and the world around us doesn't change either. The *after* won't be so different from the *before*. Expectations of a rosy future, after xyz is accomplished, rob us of enjoyments we could have right now. Don't wait. People's conviction that life will be fantastic after solving a huge problem describes the void they will be falling into. Waiting for a better life creates emotional potholes today, and the same frustrating void will accompany you from now until *the great then*. Good luck!

    Have fun today with productive activities and you will also experience fun and productivity after long-awaited solutions are accomplished. Often I have seen that the solutions we crave can take ten, a hundred times longer than we thought originally. Waiting for solutions to improve your life, hoping for a greater thereafter, will put your life on hold at best, and end it at worst. There is no real before and after; only a before, and it'll last longer than you think.

    Order cannot be had. Temporarily life may look as if everything is in order, peaceful and perfect according to our ideas and ideals. Most of the time, however, life is messy and out of control. Reality couldn't care less how we think it should be. The markets don't behave obediently like a German Shepard. Time moves too slowly or too fast. The damn children misbehave like the markets, and the grandparents certainly can't be taught what to do. Once more, life is an ongoing mess and if you want to enjoy yourself as much as possible, you may want to say good-bye to the notion that things should be in order--in your image of order to be exact.

Tension is needed to run an internal combustion engine and it is equally indispensable as the driving force of a person's life. Tension is good. Yeah, yeah, people desire peace and relaxation but trust me, if they had that all day they'd be bored to tears. Computer games or hockey aren't fascinating because they're inducing a peaceful, meditative state in their fans. People wish to be grabbed by their lapels. They want to be thrown into action. And even if it's just secondhand action, it is sufficient to get emotions boiling. Peace is a fine and noble idea, but none of us can live without tension. Not even peace can be negotiated or upheld without tremendous tension. We love flying sparks, friction, unpredictability before and during our activities.

Reason causes happiness? I doubt it. Our actions are rarely initiated by reasonable thoughts. Neither are our moods or emotions founded on reason. Reason is an instrument we may use to sort out the human environment around us. A looking glass to detect insanity. Reason can help in making important decisions. Until you find out five years--or three days--down the road how unhappy you are with your reason-based decisions to marry that man and in choosing your profession. Nothing wrong with reason, but our use of it is heavily bungled. Chimps will memorize the U.S. tax code before homo sapiens figure out how to fully apply reason.

We pretend to be reasonable and we know how to make a serious enough face to look believable. However, we are insane-- all of us--in different departments and with varying levels of intensity. On your daily commute home you have an opportunity to see ample evidence of human beings being run by anything but reason. Just like money, cars don't cause our insanity but they make it visible to everybody else. Reason can support our happiness or it can be used to destroy it. Luckily for us, we don't need reasons to be happy nor reason to get there.

Afterlife is not a term exclusively reserved for a non-existent life after death. There is an equally unrealistic expectation that life after success may be special and better than what we're experiencing today. I am afraid there will indeed be life after success. However, it's not going to be much different from your life as it presents itself to you right now. Life as you know it, with all its flaws, doesn't end with success. In that regard, the greatest success you can imagine may be your greatest disillusionment and frustration: nothing changes. You will still be there and success has no magic powers to mutate your world into something else just because you wish or hope for such a thing to happen. You are the bloody same, before and after your successes, and your hopes and expectations for something grand to hide behind the curtain are a waste of time. You might just as well decide to be happy today. It's much easier and also cheaper.

Got a minute? Then please read this last paragraph again-- twice. It may save your life at some point. I have personally known individuals who worked hard for decades toward their life's goals. Within days or weeks after achieving their greatest accomplishments some of them committed suicide. One person murdered his wife and children first before he blew his own brains out. What happened? He had everything and now this. Exactamente. No, these people did not kill themselves because they *had it all* or they had *too much*. They ended their enviable lives because they expected too much from getting there, and what they really wanted wasn't in the bag.

Because NOTHING will change with the most fabulous success. Nothing that counts at least. And the shock wave of that realization can kill people, literally. The sooner you realize it, the healthier and the happier you'll be. Once more, there is nothing wrong with success and all the toys you want. Just don't expect for any of that stuff to turn your world into something it's not already today! 'Nuff said.

Mind over matter? Really? I have yet to meet a mind that would function autonomously without being attached to a body and matter. There is no mind without matter, and even though we would love the idea that we could steer and control matter with our bare minds, it doesn't seem to work that way. Our matter moves and then our minds have the hardest time to catch up justifying the latest move by our matter. Truth is, mind and matter enter existence simultaneously and, as much as you may despise the fact, both will exit existence at the same time. Mind over matter, matter over mind--it really doesn't matter. It's one unit, incredibly sophisticated, incredibly capable, and incredibly flawed. I can't see what could be gained by one theory winning over the other, except some people insist on losing their minds over things that don't really matter.

Messy is good and making yourself feel at home in messy environments is an even better idea. Why? 'Cause it's going to stay that way and it will be messy for a long time. Oh, and if I am wrong and your life is in perfect order, you'll have to deal with messes around you in your relationships, friendships, the marketplace, and in your extended socio-political surroundings. There is always a grand mess nearby. You don't have to look for one. Instead of running away from it, face the challenge and scare up the fun in the heap. Gems can be located in any pile of garbage, and in the middle of muddle hides entertainment, guaranteed. Life is not in order and that's fine: you won't be bored.

Reality can be nasty. Especially when you expected something else to happen. In fact, reality is almost never as it should be. What *should be* is a figment of people's imagination, a disturbance of their minds or better yet the sign of a disturbed mind. One definition of growing up is taking reality precisely as it presents itself, without making a fuss. You don't have a choice. For the moment things are as they are. It is a waste of everyone's time to complain about reality. It's insanity trying to *teach* the world how it should have behaved properly a minute ago. Worse still while you're pissed off you can't do what you want to do. Your freedom is on hold. Anyone in a wheelchair is better off than you are in bitch mode. Chill for a minute, will you?

Reality is the realm of facts. You can't change it in retrospect but you can own the moment, your personal perspective on what is, and you've got approximately a second to recognize the smell of your reality as yours. Claiming last minute's events as yours, bungled as they may have been, you are free again to do whatever the hell it is you want to do.

Envy grants us the idea of what we could have *too*. Envy is me-too lala-land. The glamorous have it. That damned rich guy has it. Why don't I? Observing someone else's good life, we only look at a select small section of that person's reality. Our picture of that *lucky man* conveniently leaves out the price he pays for the stuff we're jealous of. The *dark side* of his acquisitions is unknown to us and never makes it out of the shadows into the media. I'm not talking about his monetary expenses. The subject of our interest resides in a 10,000 square foot home on top of a mountain, overlooking the ocean. We love that place. Would we equally enjoy putting up with his Xanthippe of a wife, this shrew, and her brood of relatives? Would you also prefer to have had his son who folded himself around a Carpathian Walnut tree on the eve of his 23rd birthday, neatly mingled in a threesome with his girlfriend and your new Arctic Silver Porsche? I am confident thousands of imbeciles envied Kenneth Lay in, say 1999. Some of them may have renounced that emotion meanwhile.

Relaxation can be fantastic, yet not more valuable than a shot of good Bourbon. What most people call relaxation is artificial, an exercise and no more. Meditating on a Pilates mat may be training your relaxation muscle a bit but it's not real relaxation. When everyone around you has to be quiet you know it's not a realistic situation, and the relaxation is just as fake. It may feel good to you and it may look good from afar, but from up close everybody can spot a toupee.

Relaxation is next to worthless if you can't relax in the middle of an intersection, or in your office while three phone lines are flashing, your boss is barking at you, and your colleagues are asking you to join the company funeral fund. True relaxation can only be had in the midst of chaos. How do you let chaos and bristling tension affect your countenance? Are you having the time of your life or are you anxiously awaiting Friday afternoon and your damned meditation pillow to pacify emotional turmoil?

Relax in the urban wilderness! Any fool can breathe softly on a Yoga mat while the brats are locked away. Invite the noise, the crap, the chaos, and don't let them steal your inner peace. It'll gain unheard of levels of quality.

Creativity is not as dependent on stimulation as it is on your ability to choose. No muse needed. Nothing provides a more perfect environment for the freedom of choice than an utter mess and complete confusion. Where there is a mess you can mold it into order, any order, or you can transform one type of chaos into a new kind. A mess was the ideal spring board for the God of Genesis to form a world of his choice. What more do you need in order to do what you want? A state of confusion, when you don't know anything for sure, is the best inspiration for freedom of choice. The child who destroys a wood block building has the fresh and exciting choice to pick the first block out of the ruins as the foundation for a new construction.

Before and after is a great myth. We believe in preposterous changes that will supposedly happen between now and then. Then, life will be easier. After winning the lottery, we'll be in such an elevated financial state that we can relax for good. Our money will be making more money and we won't have to worry about the bills in the mailbox as we do today. Horse puckey. As difficult as it can be to come by a decent pile of cash, it is even more difficult to keep it and to keep your pile growing. The more money you have, the more you'll have to think about what to do with it next. It will never take care of itself. Same with higher aspirations and wishes: there is no magic line dividing the before and after. Sure, some things will change gradually but you will remain the one inventing your life against a ton of odds.

Happiness does not depend on your accomplishments. We believe we'd be happier were our dreams realized and all sorts of things accomplished, but that is not true. It may prove difficult to impossible to control the time it takes to achieve a particular goal. There are two ways to do this. Work like crazy toward that target, not caring about yourself or anything else until the goal has been attained. You may be the most unhappy bastard in the meantime but then, oh, it'll be the gateway to paradise on Earth. Rubbish! Neglect your health and your emotional balance today, sacrifice everything for your important objective. Worst possible outcome; you won't ever accomplish your goal and you are miserable now *and* then.

Second approach: keep your aim in mind but detach your physical and emotional well-being from the expected outcome. Worst possible result; you don't reach your goal but you are healthy and happy now *and* then. The more relaxed you are during the process, the more creative you will be, the more people you will meet and befriend, and the more you can accomplish in a shorter time span. Your happy and relaxed state increases the probability of completing your mission. If you don't get there, it won't matter that much. And you may come across new and interesting ideas, more appealing solutions, rendering your previous objectives unnecessary.

After will be better than the *before*? Think again. It's the typical positive thinking dilemma, "Every day in every way, I'm getting better and better." (Emile Coue, 1857-1926) That's just great! In other words, you are today in worse shape than you will be tomorrow. Your present will always suck compared with the future. If that doesn't have the power to chip away at your self-confidence, I don't know what will. Positive thinking is the most negative garbage people can fill their minds with. It's destructive stuff. Positive thinking and the before/after hysteria are detrimental to your happiness and to your overall well-being. I do not look forward to rosy times replacing what I'm experiencing today.

"My wedding day will be the happiest day of my life!" What a sad sod one has to be to think such fiddle-faddle. The schmuck she's going to marry has no clue that this dumb cow just cursed their marriage. Obviously she knows how to make sure it won't be a real happy one. Anyway, your best bet is to have fun today, allowing today's enjoyment to grow into tomorrow's. Today's happiness permeates activities and goals you are going to busy yourself with at a later date. Goals, in dream state or completely realized, don't make you happy. They can't. What you can do easily and immediately is to impregnate your activities and goals with your happiness.

Problems are certainly not our favorite things to deal with. While longing for nonsense like peace and sunshine, we don't care for cars or refrigerators breaking down, begging for repair at the worst possible moments. I have news for you: you and I, we will always have problems. ALWAYS. Don't spend too much time in reaction mode or it'll ride you straight into a state of permanent uselessness. Choose to do what you want to do regardless of the circumstances. Easy for me to say? No, I had to experience years of chaos and misery, longer than a decade actually, to discover what I am suggesting here, as arrogant as it seems. I have tried it, it's impossible to care for each new occurring problem properly and to have something that resembles a life.

You may not be able to do all day what you really want to do, maybe not even for a few hours each day. Steal a minimum of an hour everyday for yourself. No spouse, no kids, no chores, no reaction to the crap that sets out to bury you. Spend that hour as you please for fun _and_ profit. You are it, and you are its architect. From there, you may develop an understandable interest to expand upon.

Chapter Four
Poverty and Prosperity

"The poor man is happy; he expects no change for the worse."

Demetrius

"The cure for admiring the House of Lords is to go and look at it."

Walter Bogehut

Poverty is relative? Nope. You may have been penniless in your past or outright broke, but you haven't been poor. It's impossible for you to be poor. Being poor is not one of your options, because being poor means not having any other choice for the rest of your days. You've got nothing left to lose? That's tough and it can happen. You have alternatives still, an unlimited supply in fact. I can't help it that you may be lazy or that you may choose not to be aware of your freedom to choose. Perhaps you do know possible 'escape routes', you have preferences of course, unless your brilliant noodle is entirely caked shut. You just don't want to go there now. Fine.

You're agreeing with me, finally? You are not poor? You know what you could do, where you could go, or whom you could talk to? Fabulous! Then stop pointing your stinky finger at rich people, judging them for doing something you don't want to do. The ones you call rich are people who decided to do something that you decided not to do. I don't know whether you're pissed off about *them* doing it or about yourself not doing it, but pissed off you are when you are getting serious about the rich-poor distinction. There is no definition of being rich two people on Earth would agree on.

According to Webster's, being rich means "having abundant possessions and esp. material wealth." The Oxford American College Dictionary defines rich as "having a great deal of money or assets." You fit the description perfectly from the perspective of 97% of this planet's population. More than six billion people are convinced you are rich, but you insist on faking poverty for the sole purpose of bitching at and about the *real rich* people, the evil ones? You can't even fool your pooch with such nonsense. As I said before, we love to hate something, and what could be worse than not being poor anymore? Deprived of hatred for the rich, what would we do?

Oops, I forgot to tell you: you cannot be rich either. Yeah, but what about being rich as a state of mind? Isn't it important to feel rich spiritually? Nice cop-out, but since it makes me want to puke we won't pursue this train of thought any further. First of all, you can't get rich. How would that look? How much would you have to have or make? We have established the fact that the idea of being rich--especially rich in material terms--has no number attached to it. Apropos, what's wrong with an appetite for large numbers of money? If you don't make as much money as you'd like to make, seek to increase it instead of losing yourself in the idiocy of how-to-get-rich-and-happy or how-to-stay-poor-and-self-righteous objectives.

Forget getting rich. It's bait for ninnies. Make money instead and lots of it. Oh, and one more helpful hint: quit comparing yourself with others. That's where the rich thing comes from and that's what kills it. In that paradigm--God, I hate that word--the poor want to get rich. The poor hate where they are and at the same time they hate the rich. They would like to punish them with exorbitant taxation. Go figure. Hence, the ideal solution for the poor would be to make more money without having to get rich. Bingo! You can have that. It's called BP, as in Buffett Poor.

When you realize you aren't poor, you will find there is no state of being rich on the other side of the fence. The notion of being rich, and everything you used to associate with it, will dissolve also. Once you leave the illusion of being poor behind, the idea of being rich loses its meaning. Poof! After poor there is no rich.

Impossible is a word we don't want to hear. Especially baby boomers don't like it so much and they've been telling their brood, "You can be anything you want to be, honey!" B.S. You cannot be anything: you must choose. And then, how unfortunate, all of us face certain limitations. At least it gives us something more to hate. Take choosing to be rich for example. It's one of those *anythings* you and anyone else can be supposedly. Being rich is an ideal. We imagine lavish surroundings, a relaxed lifestyle--whatever the hell you think that means--butler, cooks, maids, chauffeur, and handsome well-mannered brats populating Ivy League universities.

We don't imagine having the flu, extensive root canal work while cramped in the dentist's slippery chair, or the abrupt end of it all. Phil Specter, O.J. Simpson, Ken Lay, or Michael Vick were rich guys once, remember? From rich to wretch or dead, in 60 seconds. How rich were they really when everyone else thought they were? Oh yeah, you can get there also and your hired bean counters may show it to you in black and white. But, you can't get rich. You can't reach the ideal, the shiny and fabulous state of eternal lala land. It'll have a dark side attached to it, personally tailored, including monogram, to your specifications. Drawing a line between rich and poor, fantasizing about it and thinking it's real, is a pretty dumb idea.

Positive thinking is so 20th century. In fact, I'd think you would be over it by now. What is positive? It's a fickle thing for sure. "Nothing is either good or bad, but thinking makes it so," said good ol' Willy Shakespeare and he was spot on. You may wish to have ten million dollars and you may call that a vastly positive idea. If ten million dollars were all that Billy Gates had left tomorrow, he may not shoot himself but the thought will cross his mind and everything else he'd think about that day is not likely to be found in the realm of the positive. You need positive thinking as desperately as a hole in the head: not at all. Being optimistic helps, but if that's what you want, having an optimistic outlook, why become a militant fundamentalist?

Positive thinkers believe they are superior to negative

people. There you have it. Positive thinking is just another form of fascism. *Half-full water glass Nazis* aren't more positive than their brethren and I'll stay out of their gloriously bombastic positive paths.

Exchange is the magic word. Most of us cannot see money in any other context. We expect to receive money in exchange for something: time, goods, services, ideas. How simplistic! That frame of mind will always be limiting. You can do better. A certain type of person appreciates money only when it is hard-earned and exchanged for blood, sweat, and tears. If you are like that, I'm not the one judging you. You've got to admit, though, your income will be limited by your willingness and by your capacity to bleed, sweat, and cry in your merry line of work. When you pride yourself with money being a measurement of how hard you work, you are close to the end of your rope. If the hard-working person increases her income, it means she didn't work all that hard before. She can't make more money until she allows the illusion of hard work to collapse.

Contrary to common belief, money is not by definition a measure for exchanged value. It can be used for that purpose but possible applications of money are fortunately not limited to exchange. Of Leonard Davis' seven-year contract with the Dallas Cowboys for $49.6 million, $18.75 million were guaranteed. How hard does one work in exchange for a $16 million signing bonus? Sure, Mr. Davis will play football but that's what he wants to do anyway, is it not? How many guys play football--hard and sweaty, broken bones and all--without ever hoping to see 1% of Leonard's paycheck? I didn't rub this under your nose because I begrudge Leonard Davis his income. I don't. I love it! I brought this up for you to see one of thousands of examples that the exchange theory holds no water. Not to mention the silly calculation how much harder one has to *play* for $50 million when thousands of kids play hard already in college, for free.

Another example: Goldman Sachs Group Inc., the world's biggest securities firm, awarded Chief Executive Officer Lloyd Blankfein a record $67.9 million year-end bonus in 2007, and he worked hard for every penny, I'm sure. Let's consider he labored 50 weeks in 2007, 6 days per week, and 12 hours each day. That translates to an hourly *wage* of $18,861--not even counting his basic $600,000 salary. If you are making 38 bucks an hour, you'd have to work 500 times harder to keep up with Mr. Blankfein. When every minute of yours is worth $314, you may think really hard what to do next.

Prosperity is no different than poverty. There is no demarcation zone between the two. Prosperity is a new age idea of the 1970s and '80s. It has no relevance for you or me in the 21st century. Look at individuals you consider rich. The closer you get, the more obvious it becomes--with exceptions, of course--that the ones we thought to be rich are poor people loaded with cash. Some of them are poor wretched idiots with tons of money. Jealous? Really? Do *you* want to be married to Tom Cruise?

In our more altruistic moments we hope to eliminate poverty in the world. I have zero respect for such endeavors because it's just another smoke machine. Getting rid of malaria: that can be done. Fight aids. Feed the hungry instead of contributing to their corrupt governments. Establish an environment permitting free enterprise to flourish. Very possible. Trying to defeat poverty, however, is like fighting a ghost. The *dividing line*, as far as developing countries there--or developing individuals here--are concerned, is not between poverty and prosperity. How determined are we to tackle issues that are obscured by the simplistic perspective of dollar amounts? As long as people argue about rich and poor, they don't give a damn about reality: they fight to remain in the dream world of good and evil.

How do I know they don't give a damn? Take a job from someone who hates it and outsource it to someone in a developing country. We don't even want to give these people something we hate. How much less excited would we be about supporting them with something we care for? What *do* we care for? Making a shit load of money without the IRS, our friends, and our hunchbacked in-laws ever getting a whiff of how rich we have become. Yeah sure, we don't like having poor people in the world. It's no fun hearing about North Koreans gnawing tree bark for lunch (even they get free lunch, see). We don't want them to be poor. But sure as hell we don't want them to get rich either.

The average hypocrite in his poor vs. rich thinking has the blurred idea that people in developing places shouldn't be as poor as they are. They should be as poor as he is. Well, almost as poor. Preferably a little poorer. We don't enjoy hearing about sweat shops and neither would we allow them to take our hated jobs. Ergo, they shouldn't be as bad off as sweat shop slaves but definitely our own hated jobs would be too good for them. There's got to be a balance. Don't we have something in stock they can hate a tad more than what we do?

For people in the developing areas of our world we need to find the balance of hatred. Hatred is where we feel home and so should they. God forbid these pooroids take off, make real money, and surpass us. Come to think of it, that is sort of what government employees are afraid you might do. Do you know what's worse than seeing a couple hundred million people getting malaria each year and almost three million of them dying (a type of genocide and infanticide that could be stopped relatively easily, except that the discussion of abortion / no abortion is so much more important, since we care about human life so much)? Seeing the same couple hundred million people in the Third World getting rich and turning into millionaires each year! Boy, you couldn't handle it, could you? It would drive your neighbors up the wall. Dead Africans are easier to live with than rich ones. The most we would ever allot them is jobs we hate more than ours.

For the artificially poor here in America, the truly poor are not as much a problem as the rich. And here we see *the line*; not between poor and rich or between less money and more money, but rather between dependency, employment, group thinking on one side and a free market, free enterprise, individualism on the other. Those who hate the rich--and the jobs they provide--find more satisfaction in the prospect of seeing the rich get poorer and restricted by laws, than seeing poor people getting rich and breaking free from dependency. That's why the entire poor-rich idea is a blatant lie, protecting the sheltered but hated life of an employee-oriented society. We talk about freedom a great deal, perhaps to hide the fact that freedom is our greatest fear--freedom and individualism.

Wealth can't be obtained by stashing money away for a single reason: money per se doesn't cause anything. Money won't magically turn one thing into another but it will do what you want it to do. Well, for the most part. All the cash in the world can't buy you the guy you want, or the girl--unless she's like Heather Mills and missing a leg, or like Tyna Marie Robertson, missing a brain. You can't buy wealth with money either. Ideals cannot be purchased. Dreams don't have price tags. Whatever it is you associate with wealth, money is of little help to get you there.

You can change your lifestyle to enjoy more of what you are after. No, I'm not talking about buying a bigger car. But if relaxation is part of your damned wealth idea, why don't you relax more often? Play a game of chess, dust off your yoga mat, or meditate the crap out of your navel. Relaxing is free, and hell, some people actually make plenty of money with it. Here we go, you can make a nice pile of dough by selling the idea of wealth to other suckers. But you can't make enough money to turn your illusion of being wealthy into reality.

Lack of money is just that: lack of money. It's not poverty. Needing an extra $800 by Friday because your rent is due is the same perceived lack as somebody else's desperation to get an additional $35 million by the end of the month to fulfill a contract. Both kinds of individuals exist and neither of them really lives in poverty. As old as you get and as loaded with moolah as you may become, you will be able to feel pressure. Your emotions will be triggered by stiffened circumstances perhaps, but they are yours. They are your emotions. Money or the lack thereof can't *produce* them.

Your ability to feel whatever the hell it is you feel all day has been part of you since the day you popped out of mom. That was years before you became aware of cash. And if you are honest, you will recall that the first times you experienced that type of panic--the kind you are now connecting with lack of money--were not related to money. What I just called panic may be something else for you: sadness, emptiness, anger, or the old fight-or-flight response. The emotion you connect with lack of money has been part of the spectrum of human experience for a couple of hundred thousand years. To say money, or too little of it, makes you feel this or that is ridiculous.

Money can't buy you out of uncomfortable feelings into comfortable ones. Sorry. Neither can absence of cash get you from comfy to miserable. You are generating your emotions and THEN, you are using your financial status quo to explain what you feel. Or you're using your messed-up relationship as explanation, the news, the weather, your job, or whatever crosses your mind next. Stress and other highly unpopular feelings are not caused by lack of money. We are used to connecting events and physical sensations with moods and feelings. I know, it's not the brightest thing we are capable of.

Lack of money does not cause hunger and starvation. Lack of food may cause hunger. In your and my neighborhood, however, hunger is not caused by lack of food; it's caused by boredom. And poverty is not caused by lack of money. The term 'poverty' expresses the helplessness we feel when we witness a person's dire situation. Poverty is vague, it's not true, and it allows us to escape from taking a hard and clear look at what we really see. Once something is called poverty, it cannot be dealt with anymore; it's been dragged from the factual into the nebulous.

The end of poverty cannot be induced by money nor by anything else. Just as poverty is nothing but an idea, so the end of poverty is nothing real. Each of us means something different when we speak of poverty. Poverty will never be ended. Symptoms and elements you connect with what you call poverty may very well be eliminated eventually, and I am all for it. Money won't be the *cause* of anything. A few hundred years ago, no one was thinking about money as the magic wand to solve personal or collective problems. Our ancestors were after gold.

The alchemists were serious about discovering processes to manufacture gold. Gold to get rich, to empower governments, to end poverty, in a word: to solve everybody's problems. Meanwhile, we have managed to replace our desire for gold with an urge to get our sweaty little paws on money. There are more people who have plenty of money today than there were individuals owning a few nice sacks of gold back then. Obviously, screaming for more of that stuff to fix the world hasn't slowed down our ability to live complicated and problematic lives. It is childish to expect that some beautiful day we will have accumulated coffers filled with gold or mountains of cash high enough to solve our problems.

Hating rich people while not wanting to be poor is a common phenomenon. Littered with inconsistencies but as common as the flu. People desire to be comfortable financially, and once there they'd rather bite their tongue than consider themselves rich. Otherwise, they'd have to give up their irrational hatred for the true rich. Insane! Who am I talking about? Not you, of course. Those of us who can't wait to slap the rich with higher taxes than we're willing to pay ourselves somehow have the weird wish to punish the rich for having so much money. The very people who hope and pray to win $300 million in the upcoming Powerball drawing are angry, A N G R Y as hell, at those who already have various assets adding up to $300 million.

The worst about others who bathe in hundreds of millions of dollars--as the dumber versions of Jane Doe believe in their silly visions--is that we don't have the same. They ought to apologize at least, shouldn't they? As much as we revere the hard way of earning money on a normal day, instinctively we know *real money* is never made the hard way. Have-nots don't believe the hard-work stories of the Haves, and to a small degree they are right.

Hard work didn't get the Haves to their status quo and hard work won't do it for you. But make no mistake: average Haves do work hard and average Have-nots don't want to work. Sounds like a riddle? It is. Many hard-working people who want to strike it rich some day, want to get there with ease and then retire. I admit, it's puzzling: if money isn't worth much for you unless you've worked hard for it, how can you expect to get it easily? And if you can get money easily, how come it's so crucial for the average Haves to work hard? Anyway, since they--the ones on the get-rich trip--haven't discovered the recipe, they're pissed off that they haven't and even more pissed off that others apparently have found it.

Of course there is no recipe, no how-to, and no system, and any quest for such nonsense will be futile. That's the wrong stuff that people are trying to understand so desperately. What I like about the rich vs. poor issue is the wacky behavior it exposes, the impossible mindsets: "How can I continue hating the rich while not staying so damned poor?" Another S/M type situation, isn't it? You cannot find an answer to that, ever, and most people don't want to because the pain is too enjoyable. Ask WTO demonstrators.

What can you do if you are indeed getting tired of the game? I thought you'd never ask. Apostasy! Switch camps. Defect from the sacred cause of being so zealously poor. Join the camp of the ones you thought were rich, and the idea of poor will disappear. Edward Kennedy won't give up and he'll be the only lonely poor man left, but you can do it this minute. Poverty exists because it's been fought for religiously and violently. No, this is not a matter of affirmations. It's not about you plastering *I'm rich*! post-it notes over your fridge, bathroom mirror, and the dog house. Hogwash! Big question is, are you willing to think and speak for individuals who have money and for their--your--interests? Will you make life easier for the Haves--politically, socially, and personally? For starters, do you have the spine to defend tax cuts in conversations with friends, family, and colleagues? Tax cuts beneficially affecting the wealthy, that is?

Corporations are evil? Really? I am amazed to see the same individuals, who are addicted to benefits and false job security, hating the corporation that provides those goodies. How is it possible to despise the very source of everything an employee is seeking? You don't get the same level of benefits and security, or career opportunities, from mom and pop operations. Corporations are considered evil when they don't provide as many job offers as they *should*, and they are even more evil when they do and you *have to* work for them. Crazy.

Corporations are what they are but truly devious are the employed and the unemployed, hating corporations for literally every step they take. You hate them when they don't hire you and you hate them when they do. You hate them for the benefit bait they sucked you in with and you hate them when the benefit package doesn't live up to your expectations. Apropos benefits: that stuff is only a benefit when your life is in the crapper and you have to see a doctor. For the normal person, so-called benefits are suckerware, and the individual selling his life for the benefits has to be bonkers on some level.

Poor and rich--we can't solve that problem if we continue sitting on opposite sides of the table. As long as we recognize *the other*, we are the cause of the problem we are trying to solve. Dividing societies is the root of the problem. Rich and poor, developing and developed countries--we are causing the divide we then can't overcome. Abandon the idea of poor vs. rich in your society. Drop the distinction between developed nations opposed to developing ones. What arrogance! We are proud of mass job slavery and we call ourselves developed? Most people in developed countries hate what they do, and that's why we want the developing parts of the world to adapt to our ways? An advanced idea, indeed.

It behooves us to tear down the walls between developing and developed, between poor and rich. Once the fence is gone, *the other side* will be gone also and we can no longer define ourselves and others with labels we didn't like in the first place. From there, who knows what we can accomplish?!

Poor people get poorer and the rich get richer because the bible said so, "I say unto you, that unto every one that hath shall be given; but from him that hath not, even that which he hath shall be taken away from him." (Luke 19:26) Hooey. Of course that is not the reason. It's actually not true that the rich get richer. I know of a bunch who got poorer over time, and the history of business is littered with unfortunate people who lost every penny they had made or who couldn't increase their assets no matter how hard they tried. William C. 'Billy' Durant, for instance, founder of General Motors, was wealthy twice but lived the last years of his life on a puny pension, managing a bowling alley in Flint, Michigan.

The poor don't get poorer either. The saying that the poor get poorer is part of the rich-poor contrivance, part of a self-fulfilling prophecy invented to keep the cross hairs trained on the enemy: the evil rich. This tripe--the poor get poorer and the rich get richer--doesn't really hurt those who have more than you do, but it pulls the rug from underneath YOU. It's as immature as a four-year-old blaming his pain on the parents: "It's my mom's fault my hands are freezing; why doesn't she find the gloves I lost?" The childish media love you as long as you are in pain--pain sells copy, you know--and they will gladly help you to pour gasoline into the flames of hatred against every damn thing you so fervently desire for yourself: a free market, money, freedom.

Alternatives to poverty vs. prosperity thinking? Easy: just don't judge individuals--yourself included--by the money they have, or even better, by your perception of what they may or may not have. Money is a crude and cruel tool with which to judge and to individualize human beings. However you attempt to categorize people with a rich-poor view-point, I'm afraid you will be wrong. You will hurt other individuals and you will get hurt in the process. Measure others, compare yourself to them, and you are limiting your financial future. No doubt, it is one sure-fire way to butcher your happiness. Instead of seeing black people and white people as in decades past, now we are able to just see people. Well, instead of seeing rich people and poor people, maybe you can manage to see just people ... eventually. When you do, you will win. If you don't want to, go to hell. Oh, I forgot; you're probably there already.

Unhappiness is often the result of poverty-prosperity

thinking. What began so promising in the 1970s as a positive thing has deteriorated to misery. Prosperity thinking was never really positive. Constantly proclaiming, "You can have it all, baby," can be a burden and negative in itself. Having-it-all in the mind turned out to be stressful and immensely boring after a while. Being rich wasn't easy and besides, it didn't work as anticipated. What happened? The pitiable prosperity-evoking crowd got kicked in the nuts by their own confusion. Confusion is the obvious aftermath of judging *the rich* as not being rich the right way--our way, naturally--feeling compassion for *the poor*, seeing ourselves as poor but not THAT poor, and finally trying to get rich enough, but not as rich as the real rich. We were aiming to be less poor and more rich without ever belonging distinctly to either group, because that would have made us subject to our own merciless judgment. Eventually, we ran out of breath and out of post-it notes before we saw any cash.

We don't do prosperity anymore. Still, we haven't dropped the mind-numbing discussion nor the witch hunt to see the rich burning at the stake. A liberal trance dance. Dancing on egg shells will prevent the best of us from making decent piles of money, and it will drive the most capable mind to insanity. It's not money nor the lack thereof that makes or keeps you from happiness. Both poverty and prosperity, the dividing line between, the bridge that should bring them together--will always be undefined and confusing, source of fights and frustration, and entirely hypothetical. Not even gods and money can help you if you choose to continue persecuting *the rich* and commiserating with *the poor*. You will be unhappy. I promise.

Chapter Five
Fairness and Freedom

"The middle of the road is where the white line is, and that's the worst place to drive."

Robert Frost

Freedom has not been too desirable an objective for most of us. Sure, we have talked about it for centuries, if not for millennia. Yet even in developed countries freedom is a strange animal. Exhibit A: the majority of people spending the majority of their lives hating what they do. We can smell freedom in the air, at times we think we are close, but the real thing scares the bejeezus out of individuals and their governments alike. Freedom is perhaps the most threatening enemy we have to face. And you thought fighting terrorism is difficult and expensive. Freedom can't be financed collectively: you've got to do it on your own. That could be the reason we believe the expression of true freedom requires oodles of money. "I can't do what I want because I don't have enough money." Rubbish. Freedom means there are no strings attached. If you had the balls to claim freedom for yourself, you could do what you want to do today. Naturally, that would have consequences. Circumstances are not stopping you. You are. Wait a moment. Freedom as the enemy?

Fairness is often seen as the conscientious brother of freedom. Fairness is the stuffy step-brother. You can't do what you want because it's not fair to your fellow 'free' citizens? True, fairness does have its merits in the sandlot. Certain situations can more easily be explained to a five-year old using the concept of fairness. In the adult world fairness has no place. Oh, now you think I have no morals? You are right but I did not invent reality and its rules like, *Life is not fair*. Here's another fact not likely to come out of the lips of school teachers and politicians: *Fairness and freedom exclude each other.* Figure it out for yourself.

Listen up: No, I did not say you shouldn't hesitate hurting other people while expressing your questionable perspective of freedom. DO NOT HURT OTHER INDIVIDUALS ... or dogs, or fighting gerbils, etc.! Jesus! It's pretty sad that I feel compelled to say that but if I didn't, some half-wit somewhere would love to accuse me of instigating mayhem. Hurting people is simply not what 99% of individuals have in mind when they think of freedom and what they truly desire to do with their lives. And for the 1% of asses who can and would hurt others for the sake of personal gain: it's illegal, and I like it that way. Besides, hurting another person is not necessary for you to act freely.

On the contrary: if your freedom damages or limits someone else's freedom, your *freedom* will be extremely temporary and it is subject to powerful limitations. Your personal freedom can expand only when it's contagious, when others are free to either hate you or to feel inspired to do what they wish to do. Freedom will always be controversial and it'll heat up little minds way too much to be considered peaceful. Peaceful freedom is an oxymoron. Anyway, it may pain you but fairness, like lack of money, is a lame excuse holding people back from being free.

Freedom is not without rules. Any game worth playing gains spice with rules. I'm afraid you'll have to deal with gravity for a long time to come. Laws of physics, the legal landscape of the country you live in, and a sense of good taste can propel you to explore your freedom. So what's so scary about freedom? Lack of structure! We have not much to hold onto. Our admiration for philosophers, for instance, can't hide our fear to end up like Friedrich Nietzsche or Socrates. We prefer to end up dull and boring. We don't want to offend and upset anybody, least of all our own stomachs. For some strange reason, however, we don't shy away from boring ourselves to death. We mistake unusual paint jobs on cars and tattoos in weird places for individualism. In a sense, that describes the dimensions of the freedom we're willing to handle. You think that's funny? The tattoo and piercing culture is proof of how scared we are to live free. Too fearful and immature to make it past the idea of futile rebellion. In 1918, fearful and immature rebels murdered the Czar and his family. Today, they run bloody attacks against their own skin. I call that evolution because nobody else gets hurt.

I am making it all up, you say, and freedom is what everybody wants? Then, please explain to me why groups, unions, and wannabe individuals instruct their political representatives to negotiate shady rules of fairness to curb free markets and free trade? Since I may not hear your answer soon, I'll tell you why. Remember the rich/poor issue? We like for the evil rich sons of bitches to pay higher tax percentages and we want them to choke on their success because we would hate to become one of them. The artificially and politically poor are fighting for their privilege to hate. Same here: count the individuals you know who would trust free markets and free trade. In the freest country on Earth, more people are afraid of freedom than of terrorism. Ask Alan Greenspan. Hostility against truly free markets equals pathological affection for crooked fairness. Those who demand fairness DO NOT care for freedom, not for themselves nor for anybody else.

Job environments are far from becoming institutions fostering fairness--or freedom for that matter. Deceptive terms like teamwork or performance related salary are meant to evoke the spirit of fairness, but you are painfully aware that there is no such thing at work. Certainly, there is no freedom either in the average company. The typical work environment has nothing to do with real life. Your possible interest in fairness or freedom are ignored intentionally. No wiggle room for that type of luxury. Team members are anxious to advance after the team work is completed and, if backstabbing helps, preferably sooner than later. There are more I's in a team than team members. You will never know how many selves and personalities your fellow slaves drag along, and ever so subtly yours and theirs are all at each other's throats. As long as you care for your career or one of your esteemed colleagues cares for hers, fairness is a sweet yet empty cliché.

Gratefully I am embracing the fact that I'll never be treated fairly. Nothing better could happen to me. Absence of fairness allows us to live life as we please. Once in awhile someone won't like it. So what! Do you believe two children, siblings of the same parents, are treated fairly? No way! Treat them equally, or give it a try, and within five minutes at least one of them will complain that you are unfair. Treat your brats as you think they should be treated according to their age and their level of development, and they will scream, UNFAIR. Children are individuals and they must be treated individually. As you know yourself they will always think you are unfair, no matter what you do. Surprise: so will you. You, too, will always think life is unfair. It's up to you to call that either bad or good. As long as you believe it's bad, you will be inhibited in your actions. If you make it through to the perspective that fairness is a myth and that neither you nor anybody else can expect to see much of it, you are free at last to live as you damned well please.

Insecurity calls for structure. Unsure of what to do and where to go, a concept of fairness comes in handy. It seems to be a practical tool when we feel in need of something to hold on to. Yet it proves to be useless because fairness is hard to come by. No fairness in sports: how often have you seen that a referee's final decision was not motivated by fairness? Are the Olympic games fair? And good luck with your relationships if fairness is important to you. Fairness doesn't make it easier for us to master our lives. On the contrary, it leads to greater instability. If you really care for peace--anywhere at any time--the cry for fairness is counter-productive. You can't have both. Values such as fairness are ill-chosen as the dominant structures to live one's life by. What's so bad about reality, facts, the things that are happening in the world around you? Seeing the world 'as is' instead of yammering how things should be provides a firm foundation for any person to act and respond with sufficient relevance.

Fairness anywhere? Anybody? Rules are a nice compensation for lack of fairness and then again, it depends on who interprets and enforces the rules. What perspective will the rule enforcing person or party have? Will they be willing to bend the rules a little here but not so much there? Is this a game of chance? "Not the way I play it," said W.C. Fields. Each one of us has ideas and ideals of how *fair* looks. We apply our fairness template and it works smoothly at times. We can even recognize our home-grown patterns of fairness in plenty of circumstances. Until we hit a brick wall; sooner or later people will disagree with you. Your concept of fairness is not congruent with theirs. At least one of us is wrong and maybe both of us. Belief in fairness is nice as long as it lasts, but it's not real. If we could agree on what's fair and what is not, we wouldn't need law professors or the Supreme Court. We can't agree on fairness and the justices of the Supreme Court won't, because there is no such animal. If there was, it would have five feet--believe me.

A belief in something seems to be needed by those who are not happy with their lives. It's easy enough to see the desk in front of you and to feel the chair under your buttocks. Feeling air flowing through your sinuses, noticing how it fills your lungs, and the sensation of exhaling is not enough for most of us. It's a bit too down-to-earth. To feel safe, we crave something that is not there. Only beliefs give us solidity we can hold onto.

How silly! Direction is supposed to come from the outside. Really? If you follow belief systems, you are afraid of your own freedom to determine the direction you want to take in life. Beliefs don't help us with our insecurities. Our beliefs are manifestations of the very insecurity we desire to leave behind. We use beliefs as a form of escapism, to raise ourselves above the rat race and its mundane problems. Yet beliefs race far ahead of reality--faster than any rat race--causing unsurmountable problems that dwarf the worst possible dispute with the tax man. Believing in *things* that are not verifiable is the ultimate rat race to me, exhausting, and no better addiction than any other. How unfortunate. We mean to expand life and freedom with our beliefs, yet our world and the range of our actions are limited by our own remedies. Beliefs control the fences.

Employees want fairness as a confirmation of their

security, however fake and hollow that may be. Jobs are income sources for insecure individuals to begin with. And fairness, or the delusion thereof, is the second helping of something that poses as a solid structure. The typical employee wants someone else to bestow order on her world. Tell me what to do. Tell me how. Tell me when. Tell me how much I'll get paid. Tell me what the consequences will be if I don't meet your expectations. A sense of fairness is the last straw of your baseless belief that you count. And then we feign surprise that jobs are subject to hatred. Guess what, your job hates you too.

Self-employment is not freedom by definition. You and I, we both know self-employed folks who are slaves of their own businesses, and from the outside they don't look much better off than the average employee. Even though the self-employed person may not find freedom at first, at least he is willing to try. Trial and error are crucial to unearth your freedom. Look for error. Embrace error.

Total freedom translates not so much into a life of ease and success; rather, freedom leads to a life of error and failure. The truth will set you free? I doubt it. Error, failure, and mistakes will get you on the road. As long as you are willing to fail again, you're as close to freedom as you will ever be. Freedom of the self-employed takes shape in the freedom to make mistakes and to fail. Success emerges from that freedom, from a small percentage of those failures. By the way, if you are a victim of your own self-employment, you owe it to yourself to stick your ugly nose between the covers of Michael Gerber's *The E-Myth Revisited*.

Reality is what exactly? Two witnesses of an accident file two different police reports. Each of these two people are likely to differ from their own position an hour later and definitely the next day. In short, we don't have a clue what really happened and we aren't sure of what we saw. Similarly, fairness is a different animal for two individuals. Next week you will think differently about fairness than you do today. Fairness is more or less an illusion and, since we're at it, so is freedom. Both are meaningless. It doesn't matter what you think freedom or fairness may be today or a year from now. They're ghosts you are evoking from time to time, and they matter as much as blowing leaves. Question is, what do you do? How do you express what you call freedom this minute? I don't care how you express it and what you call it, but *you* might.

Randomly, our judiciary system is unjust. Not only is our world not fair, it is anything but just. I recommend giving up the notion of a just world. We will never get there. Not here in America and certainly not in any other country. Have I mentioned life is messy? It is. There won't be any justice for your causes--noble or otherwise--except sometimes. Yes, it is childish to hold on to the belief that justice will be served, sooner or later. It may happen and then again, it may not. Randomly, good things happen and again randomly, something happens that you really love. So what?

Wild ideas of good and evil have been ingrained in us as if there was such a thing. What is good? We don't know. Preachers bless weapons one day and condemn war the next. The same people are against abortion *and* for the death penalty. Thou shalt not kill? Yeah, but ... It all depends. Religious leaders aren't any more clear about their intentionally foggy messages of good and evil than the rest of us. As Billy Shakespeare pointed out, nothing is intrinsically good or evil. Your thinking makes it what you want it to be. From moment to moment we decide whatever best serves our interests. Our values are so blurred and even interchangeable that we may switch from one side to its opposite. What's good today may be bad tomorrow and vice versa.

We keep parallel worlds and realities going? You bet we do. If you dare you can see both at the same time. Hey, I too would have advocated Hitler's and Stalin's assassination. Would I have done it? Don't ask me questions I don't want to answer! Realistically, we have more than two versions of good and evil theories operating in our minds, simultaneously. It's silly to think there is good and evil, a moral anvil objectively separating the two throughout the time of man. No, even a hot issue like this one we make up as we go. We all do and we always have.

Choice is on your side. There is nothing you can do about the fact that life is messy. Temporarily, and sometimes for excruciatingly extended stretches, your life will be on the fritz. Normally we hate when that happens because we have been groomed by our dear parents and by the rest of our dysfunctional families that life should be in order, peaceful, and neat.

Life can be EVERYTHING. Duh. We'll be happier the more willing we are to respond to every possible experience with a warm welcome. I must be nuts? You are correct, I am. Anyway, expecting order and perfect circumstances will have you hating your life more often than you care for. When messy is nothing out of the ordinary, it may turn out so much more adventurous and enjoyable. How do you get there? By choice. This may be the only time multiple choice is not a stupid idea.

Fairness is never in your favor, especially not when you think it is. All isn't well. Ever. Instances of accidental fairness can be measured in split seconds. Great perhaps, but if you dwell on it for too long you are missing out on the next round. Your celebration of a victory of fairness is actually the perfect moment for you to get screwed over. Self-righteous people are so unassuming. Fairness works against your interest most of the time, even when it appears to be working for you. Those moments nourish the illusion that all is well. You may want to stick that note on your bathroom mirror, instead of cluttering it up with positive affirmations on pink paper about how pretty your world is in your cute and girly imagination. Since you can't have both, which one of the two is more attractive to you: freedom or fairness?

Expectations are the death of happiness. Expecting fairness in your immediate work environment is a setup for misery. Expecting justice in society will do the same. It's not going to happen, not any time soon. What's more important to you? Trying to control your world or your happiness? The world is not that interested in your respectable input and nobody cares whether you are miserable or happy. You cannot control the world. Too many people and all kinds of factors *put it together* day by day. The best and easiest thing you can do, really, is to be happy. It hardly requires any effort. Don't expect your environment and the individuals around you to be different than they are, and you are already there--happy. Where there is no fairness, there is room for happiness. Yours.

Tolerance gets the booby prize. Don't tolerate other people. It's a shameless insult! Do you want to be tolerated? I don't think so. That stuff will destroy any individual's dignity. 'I can barely keep myself from getting rid of you, but I'll manage-- for the sake of tolerance.' You are teaching your children how to properly perform that trick? Good luck. Tolerance is latent hostility, ready to erupt at any given time. Tolerance comes with grinding teeth and an expiration date. We tolerate an itching nose only while our beloved dentist has both hands and pointy instruments down our throats.

Of course we tolerate dentists also, temporarily. We may tolerate an alcoholic spouse for quite some time. We tolerate a horsefly on the wall during an important business conversation. We can tolerate a lot of bull ... until a certain point is reached when brisk action is required. It may be new to you but human beings HATE to be subjected to tolerance. Calls for tolerance stem from the strange idea that most people are like us, at least they *should* be like us, and if they aren't the differing minority needs to be tolerated for their own safety. What arrogance!

You are always the minority because nobody is like you. I am happy because I didn't get eaten alive today. Nobody is like me, and there's reason enough for people not to like me. So what? I don't ask for the tolerance of others, and I don't tolerate anybody. Thankful that no one bores me by being just like me, I enjoy people's individuality. I am glad they are different and delighted that they're disagreeing with me. If you are having problems letting other people be different, you will soon run into serious difficulty in allowing yourself to be uninhibitedly you. Tolerance appears to be the fair way to castrate freedom responsibly. Yeah. No. Thanks!

Messed up work conditions can't be tolerated either. If

you've had enough of it, you've got to take action. No, don't go postal! That's what the tolerant people do eventually. Change your current job or change jobs within your company, if that's what you want. Go elsewhere. Or if you're truly after enlightenment, decide to hate your job with more passion than you have ever invested in anything, and you will discover there is no end to it--to your hatred, to your love of your hatred, and to your freedom to explore such a crazy phenomenon. Tolerance is socially accepted mediocrity. It can't be good for the simple reason that it's politically correct. Hating your job with all the love you can muster will be an experience of unlimited and unadulterated freedom.

In case I haven't warned you before: do not do as I say. Beware of my advice!

Chapter Six
Strength and Weakness

"If you hear a little voice within you saying 'I am not a painter,' then, by all means, paint ... and that little voice will be silenced."

Vincent van Gogh

Matisse followed his strengths and studied law in Paris. When he was 21--during a period of convalescence, recovering from appendicitis--his mother gave him a box of pencils and Henri Matisse discovered *a kind of paradise*. Before paradise, law was his strength. After finding paradise in mom's pencil box, Matisse discovered Matisse.

You have a chance to discover yourself. Your strengths may or may not be what makes you so authentically you. Strengths are good for school teachers and employers. Perhaps your strengths can pay for the roof over your head and provide for your family, but that's it. Screw your strengths and find your kind of paradise!

Nazis didn't like weakness: "What doesn't kill you, makes you stronger." The weak, whatever that meant for these freaks, were radically euthanized. Companies don't like your weaknesses either. If you fall into the interviewer's trap and you reveal too much weakness, they're likely to euthanize you on the spot also, letting you go painlessly before you smuggle your contagious disease into the inner sanctum.

People despise their own weaknesses, try to overcome them, eliminate them, cover them up, or limit them to a life in the closet. As far as weakness goes, most individuals treat themselves like Nazis treated the handicapped; with murder in their hearts. If freedom is what you are after you've got to let your weaknesses breathe and live, in the face of the strength Nazis. Amidst your weaknesses you may find Matisse's kind of paradise, while your imposing strengths may prove to be debilitating limitations.

Weakness does not require effort. You are engaged in it whether you like it or not. Weakness is so much you. Hell, we are all addicts of one kind or another and usually we trade one addiction for the next. People quit smoking and then they chew gum, or they take to eating as if the next famine started Tuesday at noon. There is something everyone of us is nuts about. You may want to tone down your greatest weakness a bit so that it doesn't kill you, but each weakness comes with a tremendous profit potential. You are not the only dissident, you know, and serious money can be made by catering to those who cultivate the same weakness AND to those who want to get rid of it. Cash is spent on both sides of that fence. There is hardly anything as exciting in life as your weaknesses. Treasure them!

Strength is not worth much once you have begun hating your job, just as your weaknesses aren't really helpful when you neglect and despise that part of yourself. Value does not automatically result from strengths, and weakness is not worthless by definition. Your hatred destroys the potential value they both can develop for you and for the market. Hence your finest strength is useless, perhaps producing mediocre or even poor results if you are not happy in your work environment. Strengths need supportive environments not only to remain strong, but to unfold and expand without limitations. Strength *in a cage* deteriorates.

Retirement is a pleasant alternative to cardiac arrest, the other method to escape a lifestyle you desperately want to leave behind. When your life sucks you consider ending it. If you shy away from blowing your brains out tonight, you just start thinking ahead a couple of years or decades and daydream of what exciting things you will do once you are retired and senile. Nice! You tell me - what else is a retirement plan besides time-released suicide? It's a weakness? Good answer! That's why financial advisers multiply like rabbits, helping with your retirement planning. Alas, so many of us die shortly after retiring and reaping the benefits of your hard labor was a pipe dream. If you know now what you would do then--after your retirement--you may want to ponder ways to do exactly that, but NOW, in the nearest of futures.

Manipulation is one of our favorite pastimes. Since we are so good at it no one is easily manipulated, and for the most part we manipulate ourselves. Stuck with strength, we're trying to intimidate and dominate our human environment with whatever we think is so amazing about ourselves. Keeping weakness in the closet--or so we believe--we hide our ugly step-children from society the best we can. Naturally, the results aren't as desired. Our friends know our weak spots long before we want them to notice. Silly hide-and-seek games become utterly annoying at best and tasteless charades at worst. Nobody who knows us takes our strength seriously. Your wife isn't that impressed by it, is she? Rigid and incorrigible, our best sides have become the laughing stock for all who know us closely. Tell me, what is so strong about strength?

Dividing yourself into weak and strong parts is painful in itself. Being reminded to do so on a demanding job intensifies the negative experience. Of course you hate that. Pretending can be fun as a game, but being required to pretend to be strong is stressful and a major turn-off. Especially when you are not feeling the strength you're supposed to display. Let's face it, if you really were that strong, you wouldn't be working on that job. You would have decided to turn your real strengths into real money in your own name. Since you haven't, seeing your strength--true or pretend--being discounted in the service of the douche bag you're working for ought to piss you off.

Strength may or may not be a way for you to gain influence. Personally I doubt the average human being is lusting after power, as we are accusing each other of. Those of us who need power to prove to ourselves who knows what, definitely show more weakness than power. You NEED something? That *something* instantly has power over you, even before you acquire it. It illuminates one of your vulnerable weak spots.

Weakness is our true power. The newborn who screams

the house down at 3:24 am has power over every single household member. The poor and weak beggar on the sidewalk wields tremendous power over almost everybody who steps aside to pass him. He controls the emotions--from feelings of guilt to arrogance, from pity to compassion--of those who see him. It's hardly a good idea to underestimate the power of weakness or to overestimate your silly strengths.

Responsibility has the modus operandi built into it to experience a real form of strength. I am not talking guilt, I mean responsibility. When you overdose on responsibility, like a bunch of aging new-agers, and you believe "Everybody is 100% responsible for everything that happens to them," you have gone off the deep end. However, assuming 100% responsibility for your response to the things happening to you pulls you out of the morass of mediocrity. Responsibility is less a weight on your shoulders than a chance to try a new approach. We all experience crap in our lives that we neither invited nor agreed to. Responsibility can't prevent that shit from happening, but it prevents us from getting comfortable in the role of victims. In that sense, responsibility is a new doorway to freedom. Not an obligation but an engine driving us to new discovery.

Weakness is a great thing. Smoking two packs of cigarettes a day for twenty years straight is proof of formidable willpower. Don't you think? We blast ourselves for not mustering enough willpower but we neglect to acknowledge our use of it in areas we are not so proud of. Trust me, you've got willpower and lots of it. I have never met a person without it. Trust your weaknesses and how you have handled them. Poorly, you say? Don't be too sure. Every addiction that costs you horrendous amounts of money is a potential money maker, possibly a money machine on autopilot. In fact, your weakness is generating mountains of cash for other people as you are reading this. Yes, your strengths are nice to have, but your weaknesses-- the worse, the better--demand your true respect and full attention. They are cash cows and it depends solely on you to milk them.

Freedom to be uninhibitedly yourself requires recognition

and more than forced acceptance of your so-called weaknesses. I have observed a romance some individuals have with *the weakest link* in organizations and elsewhere. They want to get rid of it. Living your life in awe of strength and in disgust of weakness elevates you to a member of honor in an illustrious group of people: you are the newest fascist dictator over your faculties! Since it's all yours, you can have your way with it. Right? Forget what part of you is weak or strong. Both, and everything in between, are sides of you and it won't be easy or painless to eliminate any of them.

As I think it is utter nonsense to distinguish left-brain and right-brain functions, male and female sides, it is not helpful to point out your weak and strong departments. Who cares? Demonizing and splitting off your favorite weakness--good luck with that!--practically ends your dreams of life in freedom. Without your weakness, your freedom is dead.

Strengths are addictive, like other potent substances. That alone predestines your strengths to be in line to turn into strong weaknesses. The doomed myth of strengths has been invented to keep you in slavery to nasty jobs. Who needs that stuff? You? Instead, ask yourself what do you want to do. Perhaps you're not too bad at things you really want to pursue and maybe, as was the case for Henri Matisse, you have never tried it before. *What do you want to do?* inspires one to experience practical freedom and responsibility for action. Of course the outcome is uncertain, but you are in control of a new start--again and again. There is no future without *What do you want to do?* Just silent suffering and retirement ... eventually.

Structure is what people hope to get for their lives from strong beliefs. We like something to hold on to. Freedom is too scary. Patterns, beliefs, and habits seem to provide a minimum of safety. Strong beliefs are designed to make life more predictable, but does it work? Beliefs limit our actions and certainly limit the way we think. In other words, the believer becomes more predictable. Not her life. Life and all the things that can happen to you will never be controlled. Neither will you be able to predict it. Beliefs limit the variety of possible moves, our freedom to act and react in the real world. The more rigid the structure of your belief, the weaker it will be. The safer your structured thinking appears to be, the narrower is what you call freedom. Nothing against clear principles by which you choose to live your life. On the contrary. But believing in something deprives you of a hefty chunk of power over that area. If you don't enjoy weakness, reconsider your strongest beliefs.

How can you make money with your weaknesses? Take an eye-opening look at collectors and sports fans. Golfers, cigar aficionados, baseball fans can teach you about lucrative addictions. Collectors go insane over dolls, coins, kimonos, vintage weaponry, pottery, books, antiques, pocket watches, stamps, teddy bears, records, corkscrews, depression glass, art nouveau, porcelain, netsuke, shabby chic, and thousands of other things. The list is literally endless and brand new weaknesses are invented every day. Can you faintly smell the potential? Hey, even money itself is a wonderful weakness to have and you could cater to those who collect it.

Amazon's and Ebay's multi-billion dollar businesses are not the only possible options to profit from the strong tie between money and people's soft spots. Hell, don't tell me the cellphone and wireless industry is based on our *needs*. We go gaga about iPhones. That's why they're made. Two billion dollars in ring tone sales per year? You care to peddle basic needs, like diapers and toothpaste, or juicy weaknesses, baby? I thought so.

Truck loads of cash change hands in relation to our addictions. We are willing to pay higher profit margins for products we don't need than for soap and toilet paper. The existence of The Apple Store has more to do with religion than with need. Ever been inside one? The Church of Mac elevates its congregation's addiction to the level of something sacred. And boy, it works: nobody compares prices or looks for cheaper alternatives. No, the faithful are proud of the money they contribute and donate.

The question is, how do you intend to jump into the

stream of weakness to participate? First you need to learn a lot? Rubbish! You have a weakness you have been practicing for years, you are a professional. That alone makes you proficient enough to present yourself as an authority in your field.

Strength cannot guarantee greatness. Maybe you are good at something and it bores you to tears to do that something all day, everyday. Need motivation to continue doing what you are so good at? Of course you do. It's a big problem and the upcoming mortgage payment may not be motivating enough. Lack of motivation will cost you consistency and the true potential of your great trait is out the window. Now, your weaknesses won't guarantee greatness either, but you don't need extrinsic motivation or your wife's kick in the pants to perform. Weakness has incredible motivators built into it. More than you need, in fact. You may look like an idiot or maybe some people can see the genius in your obsession, but the possibility and the probability for you to succeed with your weak sides is greater than hobbling about on sporadically impressive strengths.

Chapter Seven
Individual and Independent

"It's easy to be independent when you've got money. But to be independent when you haven't got a thing--that's the Lord's test."

Mahalia Jackson

Freedom cannot depend on income. The more money you have, the more free you'll be? Pathetic kind of freedom. Freedom can't depend on anything, by definition. Not even on money. Your freedom exists practically today, this minute. It can't be worth much, goodness, there is zero value in freedom you will buy in the future with money you will have to make first. Freedom in the future? That's as exciting as free beer tomorrow. It's now or never. Delaying freedom to *a time when ...* is an expression of fear. That doesn't mean you aren't free. It means you can't handle your freedom. And if you can't manage the freedom you possess today, you won't be able to handle freedom in the future. How much money you will make in the future won't have any influence on your freedom or on your willingness to be bold.

Independence means exactly that: independence. If you need to finance your independence you are quite dependent. Get your finances in order and you'll be financially independent? Cute, but no, most people's definition of financial independence is a description of dependency. Financial independence is a bloody lie! As a matter of fact, there is no such thing as financial independence. Better yet, your independence can be had today. Independence depends on nothing, not even on your financial situation. Oh, I am wrong and it does indeed depend on finances? Then again, even if you have the funds you deem necessary to guarantee your independence, it would depend on millions of factors you have no control over whatsoever. A bit of a stretch to call that independence, don't you think?

If you want to be independent, hell, be independent! Customize your life. Custom cars are popular but as far as jobs are concerned, people settle for mediocrity too easily and worse: we allow others to customize us for the job we are supposed to *fill*. We are willing to work throughout our entire lives on some thing we despise working on as long as we can have custom wheels on our cars? Good God! How amazingly stupid are we, really? The most atrocious crimes we commit against ourselves appear to be so normal. It's common that we are the most vicious threat to ourselves. No one else treats us as poorly as we do. Still, to murder yourself on a despicable job? That's absolutely phenomenal. Refusing to customize an enjoyable life, we become experts at customizing life-long suicide. By the time you retire you are already a vegetable, at least the parts of you that count.

Politicians promising more jobs promise more pain and less individuality. That's why we love them, or at least we hate them with more love and understanding. The permanent job promise on a politician's To-Do list turns into a reminder eventually that voters demand the loudest what they want the least. Thy will be done, baby! Nothing is easier to deliver than that, even for the most incompetent government drone. You shall have more of what you don't want in the future, near or distant.

What good can come from the sheer quantity of more jobs? Freedom and individuality are both threatened by such a promise. Independence through slavery? Yeah, I would hate myself too if I fell for that. More jobs mean additional opportunities for self-loathing. Do you really believe the more people hate themselves and what they do, the more productive a society will be?

Retirement is the opposite of independence. You don't enjoy your job very much? Since jobs occupy most waking hours of our day, it's relatively safe to say that people who look forward to retirement don't just despise their jobs; they hate their lives. And if you hate your life, it is no surprise that you are dreaming of and planning for your retirement to gain independence.

Independence, however, is NOT the engine driving you towards that goal, unfortunately. Your hatred is. Loathing what you currently do gives you the idea of retirement. Not only that, add a decent portion of self-loathing. You may despise your job but you hate yourself even more for being so corrupt that you can't let go of your job because you'd lose all the benefits you have accumulated with your impressive seniority.

You gave permission to be bought into corruption and out of the independence you once possessed. True independence lies in your past and naturally, you want it back. Now you're thinking about the conditions you may be able to purchase independence with, called a retirement plan. It's a hostage type situation and you suffer through it as the abductee. Alas, the decades of futile negotiations to agree on a ransom have been such a drag because you are not the victim: you are the hardass abductor.

Retirement may look like a golden doorway, like a departure from the throes of your daily grind, but it's burdened with too many *ifs* and *whens*. You can hardly call that independence. Most people's retirement doesn't look like their golden age at all, and why would it? If you insist on calling it freedom, then freedom is flawed and fraught with more conditions and limitations than the disclaimer of your homeowners insurance.

Retirement as an equivalent of independence is a fraud. No wonder you hate corrupt people so much. You are one of them, if questionable benefits entice you to aim for retirement instead of establishing and living your independence today. Nah, don't quit your job! Keep it! You deserve each other, and the inner turmoil that comes with it keeps you on your toes. But if it's independence you desire, you better quit waiting for retirement. Do what you want and more of it, every damned day. If you can't, shut up and grind your teeth some more. Perhaps retirement is the only thing that will save you from yourself.

Self-help is anything but helpful as far as individuality and independence are concerned. Improvement sounds like a nice idea, but if someone has to tell you what to improve and how, it takes away from your freedom to unfold your capacity as you please, doesn't it? The self-improvement industry is a religion, to a degree derived from the new age movement and in no way more efficient. I don't expect to see hard evidence of improvement anytime soon. Neither have I met large numbers of improved selves. Selves don't improve per se, but you are free to use different ones as you see fit. The supply is endless. You are independent from limited or inappropriate selves, and free to engage the selves of yours that are better suited for the tasks at hand.

Independence is what you can work with today. You can't have more of it or less. Self-improvement for the sake of gaining independence is a joke, it limits that very independence.

Snake oil is as old as the world and we still love that stuff. Miracle cures are always en vogue for health and wealth issues. Hope is raging. People go blind on it as they used to on bootleg booze. Give me the quick fix whether it helps or not. Individuals appear to love snake oil more than individual solutions for individual situations. Sell me a system that comes with an iron-clad guarantee, a no-brainer that solves my problems. I've got the rims, I haven't got the brains. So tell me what to do. The idiocy of hope is mind numbing. Age and experience--I almost said wisdom--don't matter, we continue to fall prey to things so abstruse, they can't possibly work. But, what if it works for me? Well, if you're so damn special that it works for you only, it wasn't a system. A true system works for everybody alike. Except the ones you desire to unearth for your monetary gain have never turned up an additional dime for anybody.

Holy water from Lourdes, crystals blue and white, the system that beats the thoroughbred races, fills your mailbox with checks, picks the next miracle stock, the potion that dewrinkles grandma and heals uncle John--these things do not exist. They cannot exist, as certainly as nobody will invent perpetual motion before June. We do have a soft spot for the impossible, but belief in the next hoax is anything but cute. Confidence in our own abilities is sadly rudimentary and negligible if we're desperate to hope for super quantum velocity and frequency of electromagnetic energy, in combination with incorporeal substances, to get us places by simply tapping that other realm of negative entropy. Say what? Exactly! If you don't grow the balls in the next five minutes to be an independent individual with a serious spine, nobody and nothing will ever help you.

Independence threatens us. That's why we hate it so much. We hate freedom, independence, and individuality? Of course we do. How else would you explain your obsession to put that stuff off until retirement? We know damn well the importance of keeping crazy and dangerous things like independence and cookie jars out of reach, just as we try to prevent matchbooks and money from mingling with our children. Independence is more hazardous than anything we have encountered in life. It could replace our boredom with excitement and possible chaos, and we are not prepared.

Our society invented the oxymoron *financial independence* as a safeguard <u>against</u> independence. If you really cared for independence, you'd have to admit that all you do all day is already based on your independence, entirely. You do what you do because you chose to do so. Of course you could choose differently, but for your own sake and safety I hope nobody will ever tell you.

Individuality is not meant for individuals, you know? If it were, some of them might claim it for themselves. But most never do. Group-think proves to be safer and supports inherent laziness. If we were delighted to be individuals, wouldn't large chunks of our day look somewhat different from other people's? For two decades of our lives we try to copy other people's choices that didn't pan out for them either. Make no mistake, rebellion against parents (or the evil *system*) is a reverse type of copying— not the slightest trace of individuality there. You don't believe me, do you? See, when rebels raise rebelling kids themselves, grandchildren and their grandparents will think alike. Oh my God that's so unusual! Not. Rebels are the most pathetic kind of non-individuals. They aren't likely to be more successful or happy than their messed-up moms and dads. The typical rebel is just a more radical bore.

Independence requires time and money. Simply money? Probably not: funds and assets sound better suited. It's got to be something on the substantial side. How much? Nobody knows, but instant gratification is not an option here. Hmm ... are you sure?

I beg to differ. It takes no time whatsoever to develop your independence and not a penny of your hard-earned capital is needed. You can have independence right now. Will it have consequences? Absolutely, everything does. Of what sort? That depends. For instance, if you claim and declare your independence next Wednesday morning at 8:15 am, but you don't alter your plan for the day, the only immediate consequence may be that you won't feel like a slave of your calendar. From one minute to the next, you are master and maker of your day. And it is of no importance whether you are self-employed, employed, or if you happen to suffer through a meeting you allowed some ass to coax you into. Now, if you tell your superiors or your customers not to bother you anymore with their problems while you're taking extended mid-day naps, the consequences are likely to differ somewhat.

The time you take to claim your independence is prolonged only by your difficulty in accepting consequences as a normal environment for you as a free person. Negative connotations of the term *consequence* may hold you back. How about benefits? Warm up to perceiving each consequence of freedom as a benefit and there may be a time in your future when you won't use money you haven't made yet as a safeguard against instant independence.

Slave and Master appears to be a popular game. The majority of people dedicate their entire lives to playing it. Except, it's not really a game. It's dead serious, it's a job, and it is their life. What is the difference between employment and slavery? Your boss can't beat you physically, but you can be abused for fun and profit. No one owns you as an employee? Who schedules your day off and what part of the day you do have for yourself? Your owner can't sell you? Says who? In fact, being sold to a new owner is considered a better fate by modern slaves than being kicked out and into the gutter.

And funny, yet not surprising: so many slaves dream of being a master one day. No, there is no reason to blame today's masters or employers for the slavish nature of our society. That is the real difference between slaves and employees. Slaves had no choice. Period. Employees on the other hand BEG for their servile lot while trying to make the world believe they have no choice in the matter. Corporations, and the government as the largest employer, could not play the game of submission without hordes of obsequious slaves eager to please their master. Now the masters, in turn, almost have no choice but to enslave the willing. Be proud of yourself if you have successfully reached slave status in the 21st century. You are a privileged creature indeed.

Network marketing is considered an alternative income source by numerous employees. I don't comprehend what one can possibly like about it. MLM is a system and, as we have mentioned before, that makes it snake oil. Sure, some people are cashing in on network marketing, but they are less than 3% out of all who try. 3% out of any group of people in any profession strike it rich--if we want to use *rich* for the sake of simplified communication (and MLM'ers aren't that sophisticated anyway). The system has nothing to do with it. It depends entirely on these people who chose MLM as their work environment. Network marketing doesn't make them rich. *They* are making that particular MLM-based company rich. You know, a network marketing company is *not* your window of opportunity. *You* are that company's window of opportunity. MLM doesn't work for you. It will always be the other way around.

MLM is snake oil. Fine. I have yet to meet a networker who will readily tell me how much money she is making and how much of her own money and time she has invested so far. Difficult, because networkers lie so excitedly. They'll report about future expectations, hopes, and about *another guy* who is already there, supposedly, but they'll be mum about their own pocket book. Network marketing is not an occupation. It's a religion and hence lying is not lying. It's called positive thinking and is a common practice in the industry. You think that's bad? Not at all and rather harmless compared with the real nasty MLM illness. What's that? Hitting up all your friends to either join or buy? Network marketing is indeed one of the most rotten treatments for friendships but its side effects are equally lousy for you:

Even if pyramid schemes work out for you financially--they are not really pyramids and more respectable than Mr. Ponzi, or so they claim--and you don't peddle overpriced soap and gizmos for 85 cents per hour, they suck. In fact, the more successful you become the worse it gets. Why? Like any other job you're doing for money, MLM buries your individuality--alive! You work the system, you are dead. Not literally, but everything that makes you unique and special is useless, a liability even, and sooner or later 95% of networkers are as unhappy as they were on their old jobs. Except, you can't leave easily when you are making decent money.

May I ask you an innocent question? Will you give me--and more importantly yourself--an honest answer? Would you engage in any network marketing job without getting paid? Exactly! That should answer all your questions about MLM. If you wouldn't consider doing it for free, or for the fun of it, it may serve as a temporary support but it is working against you in the long run. Anything you are not willing to do freely, you will want to retire from one beautiful day. If you are working for money only--oh yeah, or to build *residual* income, you dork--it sucks ass and turns your life to crap, as you have undoubtedly experienced before.

Copycats don't get very far. A bunch of people believe they can succeed by learning about successful individuals' paths to money. We are stung by the glorious idea of copying success and again, we fail miserably. Before we try out individuality we are tempted to settle for mediocrity. Everybody else is doing it and it seems to be safe. Just because there's no visible chain, it doesn't mean you are not in a chain gang.

Steve Jobs is not a copycat. Steven Spielberg isn't, and

neither is Richard Branson. Love them or hate them--they are originals. Copycats will rarely surpass their role model. On average, copies aren't better than originals. So, why would you want to learn the How-to from anybody? Successful individuals will never tell you the truth about their breakthroughs and how they happened. A bunch of them don't even know why things started rolling in their direction. They may recall certain actions they took but they're clueless as to what triggered positive responses and why. They don't know the truth about their own success. If they knew precisely how their success evolved, and if they were open to reveal the process to you in baby steps, you'd discover that the main ingredient is nothing you could repeat at will.

Ergo, it makes no sense to waste your and their time to figure out what has worked well for some rich person. Read Napoleon or Napoleon Hill if you have too much time on your hands. Better yet, do what you want to do and make money. Someone you look up to is more limiting than helpful for individual development and for your possible success.

Confusion is good for you. How so? Confusion is the optimal situation to be in before you choose freely. When you know what you want, your choice is predetermined by considerations, past experiences, personal preferences, advice, etc. No real independence or freedom to choose in sight. Only when you are hopelessly stuck in the darkness of confusion are you as free as you'll ever be. Not knowing what to do permits you to pick. The next best idea is IT. Throw dice. Start walking and let your feet determine the direction you'll take. Decide on a whim. What's it going to be?

I love confusion. That's when you can be yourself, innocent, at a new beginning.

Regrets pertain normally to things we have done and we wish we hadn't. As a result we become careful and we tend to do less and less of things involving risks. People get old and miserable that way. Listen, you must do things you will regret! Regrets are fuel for a fulfilled life. Once old and immobile, we will regret actions we have NOT taken so much more than mistakes we have indeed committed. Pitiful. Have something to regret. Collect that stuff. Please, do yourself a favor and keep your actions legal! But make mistakes, small ones and huge ones, do regrettable things and do them often.

      We are nothing and we will never amount to anything without accumulating a long list of regrets in the process. Independence is born that way and individuality gets a chance to unfold.

Chapter Eight
Slave and Master

"One half of the world cannot understand the pleasures of the other."

Jane Austen

Pain fascinates us. We love it. Look into anybody's life and you will find elements of deliberate masochism. Not all of us may be into S/M but the idea isn't that foreign to any of us. The enjoyment of pain is common. Publicly we denounce it, of course. Nobody likes to be seen as a weirdo, but privately we must admit we love some of what we say we hate. If all the reasons for complaints were removed from our lives, we would be quite upset, left behind with a feeling of emptiness.

Many of us find meaning in pain. We believe we can learn from it and we develop a perverted kind of gratefulness toward pain. Human beings are pleasure seeking and pain avoiding animals? Really? Such pseudo knowledge may satisfy a first semester psychology student until lunch but between you and me, it's meshugge. Pleasure seeking and pain avoidance says nothing, since each of us has a different idea of what pleasure and pain mean to us. Not only that, we have the incredible ability to switch back and forth between the two. But we are getting ahead of ourselves. On a normal day, there is not enough tension in things most people associate with pleasure. Like hanging out at the beach doing nothing. It bores us quickly, possibly driving us into the arms of pain. Once there we crank up our discerning intellect and, believe it or not, we are capable of detecting pleasure in our most painful experiences.

Masochism is an integral part of our upbringing. We enjoy hurting ourselves ... or are you not your most sadistic critic? And as we grow up believing life can't possibly be without a decent portion of pain (no pain, no gain, remember?) we think we're doing others a favor by inflicting pain on them also, or by taking their existing pain to the next exciting level. S/M is not suffering a naughty closet existence, hidden away in a few weird people's private dungeon. No sir! S/M is common in every corporate cubicle and at the kitchen table of the sweetest family. You beg to differ? Be that way, but please explain to me why the average person doesn't have these two major goals. First, to make his own life as easy and pleasurable as he possibly can. Secondly, to make everybody else's life as easy and enjoyable as is in his power-- without giving up his own ease, of course. Perhaps because we like it a bit rough, and some of us a bit rougher. Hence my suspicion we are naturals at S/M, in the cubicle and beyond. We're way too good at peddling pain to deny it believably.

S/M has something mysterious and forbidden to it, and we love that. Nobody talks proudly and openly about her practices, but we know it exists. We are aware more people are having fun with it than the general population is willing to admit. But, like little children, we aren't keen for mom to find out. A good chunk of the fun S/M provides is the fascination with the forbidden. Nevertheless, pain can be transformed to an intense form of enjoyment. Sources, claiming human beings are mostly interested in seeking pleasure and in the avoidance of pain, are either clueless or they're misleading the gullible public deliberately. It's as common as it is unpopular, the ability and the freedom of each individual to experience pain and pleasure as flip sides of the same coin.

Inferiority is as interesting an experience as it is to be in a powerful position. People's urge to gain power is overrated. Yes, there are individuals who thrive on power. They need employees and other sorts of slaves around them, as Mother Teresa needed starving blind children to feed her image and to raise a sizable pile of funds. Power is not everything: I have seen publicly powerful guys pay a dominatrix handsomely for the privilege of being slaves for an hour or two, and we don't care to know how Mother Teresa got through the night.

The dominance obsessed Nazis could not carry out their atrocities without masses of boot licking, obedient Germans who killed and died with no conscience of responsibility for any act they committed in the name of master race and their masters. During my 35 years of living in Germany, I did not meet anybody who felt responsible for the past. The old masters are dead and the old slaves are the new masters, conceptually at least. You won't believe how many Germans beg to be seen as slaves and victims of the Third Reich. Listening to this pitiful lot, there couldn't have been more than seven or maybe eight active members of the Nazi party (NSDAP) who did all the dirty work alone. Slavery can come with tremendous benefits, you see? It may save your pathetic life.

Not everyone is after power and true power is not always obvious. Helplessness may be the ultimate power position. Ask babies or your friendly neighborhood beggar. And so it happens that the caste of employees loves to control and dominate under the warm and cozy blanket of perceived inferiority.

Employers expect different things from you than you depend upon as a self-employed person. Employers want your strength, and then they pay you as if your strengths were weaknesses. Your strengths are valuable only to employers. For you as an entrepreneur weaknesses can be equally profitable. In fact, as a self-employed person you can make money with everything, weaknesses and strengths alike.

The more thoroughly you know a weakness of yours, the less you feel like a cast out, lonely victim of overwhelming forces. You understand other people better who share that same soft spot, and you may relax, especially when you discover its potential. The less you are struggling against *it* and against yourself, the easier it will be for you to see your options to freely choose your position as slave or master in this regard.

When you decide to turn your favorite weakness into a business venture, you can develop products specialized for those who feel like masters, and others specifically to be marketed to the slaves of their weakness. A candy store of options opens up to you. Employees are forced to master their weakness, while being treated as slaves. Self-employed, you have the freedom--almost the obligation--to experience both the master and slave sides of weakness and strength if you care to discover the greatest array of possible services and products in your field. Weakness may look strange at first as an opportunity, but I am confident you will triumph as a master.

Entrepreneurs aren't too keen on average to look for a job. Once you have tasted freedom and licked the blood of self-employment, you are ruined for jobs. In desperate times, a self-employed person may break down and choose to work a job temporarily. Yet pretending to be an employee long term can be quite difficult for the entrepreneurial personality.

On the other hand, enthusiasm to make things work and to make money can prove to be useless for an employee. Union members may give you the evil eye for your enthusiasm alone, and unruly thinking or--God forbid--competence blended with confidence are not appreciated by numerous superiors. Those who prefer self-employment will always experience employment as doing time, mind-numbing and unimaginative. Jobs starve human beings of their individuality. That's a generalization and entirely inappropriate, I know. Still, a self-employed individual can see the desolate situation of employees more intensely perhaps than most employees do after decades on the wheel. Typical employment is empty and geared at bankrupt minds. No wonder entrepreneurial spirits are nearly unemployable.

Victims can be arrogant creatures and by displaying this arrogance--*It is my right!*--they allow insights into the slave's exalted position. Your average slave feels she is above her master. Who would have thought?! It's called fascism of the underdog, the usual kind. No employer bests the lowliest employee in impertinence and superiority. The weakest people on Earth control everybody's emotions. Bosses have weaknesses, but the weakest of the weak may have a streak that enjoys exploiting their environment from the position of a boss's power. Don't mistake the weak for the meek, you know.

Feeling solidarity and compassion for victims can be dangerous. Well-meant compassion can get the nicest people sucked into someone's shoddy power play. MADD is a fine example, PETA, or Cindy Sheehan. The louder the victims, the dirtier they are behind their ears. Beware of control freaks camouflaged as professional victims. They don't give a crap about your touchy-feely compassion: they crave the raw power you might be able to add to their cause. Liberté, Égalité, Fraternité is the shiny French label for rivers of blood that victims enjoy literally squeezing out of the powerful. Czar Nicholas II and his family were butchered by poor and weak victims. Also, the holocaust was perpetrated by victims, as Nazis surfed to power on the wave of perceived victimhood. Germans thought of themselves as victims of the Versailles Treaty, for instance, and of the *World Jew*. You see, the Nazis didn't hate the Jews. They loved the Jews for providing such an ideal strategic tool to rally the stupid German slaves behind their grisly mission.

I shudder when I hear calls to punish the rich with severe taxation, cries against the evil corporations, or that big oil companies are gouging poor consumers. After all, corporations and *big oil* are owned by shareholders, the same consumers who refuse to feel messed-up like the typical murderous victim. Buy a couple of Halliburton shares. That may trigger inner healing.

Anyway, I distrust the suppressed, especially when they show up in bulk. Maybe the U.N. and the NY Times were right and the Iraqis deserved Saddam and his henchmen for another couple of nightmarish years. Perhaps the NY Times can also answer the question why it is indeed better for good people to have their ears cut off than to mess with a bad guy's--God forbid —sleep pattern. Historically the downtrodden have guillotines handy, they lack a decent sense of humor, and they may not shave their armpits. Ask the French.

Masters and slaves have pecuniary differences. Slaves, or employees, survive by means of obedience. An employee's greatest strength is being too weak to stand up for himself. Watch a group of employees--with their silly name tags around their necks--shuffle to lunch and back, and you know what I'm talking about. Scheming and backstabbing gets them ahead in their career, it's not performance.

Agreed, employers may use scheming and backstabbing also--after all, every weak one of us refined this effective technique to perfection during our teenage years--but underneath they, the entrepreneurial employers, are not afraid to stand up for themselves and to ask for money all day, every day. Employees ask for money once a year or three times per life. Some never. They take what they are given, like a well-behaved dog or a nice slave you might like to own.

Employees pride themselves on their stinking loyalty. "I have been with the company for 41 years." That's just fabulous! Your great accomplishment of doing time voluntarily won't deter your employer from firing your lazy arse next week before you turn into her most expensive liability. And you may want to seize a moment of reflection to realize that your damn loyalty--the dribbling source of your humble salary--has been the greatest obstacle to decent financial success.

You play the lottery? Exactly. That's what people do, deprived of experiencing financial orgasm from time to time. Lotteries and the gaming industry are the fiscal vibrators of the frustrated masses. Nothing of lasting value comes from it. Ooh la la, please forgive my sexual references, but sex and cash peaks do more for an individual's happiness and well-being than decades of dogged attempts to be loyal and a predictable bore. We have all grown out of the age of allowances by now, haven't we?

Pain and passion are rare commodities in our society. Pain is not rare at all--you have a formidable chance to find some if you like--but since we are primed to avoid pain instead of exploiting the hell out of it, good old pain is hardly perceived as a commodity. Still, pain can be joy and pleasure in disguise. Most people will never find that out and yet it is true. Emotions--like anger, disgust, fear, distress, joy, shame, surprise--are labels we use to mark physical sensations in combination with corresponding thought patterns.

In other words, the physical sensation is probably pretty damn real--except for phantom pain, for example, when my brother's thumb was itching years after it had been amputated-- and so are the thoughts we have simultaneously. But the emotional label we're sticking on that experience is subject to free choice: "damn, that's painful;" "I hate it;" "I'm afraid it may never stop;" "Oh yes, I like it." Those are our decisions entirely and not dictated by reality. Call me a pervert, but remember S/M and the flagellating medieval monks before you question my observation that practically all emotions can be transformed into sources of intense pleasure. O.K. I admit it, I am a pervert!

Pain and passion. Of what practical use are they? Do they have cash value? Pain and passion can be combined with lust. Every workaholic knows what I'm talking about when I portray pain as an obscured form of enjoyment. You have never experienced passion as some sort of pained zeal and joy? Both feed off tension, and tension is a dynamic force you can use to propel your interests and ideas. So there. You are smart enough to connect the dots.

Your strengths may be valuable, but you are a lame duck with all your impressive strengths, just as you are with your embarrassing weaknesses, until you add pain, passion, or both to the equation. The urge to get away from pain--or deeper into it, depending on your personal tastes--are gold for your business. Being obsessed and passionate won't permit you to stop. It's lust, baby--not demure love for what you do--lust will carry your business past the prophylactic resistance of the well-meaning nay sayers inside and outside your head.

Motivational speakers are not paid to speak. They're paid to shut up. Companies pay to have the select truths delivered that they want their employees to believe. Since even truth depends on lies, the hired speaker must not say all she knows. Too much truth may question simpler, more favorable truths and therefore dampen the excitement required for motivational purposes. Motivational whores mentioning Fortune 500 companies as their clientele don't intend to tell you anything new or useful. Pumping you up with old hats in new packaging secures their ordinary job with extraordinary benefits.

Oh, you mean truth questioning truth sounds a little confusing? Isn't truth, truth? I am glad you asked: I don't believe there is any truth. Period. The concept of truth contradicts the idea of freedom. One person's truth is always questioned by another one's truth. The truth an individual decides to settle for becomes for her *The Truth*. Her personal choice doesn't render this particular truth superior or absolute--just more simplistic.

Employers don't like their subjects to be confronted with exotic animals, controversial material that may crush their silly delusion of neat teamwork and empower individual development of selfish desires for fun and profit. Motivational speakers love to hate their jobs a bit longer, just as any other voluntary slave. Hence they shut up for the sake of prolonged and multiplied monetary success. We understand.

Employers hire units for their strengths and pay them as if their strengths were weaknesses. I know we said it before, but you can't hear it often enough. Of course employers have reason to do so because the average employee is not that passionate to deliver her true strength with all the energy she has. As the Gallup Institute has shown, most employees are zombies who don't care much about their jobs beyond the benefits.

I do not blame employers and corporations for the inhumanity, the idiocy, and the insult this current form of slavery poses for the human race. Employers take advantage of a perverted need for jobs, and why not? Slaves in droves are begging for jobs, banging on corporate doors, and consenting masters grant them entry. Today's slavery will take longer to get rid of because it's a voluntary agreement between consenting adults. Modern slaves submit to their masters for the sake of benefits, willfully forsaking freedom and money. Hence their sensitivity and verbal violence against those who treasure orgasmic monetary experiences and individual freedom.

Employees have no control, employers are in full control. Really? As every three-day-old baby controls the sleeping patterns of an entire household and more, the apparently weak wield more control over any system than those in power. Weakness is a power position. Unions have been built on that foundation throughout the history of industry. And I wouldn't be surprised if the typical wage slave knew on some level that he is indeed in a more powerful spot than his boss. If nothing else, the employee can leave today--or just not show up--and do something else. That single step alone is much more difficult, if not impossible, for his employer. Weakness may give you more control and power over the powerful than the so-called powerful will ever have over you. People choose weakness for the benefits it brings.

Crazy? I mean, are you crazy about the stuff you do? Yeah? Then why would you need motivational quacks jumping up and down in front of you, trying to make you dizzy? Motivation is for people who hate what they are doing. They are easy to find by looking for employees. Companies exist in spite of their hateful hordes and not because of them, or so I thought for many years.

I was wrong. By definition, slaves are not supposed to like their masters and masters are not meant to be sweethearts. People want to be treated poorly--no pain, no gain--and they crave a host of reasons to hate their employers. Companies flourish on the lunacy of employment, the symbiosis between withheld pay and withheld performance. Don't upset the slave by getting warm and fuzzy and don't piss off your master by speaking well of him, or you disrupt the balance of pain necessary to keep the game going. Oh, I did get carried away, again, didn't I?

Anyway, motivation is tailored for people not to hate their job less, but to hate it more on an elevated level. And when some motivational squeaker's references include a list of blue chip names, she's telling the world that her money is earned by coaxing those who hate their work the most into hanging on to the crap in their lives. Being motivated to hate your job is better than simply hating it. That's why. It's kind of how marriage counselors work, too. No?

What do you want to do? You don't need motivational creeps to cheer you up. If you need motivation, you don't really want to do what you are doing. And if you want to do it, you will do it and the idea of motivation is nonsense. Motivation is useless for free people who do what they damn well please. Motivation is the modern whip for modern slaves. Does it work? Of course it does, but not FOR the slave. When you choose to live in a world free of slaves and masters, motivational speakers seem outdated. Goodness, they are so 20th century. Do it or don't do it. It's that simple.

Play slave and master for your personal entertainment if you so desire, but as a way of life? C'mon, you don't want your and your dear family's income dependent on sadomasochism. Or do you? See what I mean? Jobs are for the real pervs.

Chapter Nine
Sex and Substance

"About money and sex it is impossible to be truthful ever; one's ego is too involved."

Malcolm Muggeridge

"Love of money is the root of all evil," we read in the bible. As Rev. Ike, aka Dr. Frederick Eikerenkoetter, points out, the *lack* of money is the root of all evil. In any case, we speak of love in connection with money but hardly ever of intimacy. Yet money is the perfect intimacy meter. We experience different levels of intimacy as far as our finances are concerned. Some people discuss their monetary affairs with their lawyers, accountants, or financial advisors but never with spouses or children. The money issue is taboo at many family dinner tables. We may find it easier to talk with a stranger, sitting next to us on a long flight, about our current money situation than with our parents or partners.

Detailed patterns of our intimacy in connection with money are somewhat more interesting than our love for money or the lack thereof. Money requires more intimacy than sex. You disagree? People pick up sex partners at a bar and they're willing to exchange bodily fluids with a person they met only three hours ago. We are willing to risk health and life in a sexual encounter with a randomly chosen stranger. It's quite normal.

Now, can you see yourself sharing your American Express Card and the content of your wallet with that same stranger? I don't think so. Sex and even love are close to meaningless on a scale measuring the intensity of intimate relationships between people. Money beats love and sex any day. If you want to test your true level of intimacy with any person, bring up your finances in detail ... yeah, and theirs.

Money mistakes made *under the influence* are easier

forgiven than mistakes we have made with a sober mind. Money we have lost gambling while we were drunk, for example. We may have caused damage, perhaps even totaled a car under the influence of alcohol. For some strange reason we think we are not fully responsible for things we do with alcohol in our blood. We blame a good number of our mistakes on mind-altering substances. I find that insulting to the intelligence and the ability of any individual. On a certain level we know very well what we are doing at all times. Denouncing responsibility for any or no reason is the irresponsible act which, of course, doesn't help us much in getting rid of responsibility. It's ours, as embarrassing as it may look.

Common understanding portrays alcohol induced mistakes as really bad, but I disagree. Mistakes we make when we are sober are on average more severe than the negative side effects of drunk behavior. Sober mistakes are those we commit while we're not under the influence of mind altering substances. That's what you do when you go to law school because you were born number five in a dynasty of attorneys, but all you are really interested in is archeology.

If someone was drunk choosing a job she will be working on for some forty years, I would understand somewhat what happened and why. But in general people are sober when they make such dumbass decisions. Sober people seriously plan their retirement, and retirement kills considerably more human lives than smoking. Individuals propose marriage in all sobriety, and we know roughly 50% of marriages turn out to be the costliest mistakes human beings are capable of making. Sure, your judgment is impaired when you're wasted but that doesn't mean you are more trustworthy after you've sobered up.

Money is a mind-altering substance as well. Give some schmuck a couple of million bucks and you will witness strange behavior changes, as lottery companies can attest. The outcome is not likely to be a pretty sight. To be clear, it's not the coke, the alcohol, or the money corrupting an individual's fragile little mind! People have huge problems with freedom. They can't handle it, and their admiration of freedom--financial freedom or the snorted kind matters not--is based on fear.

Disagree all you want but consider this: money is indeed harmless. It can't do anything without its current--and usually temporary--owner's consent. Yet we are scared out of our minds to give a substantial sum of it into the hands of teenagers. The idea alone gets our hearts and minds racing. We may lose the money, the teenager, and possibly both. In reality, money is not a substance per se. It is pure potential that can be converted to substance or service. But money--often just the promise of money--affects our brains in similar ways as chemical substances or sex. We go nuts? Nope. We are nuts. We don't trust ourselves as much as we trust white meat from free range chicken. The expectation of freedom puts us in a trance deeper than the daily cellphone trance, and we are horrified of possible consequences. Money, hell just the word 'money' alone, brings that stuff to the surface. Genies in their bottles are wussbags compared with the power of freedom we keep bottled up, hoping nobody will ever rub us the right way.

Intimacy with money is stranger than your levels of intimacy in other areas of your life. Loving parents may claim their children are more important to them than their money, but hardly anyone informs her brats in detail about her monetary affairs. Friends, relatives, moms and pops, or the IRS--none of them will ever have a clear picture of our finances. The most successful people as well as the greatest losers have developed sufficient smoke machines to keep their real money situation obscured. When we talk about our money, we lie the entire time.

Sex and substance relate to each other in more than one way. Ready for something truly weird? Substance--as in money and toys--can become significantly more important for those who don't enjoy an active sex life. In turn, the more important material goals are for you and the more attached you become emotionally to their accomplishment, the more difficult it will be for you to get there. The more essential money is in your perception, the harder it will be for you to obtain.

The less you care, the easier it is to get your hands on decent amounts. Happy and relaxed people don't need material goods to compensate for emotional imbalance. There you have it, sex advances to be a considerable prerequisite to money. Needy freaks, smelling of desperation, are equally unattractive to potential partners in sex and business. What? You don't buy my weak explanation? Then look into your own history of cash flow. Do you see correlations between sex and your money, or not?

Sex works, and when it doesn't the lack thereof turns people into needy little bastards. And when we are needy, nothing works. Needy people have more problems even finding a sex partner, and needy individuals experience harder times rounding up buyers for their merchandise or services. I don't believe the poor get poorer, but I have seen time and again the needy getting needier until they turn into friendly but creepy neighborhood stalkers. Money can't solve your monetary problems and sure as hell no amount of moolah can make you feel good if you don't feel grand first. Some money problems can only be solved in bed. At least, what do you have to lose by starting there?

Diversity is key to reinventing yourself, your business, and your sex life. Your business cannot thrive, not even survive, if you keep running it for years in the missionary position. Indeed, an equivalent of it may put us to sleep in every area of life. There is really nothing wrong with the missionary position, but if that's all you know, you'll bore people who have to deal with you in your office just as much as the folks populating your bed. And when boredom kicks in, the desire for retirement will get hold of you soon. Not good. It's alright to be reliable but predictability is death in every department of your life. Don't allow the people at work to hate you for the same things they hated you for ten years ago. Introduce surprise. Let the world around you hate you for something new every day. It's so much more endearing.

Submission to substance? Yep. Human beings are submissive creatures. We deny sadomasochist tendencies all day, but then we're willing to work our asses off for a silly iPhone. As I said, submission to substance. Standing in line for hours to get the damn iPhone on the first day when the chances of getting it to work are a whopping 50% describes submissive suckers, eh?

Freedom implies you CAN be submissive, by choice. However, once you have sold a good chunk of that freedom to your creditors you can still theoretically choose, but the consequences of the most appealing options have deteriorated to something less attractive than they used to be. Do you want your life to work well? I thought so. You'll have to train yourself to enjoy the entire spectrum at will, the full range between submission and dominance. Can you do that playfully? Then you may discover that there is no shame in being submissive just as there is no guilt in being dominant. It's all good, it's all fun, and it's all for profit.

Sex alters the value of your money. Without sex, your money may be much more important to you and it may seem to be more valuable, but it's actually worth less. If your sex life is nonexistent, everything else is not as much fun as it could be either. The things money can buy--and you may feel compelled to acquire--become dull and boring quickly. If you do enjoy a balanced sex life--sorry, or a wild and crazy one--the rest of your life will be more playful also. Sex allows us to experience moments of ultimate luxury: moments free of desire, when we can't think of anything we would rather do or of any place we'd rather be. Optimal wealth! Of course that might influence your stance toward your money a bit.

Acquisition of money is just as easy as it is to have sex--as long as you don't care about form or conditions. However, we don't want sex with just anybody, or some money no matter what. We have our ideas and philosophies how that should look. Sex or money are not responsible for our struggling and troubled relationships with one or the other. *We* are the problem by being so picky.

Sex is simple. Having sex with your damned soul mate only is so utterly difficile. Finding your soul mate can cost you a very long time, and if your tedious search really produces such a person, he may be a complete klutz in bed and sex-wise you're back at square one. Similarly the money issue: before sundown you can land a simple job at McDonald's or at the gasoline station around the corner and make *some money*. Making precisely the amount of money you desire could prove more challenging, and it is likely to take you longer than getting 'some' money. Generating your dough by utilizing your skills and experience can raise the bar even higher. Drawing your perfect income in exchange for *meaningful* work requires additional steps up the prickly picky people's ladder.

Don't be so sure! The frustrating ordeal outlined above proves true if you set out to find the perfect job, designed specifically for you by company X. The problem lies in the high expectation and in the low probability that your expectations will be met. Contrary to common belief, picky is good. In fact, being picky is the only way for you to determine what exactly you want to do. What about sex? Geezus! Forget sex. It was probably crappy most of the time, anyway. Doing what you want to do is better than sex, but it can only work if you are obsessed and nuts enough to sell your soul in exchange for a profitable outcome. Ready? Still got a soul for sale? I never had one, so I don't know how that feels.

Love is a wishy-washy term, especially in relationship to money. *Do what you love, the money will follow* by Marsha Sinetar, is a sweet idea but unfortunately a blatant lie. "Oh, I love to shop and now I'm trying to make money with it." "I love puppies and I'm turning my stupid puppy love into cash." Yeah right! Lots of things are possible but I'm afraid most love-based businesses will disappear faster than they pop up. "What I'd like to do is ..." Rubbish. I really like ice cream, but it would be idiotic for me to open an ice cream parlor. I want to eat M & M's: I don't care to stare at them and I don't want to sell them to other people. Neither do I have the slightest inclination to be friendly all day.

God, I hate the stuff people love. At least as far as substantial business interests go, hardly anything is as deceptive as those pink and flowery ideas somebody likes and loves. Unless you are a wedding planner or you're selling romance novels, keep business and romance apart. The only thing as devastating as being in love with your business is falling in love with stocks you buy, unable to make drastic changes or to get rid of them at the right moment. Doing what you love is noncommittal confusing bullshit. Besides, even if you do what you love, there won't be any cash showing up on your doorstep unless you ask for it and sell your love, for money. How much do you love that?

You know what I'm thinking? Love is overrated and lust, yeah good old LUST, is not that bad at all. Obsession without emotional attachment is not the worst notion to run a business on. I would bet most of us were results of lust and not children of love. Love sounds nicer but it's ethereal drivel, and when your kids look you in the eye they know instinctively love had little to do with the busted rubber. When it comes to matters of cash production, love loses the substance test also. Lust wins. Do what you want and don't be so damn coy about it.

Attachment to a certain expected outcome is counter-productive. You know what you want to do--it better be legal-- and nobody can stop you from doing it, right? A hefty portion of obsession is mandatory for entrepreneurial success. You've got that too? You risk doing what you want and I insist YOU SELL IT from day one. That will have consequences. It'll change your life. You will have less time for things you don't want. You will make less money with the things you don't want to do. And you won't have any guarantee of making more money with the things you do want. Duh.

Now, if you get scared and tighten your own thumb screws, expecting a particular outcome within a specified time, you have attached yourself to the results--emotionally and financially. Doom is upon you. Your business may have a phenomenal chance of making it, but your oafish attachment can murder the finest business operation in its infancy. Happens to a lot of I-do-what-I-love crap shops. Neediness takes over and initial confidence, motivation, and saved-up funds are out the window.

Love is kaputt, too, and the most wicked thing: the business could have worked, just not under this type of pressure. Beware of love. It can kill you, it can cost you all the assets you own, and it can bring you to a point where you have no clue which one of these two options you should favor. How to prevent such disaster? Simple: don't bank on love. Don't give up your job just yet. Didn't I tell you before? Instead hate it longer, hate it more, hate it better. It's your right.

Freedom to do what we want is more intimate an issue than money. Having sex is more common than making money on planet Earth and in our society. More people are used to making money than are willing to claim their freedom to do what they want to do. Every rabbit can have sex, every idiot can get a job and make money, but what about freedom? Freedom remains a ghost, evoked occasionally to make a point in political or philosophical discussions, but few take freedom seriously as a fact and an option of everyday life.

What does your freedom look like this minute? Too hot a topic perhaps to talk about with your spouse and out of the question to be mentioned at work. Freedom and independence are empty ideas cluttering up the constitution, unless you give them meaning and substance. Employment with benefits is a safe haven for those who are too intimidated by the ultimate challenge: Freedom.

Chapter Ten
Money and Problems

"If you think there is a solution, you're a part of the problem."

George Carlin

Money is limited. If you don't have enough, that is, and you will never have enough. Ever. Average people feel limited in their freedom to live by the amount of money they have at their disposal. A dumb idea. It really doesn't matter how much or how little you own, money will always be limited. But relax, there is not much you can do with money anyway, and neither can money do a lot for you. I am confident you disagree with me vehemently on this point, but think about it: how much of a sucker do you have to be to believe that money is the be all and end all of life's problems? Boy; parents, teachers, and preachers sure did a fine nut job on you.

The new age was wrong with its abundance trance. Did it work? Not so much, I'm afraid. Granted, you can make heaps more than you have in the past if you have the balls to let your horses run in the right direction AND IF the winds of the markets favor your products. However, the value of gold has always been determined by its limited supply. Had states been interested in abundance, there would have never been a gold standard. We would have had the dirt or the sand standard.

Today, with more moolah in circulation than an antiquated gold standard could digest, the value of this precious commodity is still based on limiting its supply. Be grateful for it because your perception of money being a rarity makes it valuable and worth pursuing. If you want money without limitations move to Zimbabwe, and Robert Mugabe will give you all you need--in a nice bag bundled with an annual inflation rate estimated at well over 1 million percent (Wall Street Journal, July

2nd, 2008).

Money has hardly any value as such. Intrinsically, as you know, it is nearly worthless. But also its role as legal tender is not worth anything until you make a decision about it. The quality of your choices gives money the value it will have for you personally. One person's $100,000 is worth more than another guy's million. Most lottery winners' millions aren't worth more than the single dollar these dorks paid for their ticket, as the adjusted reality a couple of years after hitting the jackpot proves.

If you expect money to be and do much besides covering your utility bill, you are doomed and you will have problems. It cannot help you with happiness and freedom. That's for sure. You'll have to figure out on your own what you want to do and then do it, with or without money. If you wait for your money first, not even the gods can help you. You are wasting everybody else's space and time.

Money problems are not caused by money. Money is rarely the problem, and money problems are often an *indication* of lack of money. Duh. Guess what? Lack of money is not caused by money either. Individuals are the cause of their financial situation, and money--meager or plentiful--is not going to remedy that situation. Injecting cash into someone's money problem usually delays the solution for that problem, but with certainty it won't solve anything. The solution must be found FIRST. Then, money may be added carefully and in small dosages if that's still necessary or desired.

Helping people with financial problems is a noble gesture. Often demanded but not always appreciated is the monetary support of a friend who gives you cash when you most need it. On average, months and even years later the problem still persists while the friendship may have gone down the drain long ago. No, I don't advise against helping someone in need! On the contrary. But whether you are the receiving party or the generous lender, you need to be aware of the risks you are taking. The dollar amount involved is the smallest risk. Possibly losing your friendship is the greatest potential hazard for both of you.

No sum of cash saves your behind from the consequential job of figuring out a permanent solution for your money shortage. What's the rotting cadaver at the bottom of *your* dried-up cash well? Money is not the problem, neither is it the lack of money. That would be too easy, wouldn't it? It has something to do with you or it may be an action you're hesitating to take. Perhaps you will never find the cause of your financial drought, but you must discover your way out, nevertheless. The help of your friends can buy you the time to do just that. Nothing more.

Money has power. Is that a fact? Only in your imagination. Money is often seen as the almighty solution to all sorts of situations by those who don't have any money. Money does have power over the have-nots. The perception, of course, is more powerful than the money itself. We manufacture gods and demons by ways of projection, and it is puzzling how intelligent people can fall for tricks of the mind.

The car you don't have can turn into the finest piece of metal you have ever laid eyes on. Oh my God, you'd be so happy if you could only own it! Nonsense, it's just another heap of iron, plastic, and rubber. The goddess on heels across the street remains a goddess only as long as you don't get closer. Seeing her face in broad daylight might be enough to dethrone her. The poor schmuck who's actually living with her is most likely bored out of his mind right now. Remember when Hugh Grant thought paying a hooker was a better idea than putting up with Liz Hurley gratis?

From where I am sitting it looks like more dough would not have been the end of Sigmund Freud's worry. A morphine overdose was the final answer. Sigmund's morphine was Hermann Goering's cyanide and a shotgun for Hemingway. These guys faced problems that therapy, power, fame, or cash could not solve. See? Anything, even a shotgun, beats money when you are in real trouble, and it is cheaper than therapy. Smart as you are, you get the picture. Money is the most powerful stuff and happy-making matter only for emotionally immature characters who don't permit themselves to really experiment beyond the cashless life of a money virgin. In other words, if you believe money can get you out of your hole--whatever kind of pit you may be in--you are probably pretty dumb. Don't despair, though, you are not alone.

Scared of money? Of course not. Anxiously we hope for money's amazing abilities to salvage our mediocre lives. Yet, the more powerful we expect money to come through for us, the more we become aware that money can also be an equally powerful force operating against us. So we are scared of it? No? Make up your mind, will you. Five million buckaroos could save you from a bunch of nightmares and get you instantly into your favorite dream world, but the idea the same $5 million could fall into your 17-year-old teenager's hands terrifies you. Right?

Money frightens us in direct proportion to our unfounded belief in its power. Listen to yourself talk about money. I dare you. Whatever you think all day, the opposite is just as true for you personally.

Money functions like a looking glass. It allows us to see what works in our lives and what doesn't work. Your current money situation is a symptom, not the cause of your troubles. Remedy the symptoms of any serious illness and the pain may disappear for a limited time, but the problem remains. Similarly, trying to patch up a money problem with cash is an attempt to cover up symptoms. It won't work long term.

Money increases the visibility of our affairs or character traits. Whether we are stingy or generous, morally straight or crooked--more money will make it more obvious. People used to believe that money corrupts individuals. That was nonsense of course, but if you give large sums of money to people it will become clear fairly quickly which ones are corrupt. In short, cash in ample quantities sorts out the good, the bad, and the ugly. Abundance of cash or bitter lack of money, both extremes allow a piercing look at the individual experiencing it. How intelligent would it be to hold the looking glass responsible for what you see in it?

Symptoms can show up randomly. Read warning labels

on medicine bottles and you learn side effects may occur or they may not. It's not an unwritten law of nature for side effect B to follow action A. Money is just as random in its occurrence. If money were an effect of hard work, hard work would ALWAYS cause a bunch of dollar bills to show up out of nowhere. Not so. You and I, we both know hard-working people with lots of money, and we know other individuals who prevent money from happening by working hard. Since hard work doesn't lead to heaps of money in every instance, it can't be the cause of money. Something else is, or something else in combination with good hard work. What's that: *good* hard work?

There is good air and bad air, you know. You want to breathe the former and flee the latter. You prefer to drink good water and you won't let your brats near bad or poisonous water. Then there is hard work that furthers your interests and a different kind of hard work that deludes you, destroying your objectives by keeping you occupied with fruitless labor. Before we exhaust the analogy, air doesn't cause you to breathe. If you want to breathe, clean fresh air is a great thing to have, while a public restroom can be severely demotivating for the breathing process. Similarly, if your work stinks it can't possibly be a great idea to expect a lot of money there. I'd work on something else but fortunately for you, we are not alike. You want drastically increased cash flow? Your willingness to work hard on the right things is a fine prerequisite, but not at all the cause of future funds.

Money itself cannot cause anything either, just as a lonely hockey puck by itself can't cause a damned thing. You or someone else must move money or the puck to get matters rolling. You don't hold pucks responsible for missed opportunities, do you?

The 'law' of cause and effect is overrated. Sure, we know the cause of some effects. When I was a kid, enjoying splashy jumps from one puddle into the next, my mother believed--she knew--wet feet in winter weather would give me the common cold at least and probably the flu. Today we know the common cold is caused by viruses. Rhinoviruses are responsible about half the time, and a creepy bunch of others the rest. What caused the last cold you suffered? You don't know. Where did you pick it up? Who gave it to you and when? You don't know. Unfortunately, we still don't know enough about the common cold to prevent it from catching us. The more precisely we examine causes and effects, the more vague the answers will be, often entering the realm of belief and superstition.

If there was a law of cause and effect, the same cause would result in identical effects, time after time. You do A, and B happens. Anybody doing A would cause effect B. How often is that true and repeatable? Smoking causes lung cancer, most of us believe. Some smokers get cancer, some smokers live to be 95 years old, and some people die of lung cancer without ever touching a single cigarette.

Helmut Schmidt, former Chancellor of Germany, is now 89 years old. He and his 87 year-old wife Loki have smoked like chimneys their entire lives. Their doctor told them recently that quitting smoking now could kill them. It would be too much stress, and smoking will be healthier for these two octogenerians.

What precisely causes what? We have some pretty good ideas, but we don't know for sure. We are freaks, mutations, or evolution would have never spat us into existence. What caused you to pop up? Half a bottle of Stolichnaya, a leaking rubber, or a couple of responsible teenagers? All of the above perhaps? At least 10% of us don't have a clue who our father was. We don't have a well-defined cause, just as not everything that's meant to be a cause will have the desired effect. And if there is no predictable effect, our sacred cause lacked the proper ingredients. All it may cause is that we're tearing our hair out. No cause, no effect. Just us, perplexed and loitering in a jungle of causeless effects and effectless causes.

Certain actions will never cause a thing--that's less than the dumb proverbial butterfly breaks loose with a single flap of its wing--and especially not the effect we anxiously anticipated. Some things occur out of the blue. With our brilliant theories we are sure these occurrences must be effects of definite causes but, as they simply happened, we can't connect them with any plausible cause. Settling for the best looking cause available for the sake of having one is a common habit of ours, but it's neither helpful nor particularly rational. When it comes to money, oh my God, we are completely in the dark as far as cause and effect are concerned. Let's not even go there.

Predictability is not the character trait of an attractive lover. We like predictable business partners, predictable surgeons, and predictable pilots but predictable bed partners bore us. Could it be that we love money so much because it is so utterly unpredictable? Maybe it's not the special superhero powers we find so irresistibly attractive. Perhaps we are so enamored with this bewitching substance because we cannot foresee its next step.

Money is not a math problem. Ask any pundit on Wall Street if money's next move can be safely predicted. No, it's love, baby! Money will never disappoint you by becoming predictable. Never.

Money may react to anything you feel, think, say, or do. Whatever is going on in a person's life can have an effect on her monetary situation. By ways of magic? C'mon, don't be silly. I won't peddle or ponder *law of attraction* humbug in this book. No Ma'am. Frustration, feeling elated or relaxed, headaches and the flu, happiness and excitement, love and hatred--all that stuff can have a direct and an immediate influence on your financial affairs. How so? It alters your decision making process. Messed-up relationships may affect your cash flow, decreasing or increasing it. You don't know until it happens. Depression can slow down your creativity and glowing anger may speed it up. It matters if you are tired, or awake and perky. Money will show.

"I met a friend one day in the street and told him my intentions. 'You buy the American Museum?' he said with surprise, for he knew that my funds were at ebbtide; 'what do you intend to buy it with?' 'Brass,' I replied, 'for silver and gold I have none.'" --P.T. Barnum

Individuals who consider going into business for

themselves often believe that they do not have enough money. Welcome to the club! You are in good company. Harvey Firestone, George Eastman, Henry Ford, or Thomas Edison--none of them had enough money. Most people with start-up intentions have too much money, and damned, I have learned that the expensive way. Worse and utterly embarrassing, I had to learn it the hard way AFTER I knew it to be true theoretically.

Business must start with something you sell, immediately! The average wannabe entrepreneur mistakenly believes in lists of important things he needs to spend money and time on first. If you need more money before you can start your business, be glad you don't have it. Whatever you think it is, a thousand dollars, $50,000 or a million--in all likelihood it'll be wasted and it will be a sad sight. What determines the sum you need to begin a business project? Don't slap me but commonly, we choose a number large enough to guarantee that we don't have to start. I am awful, I know.

Currency is issued individually. Not two people use the same currency. How's that, you ask? You may be using a dollar bill when you are buying a cup of coffee, but when you are thinking about money in general, you have something different in mind than a dollar bill.

The accumulation of any and all your personal associations with money and money-related issues builds up to what you summarize as *money*. Your worries, fears, and hopes. Pleasant experiences of your past and traumatic financial disasters--yours or somebody else's you have only heard of. Expensive health challenges you have had yourself or witnessed. Well-meant advice of your accountant still ringing in your ears. 50 cents you stole out of mom's wallet to buy candy with when you were 8 years old. Grandpa's grave warning not to speculate that you overheard at the dinner table decades ago. Nasty divorces you've read about in a magazine. The list is endless …

All thoughts and memories summed-up about money lead way over 50% of our society to have more negative associations with money than positive ones. THAT is the stuff you want more of? The majority of Americans associate negative experiences with money, while firmly believing a couple of million dollars more will make it all better. Nuts.

The sum of your money-related memories--mentally and emotionally--makes up what I call *your currency*. Can you handle more of it or will you have to revisit your past to make your monetary future manageable? Yeah, but we can't change the past! Says who? Hey, if you want more fun with more money in the future, you will have to change your damn past pronto. What do I care how you do that?

Sell your problems! Insane idea? I agree, but everybody who believes a relatively large sum of money will translate into an easier life with a lot less problems believes just that. *The day goes, Johnny Walker comes?* When money comes, your problems will go away? Of course, they won't. Exchanging problems for cash? Good grief, who do you think will buy your baggage? The conglomerate of your money experiences--factual, imagined, or just gossiped about--your personal currency, will determine how you'll experience your next cash encounter.

More money will bring you more experiences common for you. If money has mostly been a pleasant issue in your life, more dough is most likely going to be a pleasant happening. If money issues have been troubling and traumatic in your past, no sum of money will magically turn financial hell into a rose garden. You'll have to upgrade your experience of money one small step at a time, right where you are, before a windfall threatens to hit you SMACK! between the eyes.

You may want to make friends with the contents of your wallet. You gotta fall in love with your nickels and dimes, with no end in sight. Most of us are willing to come out of the closet immediately with our secret love for money. The real question is, are you lusting after your personal kind of currency? Are you crazy about money experiences you are known to get yourself into? Your love for money is irrelevant for the generation of additional funds without lust for your brand of financial disasters.

If your zeal for life and for the REPETITION of your greatest monetary mistakes has shriveled up in pitiful regret, more money is an unlikely event. You are too scared of yourself! When you're eager to handle more of the same trouble and worse, you may have a chance. We must do regretful things and we can't afford to regret them.

Happiness is in the doing of things. When you are so immersed in an activity that you lose track of time, the importance of your problems fades away also. No, your problems will not disappear but they are not as intimidating, grinning right in your face, while you are busy doing something that engulfs you entirely. You are gone, you are in a trance, in the zone. That's pure happiness. It's cheap, free in fact, and you have the option of making money while you are making yourself happy.

Our worrisome natures can make problems appear bigger than they are. Action, and more so active happiness, puts problems in perspective. They shrink. You, completely lost in a task, are entering a state of mind allowing you to <u>have</u> a problem instead of being owned and rattled by it. Yes, but I can't afford to do what I love doing all day! Right. I forgot. Here's where the do-what-you-love gurus have sold you dry horse puckey that's good for your rose bushes but bad for you.

You can do what you hate, and you'll be ecstatic and happy when you lose your bitching and bickering self in that nasty activity! Man, I hate doing my taxes, trust me. I procrastinate for months, and then I am shocked how much I enjoy working on it when I don't permit myself any distraction or delay. You can be just as happy doing what you hate as you can be while indulging in your favorite activities. Once you are in the middle of the action, in the eye of the storm, there is no difference. Zero.

Things we want to HAVE or everything we want to BE are not as powerful a source of happiness as DOING. Have-and-Be based happiness is extremely short-lived. You get that stuff you've been after for years and Poof! its magic is gone within hours. You desire happiness? You sure? Go DO something, and continue as long as you want to be happy. Even longer. It's free and if you do it right, it becomes profitable.

Be all you can be? I don't know about that and I refuse to make any promises about what you can be or what you can have in life. But you can do a helluva lot of things. Don't tell me you can't ride a bike in next year's Tour de France. That's simply not *doing*. It's celebrity status you crave. You want to *be* somebody. Quite alright but I can't help you with your illness. If, on the other hand, you want to ride a bike and experience everything that comes with it--exhaustion, sense of accomplishment, and joy--nothing and nobody will stop you. Sweat here, sweat in France, sweat everywhere. It's all possible.

No, you can't have all you want to have and you can't be all you want to be, but that is of insignificant consequence for your happiness. There is hardly any limit to what you can do. Some of it you can do today. Everything you need to do to be happy, you can do in five minutes. I'm not even lying this time.

Chapter Eleven
Pain and Passion

"You know that when I hate you, it is because I love you to a point of passion that unhinges my soul."

Jeanne Julie Éléonore de Lespinasse

Hatred is one of our favorite forms of expressing passion. It is difficult to be angry or hateful without being passionate, unless you are a cold-blooded school shooter or postal worker before becoming uncorked. Hardly anything offers us the opportunity to feel strongly as readily as emotions we normally try to avoid. We hate to hate, we say. We don't want to be angry and yet, once we're all worked up and we have talked ourselves into a flying rage, we don't seem to be interested in stopping our madness. Damned, we love to be enraged. We feel something, how amazing, and we can lose all perspective over it.

Hatred is beautiful and we wouldn't want to miss it. Can you remember the last time you expressed joy with a similar outburst of passion? Excitement over a creative idea you had? We'd feel mortally impoverished if we had no reason to be angry and hateful. Half the population finds meaning in it.

Pain is our secret love. What could be better suited to arouse our passions? Pain is even more intense than emotions we label as negative, like anger or hatred. People wish to die painlessly. Some of us would rather die than feel pain. Pain tops the list of everything unwanted. We may hate the unions, but even more so we hate a toothache. No, we don't love pain ... or do we?

When we are in its claws, it's not easy to escape or to concentrate on our freedom to choose. When we are *in pain*, it dominates our thoughts and actions. Pain is a 24/7 affair and as passionately as we may hate it, pain fills many people's lives with purpose. As much as we insist we despise it, some of us live for pain and for painful experiences we've had. Hardly anything is denied as vehemently as our passion for pain.

I am a cruel bastard, of course, accusing individuals of loving their pain. But go ahead and listen to a coffee circle of little old ladies. They talk about who died recently and how they died, what illnesses either they have themselves or everybody else they know. Pain sucks, but be careful not to take it away from people without their permission. For some, pain is the love of their lives.

Hurts and pains are valuable to us. We dearly love and pamper them. People in general are sadomasochists. I can't be serious? Oh yes, I am. They may not give this precious character trait much room in their sex life, but they find it particularly appealing to make other people's lives difficult. At least in traffic and around money issues we are a tough crowd. In turn, when others are making things easier for us, we're having difficulties accepting it freely without guilt.

I wonder, are there a dozen pages in the Torah, the Bible, or the Qur'an free of pain and suffering? Find a newspaper not peddling copy with pain. We grew up on that stuff, more so than on mother's milk. Pain sells better than anything else because it is more valuable to us than anything else. We thrive on it. Trust me, if you know of some pain somewhere, it can be turned into a cash cow. Time is money? Nonsense, pain is money.

Hard-earned money makes a bunch of us proud. You do not believe me that pain has cash value but you are proud how hard it is to make a living? If you think money earned through grueling toil is more precious than easy money, you <u>do</u> believe pain has a higher monetary value than fun. Our society promotes pain. Hence it is considered a supportive thing to make it more difficult for others to make a buck.

When your company cuts down on overtime, or your superior calls you in on Sunday, or you get laid off ... ultimately they are doing you a favor. I have often observed when employers reduce pay or increase workload and responsibilities, employees become *more* loyal on average. Some of them quit, sure, but most of them hang on to their miserable jobs more desperately than before, for dear life.

Sick puppies that we are, we are especially grateful when others complicate our lives. Don't you dare blame harsh work conditions on corporate leadership. They are doing the right thing after all. Heroes crave pain. Fun and cash are worthless compared to our beloved pain. Suffer some more. It's good for you. I am a negative, sarcastic bastard, aren't I? No, you are, IF you're proud about your hard-life syndrome.

Positive is not good enough. Ecstasy is preferable over positive thinking or positive experiences. Positive is rather boring and not at all what we are after. Positive, negative--what's the big difference? There's no thrill in it. What we call positive is a crude beginning, a fragile foundation for what we want. Excitement is one of those inflationary terms used by too many car salespeople and therefore void of meaning. Everybody is excited in TV commercials. How ordinary and mundane! People who say they are excited aren't really excited. They're in a controlled positive state, slightly above being bored out of their minds. Or they are acting. How many individuals--small children and Tom Cruise excluded--do you see jumping up and down over their lives' details?

Ecstasy is what I am talking about. No, not the drug! Ecstasy in pill form is still limited in its abilities and therefore useless for our purposes. Pure ecstasy is about you being yourself, being where you are, doing what you are doing, thinking what you are thinking, and best of all, without nasty side effects. Forget about the feeling part for now; it's too women's lib, controlling, and delusional. Why should anything be any different, this moment? It may scare the green slimy crap out of you but this is what you want ultimately, don't you? Extreme enjoyment of everything. Uh, not you of course. You want to leave the world a better place, for the damn children, and that is best accomplished with mediocrity and misery. Good for you, O noble one.

Oops, did I step into something when I attacked your

feelings? I am so sorry I ate your sacred cow for lunch. Brooding people demand from the world around them to respect their feelings. They want to be considered 'deep' but they are only narcissistic; miniature Gaddafis, Hitlers, Chavezes, and Castros controlling their personal relationships instead of a little country all for themselves. Dictatorship of feelings excludes happiness. Follow your feelings and not only are the people around you screwed ... so are you. If you refuse to do what you fear, you'll miss out on tons of fun stuff. For example, every sane person going into business for herself is scared. That's natural and important. Don't wait until the fear subsides. You'd better start new projects WHILE you are afraid and prepared for possible consequences. Your fear keeps you on your toes and sharpens your senses.

You eat what you feel like eating, you buy what you feel like buying on a whim, you always say what you feel, and you give in to every mood taking a hold of you <u>and</u> you want to be respected? If your feelings run your life, you have no self-respect and of course you don't deserve anybody else's respect. Watching you running your life into the ground is no fun and too painful for even the greatest S/M aficionado.

Listening to feelings--or whatever the hell you want to call it--is fine. *Acting* on feelings as a rule is devastating. Your stupid feelings are not the source of your happiness. They are just indicators to draw your attention to a possible problem area. Feelings are like warning lights on your dashboard. You have to have your car checked when you see the low-oil-pressure light flashing, sure. When you see the water temperature is below the normal operating level, you don't need to respond at all. Just drive gently until the engine warms up.

Happiness stems from your happy responses to everything that's happening to you, internally and externally. In at least 50% of instances, your response must be counterintuitive because most things that happen are not natural happy-makers. You are not responsible for everything that happens to you, by the way, as the new age religion would have you believe. For your personal happiness you ARE responsible, for all 100% of it. Hey, how are you feeling?

People are on the cute but futile mission to make the world a better place. We are compulsive fixers. Adorable! How much better is better? Windows Vista was meant to be an upgrade to Windows XP, and even with Microsoft forcefully shoving the newer and the better down our sore but patient throats, better is not always better. Quite often the long expected upgrades to our lives are disappointing. Microsoft does not have a monopoly on degenerate improvements. We are all good at it. The better job we are looking and longing for will have better this and better that, but we will hate it anyway after three, four moons. Yes, we will even hate it *better*.

Positive thinking attempts to enjoy the positive and to see the negative in an improved light. No matter how bad things are, there is always a positive side to it. Look at the bright side. Really? Sure, five years later we can laugh about almost anything. Viktor Frankl, a holocaust survivor, writes in his little gem of a book *Man's Search for Meaning* how he taught fellow Auschwitz inmates to develop a sense of humor to improve the probability of their survival. Fabulous stuff, reaching an inch deep under anybody's skin.

Here, I don't care about positive vs. negative or the possibility of improving your life. Of course, you can improve your status quo or you can worsen it. Both times you are fully intending to make it better, but you have no control over the outcome. Jocular as the universe works, we never know what's what until the final results are in. Self-improvement is a pacifier for so-called adults who refuse to grow up. Improved communication skills, another cosmetic lift of this and that, the higher vibrational rung on the spiritual ladder, a better job, the thinner you, a more environmentally conscious global warmer, the more sensitive husband--and the difference to more expensive rims is?

Both better and positive are mind numbingly boring. When my brother died of cancer at age 35, my hunchbacked relatives said it was positive: he was finally relieved of his excruciating pain. Vomiting is positive also: it gets the bad stuff out of your system and pretty soon, you'll feel better. An overall improvement, is it not? If you wish to improve yourself and better the world, puke a lot or die. That'll do and even your loved ones will approve.

Who gives a rat's pink behind about a better life? What we're really after scares the bejeezus out of us. That's how radical it is. Heaven on Earth? Did you sleep through the last five minutes? Heaven on Earth would be better than what we're experiencing and better ain't making the cut, remember? Join a cult or sign up for a Pilates class if that's what you want. I can't help you with heaven sooner or later, after you're dead. I'm selling the ecstasy of hell.

That got your attention, eh? Yeah relax, I didn't mean it. At least not literally, anyway. I certainly don't mean you should engage in heavy breathing, religious trances, and vigorous morning exercise. Do it if you like but it's not a prerequisite for life in ecstasy. What you need to do to experience complete ecstasy is ... uh, NOTHING. Baffling, I know. Savor reality, your reality. 'Why should anything be any different, this moment,' I asked a while ago. There is nothing you can do about the world and your experience, this second. It is what it is.

Spiritual lame asses want you to *accept* what is. Painful at worst and sleep inducing at best. Type A personalities prick you to *fight* what is. Sounds like the perfect recipe for a heart attack to me, exhausting at best and painful at worst. At any rate, fighting reality is futile.

When new age folks talk long and loud enough, they come close to making you believe that your reality is subject to your personal responsibility: you *created* it. Aging new agers can be quite impertinent and insulting. In fact, new age folks are religious fundamentalists. 77% of the Tutsi population in Rwanda were chopped up in 1994 with machetes, faster than Nazis ever managed to butcher Jews. According to the average well-read, but nevertheless ignorant new age dorks, the Tutsis must have created that and they were responsible for their own bloody demise? Nice! The Jews shouldn't pipe up about the holocaust because they *manifested* gas chambers, chimneys, and the German sentiment that Jews are best kept in ash trays and their gold teeth in vaults of Swiss banks? Wow!

Sometimes I wonder if the callous new agers are the new Nazis, or the old ones who traded their brown shirts for flowery ones and swastikas for peace signs on leather necklaces. Fascists they are for sure because they're convinced they are better and consciously more advanced than the rest of us who don't buy channeled garbage. Why should dead grannies know more about life than alive grandmas? It's like, duh, and not that funny. New agers prefer dead people's chatter over the gossip of live ones. You should feel threatened somewhat because they'd rather channel your ghost than talk to you in person. It's called unconditional love. I love you, dead or alive. Dead is easier. Besides, having my ears glued to the claptrap of a dead guy is more lucrative than listening to you.

But I digress. *Why should anything be any different, this moment?* Integration is the magic word. Own the world. Make it yours completely. This very second. You are enjoying your dinner? What would it cost you to be ecstatic about enjoying your dinner? Nothing. Agreed, it seems relatively easy to integrate pleasant experiences we have. Still, we don't do that. Dinner is just o.k. We take it for granted and we are not ecstatic at all. You expect to be happy owning so many toys you can't afford yet? Bull! It won't happen. You aren't ecstatic--not even happy--about the stuff you do have. Integration is claiming full ownership of your *experience*, and for now we are talking about the positive details of your life.

I can see the question mark on your forehead: why can't I just be ecstatic about my fabulous dinner? Why do I have to take this ridiculous detour and become ecstatic about *enjoying dinner* instead of being thrilled about the dinner proper? Simple: because not all dinners are fabulous! Some beautiful day, you may find yourself staring at a plate and the dinner looks rather awful. Trying to be ecstatic about the rotten food in front of you would be rather stupid. Don't you agree?

Your dinner is NOT the reality you are dealing with. Thoughts, feelings, and body sensations you have <u>in response</u> to looking at and tasting your dinner is what's real for you. You don't believe me? You hate your food and your partner loves it. Unless you are from the Pleiades, that has happened to you--both ways--hasn't it? You love your stuff and exactly the same taste triggers a gag reflex in someone else.

When our experience is negative or worse, trying to be ecstatic about the negative is precisely the wrong course of action. That was the idiocy of 20th century style positive thinking. You have a bowl of freshly plucked strawberries in front of you ... <u>and</u> you are allergic to strawberries. Objectively, there is nothing wrong with the delicious berries. Sweet-talking yourself into eating them, however, and getting ecstatic about strawberries would be a harebrained move when you don't care to spend the rest of a perfect evening in an emergency room.

Do <u>not</u> see *the positive in the negative*. Do not substitute a positive thought for a negative. Do not make garbage look pretty. That's not positive thinking: it's insanity! If your dinner tastes bad and you don't like it, that is your reality of the moment. I don't question your taste and neither should you.

One more time: ecstasy over a delicious dinner can cost you the ability to be happy while having to deal with a horrible dinner, if you don't understand this concept thoroughly. Enjoy what you do or hate it. In that very second you can't change the facts. But you can be thrilled about <u>the way you enjoy</u> something AND you can be ecstatic about <u>the way you hate</u> the present moment with all its details. Got it? Good. Enjoy your damn dinner!

How many selves do you have? Dumb question, I know. I don't intend to warm you up for a sweet personality disorder, and I discourage the notion of telling your colleagues at work that you are, in fact, Napoleon Bonaparte. However, you know you are using a <u>different personality</u> of yours when talking to your employees than when you are taking an evening walk with your spouse. Your children deal with another one of your selves, as does the telemarketer on the phone. To be precise, each of your kids may know a different you. Spending a week visiting your mom may bring a self to the surface you thought you had overcome long ago, eh?

We operate a variety of selves for a host of purposes. Approaching your boss with the who-broke-the-bathroom-mirror self you use for practical purposes in your household may not be advisable, just as it is doomed to talk to your infants with your how-about-a-raise voice. Personally, I don't believe it's a great idea to use your nipple-talk-bedroom self when calling the IRS to negotiate a payment plan, but what do I know. Voice, attitude, self--what difference does it make? We have multiple selves and that is perfectly in order. The more complex an individual you are, the more selves you are developing and employing. You can invent and use as many as you see fit.

Some people believe in having a *higher self*, handling affairs of higher vibrational importance. Or take the idea of *the observer* in the background, elevated above earthly issues. Even the old hat view of vast and powerful *unconscious* areas of our minds aren't extinct yet in Freudian circles. Woo-woo is en vogue, but that magical higher-holier-saintlier humbug is an expression of a spiritual inferiority complex. Pissed-off about a tiny dick, you start looking for something impressive elsewhere. We don't consider ourselves adequate enough and crave to be better than we actually are. At least we want to know of something better deep inside-above-around us that justifies a perceived upgrade.

We love our cats more than we love people but we don't want to be uncomplicated like cats. We want to be special, with a soul--oh yeah, and the older the soul the better--a higher self, and unloved unlike our pets. I am not surprised you don't agree with me. Anyway, the capricious soul artistics of higher self-dependence are alright and I won't talk you out of it if you're having fun with it. Keep your higher crap.

For the rest of us, maintaining a self--equal to the

multitude of selves you have in daily use already--that's thrilled all day is not a bad idea. Crazy? Maybe. You can be crazy about your life without ACTING crazy. I do not suggest you jump up and down in utter delight in public. Even a Tom Cruise can lose his job over such a display. You can keep your cool, others may accuse you of not being a happy person, and you can still be fully aware of having a blast.

"How is everything," asks the waitress. "Fine," you nod with a full mouth because that's how these beasts try to catch you, so that you are incapable of articulating the truth. At the same time you may thank the god of burgers and French fries on your inner knees for this heavenly pile of grease. Ecstasy without showing it. It affects your driving less than a cellphone conversation. No impaired judgment. Yes, integrating positive experiences like milkshakes and chocolate chip cookies looks possible and easy. Claiming ownership over the joys of a root canal procedure may seem somewhat less attractive in comparison.

Negative is just a concept. It does not need to mean anything. "Nothing is either good or bad, but thinking makes it so," said Billy Shakespeare. Do you want happiness? You sure? That is not as difficult as most people believe. You can be happy all the time. By getting rid of bad feelings and trying to do what makes us feel good? Nonsense. You and everybody else has tried that, unsuccessfully.

Negative thinking is the flip side of positive thinking and basically the same. Remember the half-full beer glass? Half empty or half full, it is the same glass and the same stale beer. I am stunned how every positive ass the world over repeats the same anemic allegory. And then what? Even the positive stinkers hate their jobs and invest in hope of a better tomorrow. If you hope and mope for an improved world, yours today isn't that positive, even with positive post-it affirmations plastered all over your refrigerator.

Frustrated, we choose the label *negative* for our current reality and try to make it go away. Oh no, we try to replace the negative with positive goals. We intend for our pink dreams to squeeze the ugly reality out of existence. Works fabulously, doesn't it? Yeah, right. Sad result is that usually and not surprisingly the awful facts don't change. Awful remains awful. Disappointment worsens instead of disappearing, and we find ourselves in an emotional downward spiral, still banking on hope since we are so positive.

Before we go on allow me to sling some more dirt around: a store clerk, maybe 22 years old, told me yesterday that hope is all she has in life. How bitter must she be, how much is she hating her present life, if hope is her only solace? "I have no hope," I told her. A terrible thing from her perspective. For me it is terrific. I have no practical use for hope. A positive thing for one of us can be negative for another. The positive thinking craze is a platitude. There's no substance to it.

Take your negative mood or a nasty experience as a foundation to build upon. For that moment in time, facts are facts and you *cannot* get rid of them. It is awful and by all means, feel free to call it negative. If happiness is indeed what you want, your only chance is to be ecstatic about the current facts. You want to be thrilled about things the way they are and feel. Nuts? Sure, there is nothing sane or sober about happiness.

When I say *you*, I don't refer to everything you are. Just to the one personality or self of yours permitted to enjoy with all plugs pulled, while the others worry about the important issues at hand. Recall a conversation you had with a child, when you had to speak earnestly and matter-of-factly to him about a *deed* while you were bursting with laughter inside, with a different self. Have you ever cried with sadness, deeply mourning maybe, while realizing how comforting and wonderful it felt? And of course, it wouldn't have been appropriate to admit the great part to others. Perhaps you didn't consider it appropriate to admit the warm and fuzzy side of your sadness to yourself. You did get a whiff of it, though, I am convinced.

See the difference to awkward attempts at positive thinking? Feeling sad or angry and overriding that with screeching laughter, re-framing negative emotions with something you think is positive, is simply idiotic. Nope, that won't make you happy. Being sad, angry, depressed and allowing another part of you to realize that it is perfectly permissable to feel sad, angry, depressed--turns the tables. People usually resist emotions that are considered negative. Fighting down tears or trying to not be angry when you are angry already is silly and futile. It doesn't work and it prolongs the emotions you don't want.

You hate getting the flu and dealing with the symptoms? I don't blame you. You have the choice to hate how you hate your damned flu, or you can be ecstatic about the way you hate having the flu. I do NOT tell you to be ecstatic about the flu, genocide in Darfur, or a sledgehammer falling on your toes. That would be a bit odd. I do NOT ask you to accept genocide and crushed toes. I do NOT suggest you find the positive perspective of starvation, malaria, and man-made atrocities. Come to think of it, starvation and malaria *are* man-made by now, also. I do NOT think AIDS in Africa is a wonderful experience to reminisce about twenty years from now, and everybody involved ought to be thankful. Continue hating what you hate. If you hate what's going on in Darfur, hate it with passion.

There it is: ecstasy and--God forbid--lust in the way we hate. We don't love the flu and we never will. We can hate being flattened by the flu and likewise, we can be passionate and thrilled about how we hate being flattened by the flu. People fight for peace with so much passion that they miss the moment when they turn belligerent and violent themselves. Allow a self of yours to admit to having a grand time fighting against global warming. I am afraid the global warming religion has gathered so much support so quickly only because it feels so good to fight *the good fight* with so many likemindless people.

When it feels good, we don't let the facts bother us too much. Greenpeace supporters enjoy the thrill of the fight against environmental evil or what they perceive as such. Hell, I understand. I hate Japan killing more than a thousand whales per year and blatantly lying about the purpose. Research? Research, my arse! I hate it and I know how thrilling it is to hate the Japanese whalers. Don't tell me PETA people don't feel lust over the challenge of a new violation against animal rights. Geez, that stuff defines them and keeps PETA in existence ... and in the money.

And now the unthinkable. I despise people murdering people; genocide, school murders, deadly family tragedies, and 9/11. Duh. Who doesn't? Terminal illnesses, the death of one person or many. Horrible! Anybody who likes such things has got to be a sick, a very sick character. You can't love cancer and torture. Can we allow ourselves to feel ecstasy and passion about the way we hate horror? It's up to you. Nobody would make a dime with horror movies if we could not and would not be able to feel lust and passion about abhorrence. Recall the simple experience of crying in sadness and simultaneously feeling comfort and warmth perhaps. My wild guess is we are--one of our many selves is--capable of being passionate and ecstatic in the face of any human emotion or experience, throughout the entire spectrum of what's considered negative and positive.

How willing are we to *integrate the world*, to claim ownership for the whole damn experience, and to be passionate and in ecstasy about EVERYTHING? Ecstatic about being excited, ecstatic about being depressed, and ecstatic about hating to be depressed. It's messed-up when your cat dies. One part of you feels passionately how messed-up it is when your cat dies. Will you let that part blossom--in secrecy, for your personal protection? Back door happiness is what I call that. We don't want that stuff, the death of our pets is not welcome, but it doesn't have to steal from us what's thrilling about life.

Don't look at me with this deer-in-the-headlights face as if I was the most cynical creep you've ever seen. According to some sources, 11 million children die each year of preventable and treatable causes. About 318 kids croak while you are nursing a beer. You know already how to enjoy life in the midst of crap, even without my complicated and long-winded explanations.

You don't need me to learn that.

What you need me for is to realize that what works for minor problems--like being happy while approximately 300 dead children keep popping up every fifteen minutes--works for the real issues in life also: you can hate your job, your life, your wife AND experience ecstatic fun. It may take a little time but you'll get there. Apropos time, what you really want to work on is called Bitch Lag.

Bitch Lag is the time it takes you from the moment you get pissed off to realizing you can't reverse, undo, or otherwise remove from existence what has pissed you off. Bitch lag is commonly filled with passionate bitching and complaining, whining and cursing, empty threats and contemplation of what could and should have been. While engaged in bitch lag at the water cooler, you are less useful than a quadriplegic in a wheel chair.

Employees can afford long, extended periods of bitch lag because their generous--or stupid--employers continue to reward the professional whiner with paychecks. Some employees live there, I mean their entire lives are a continuum of bitch lag with benefits. Entrepreneurs or the self-employed are rendered completely unproductive precisely as long as they're affected by bitch lag. While you fight a hated fact, you can't do anything about it. When you get a kick out of how you hate a certain fact, in your reality of the moment, instantly the costly and time consuming fighting subsides and you CAN do something about it. Get it? I am confident you do.

Intensity is popular. We crave adventure, firsthand from bone-splintering skateboarding, or secondhand from reality TV and the big screen. People hunger to experience life intensely and then what happens? Positive experiences are not intense enough and if they are, the excitement wears off quickly. The intensity of negative experiences lasts longer--the more we hate them, the better--and skilled as we are in getting worked up about awful stuff, we suck much more intensity out of our negative experiences. Pain is the pinnacle of negative experience. Pain is intense, and we don't escape it.

Thank God for pain! Religious sadomasochists do, every goddamn day. Ha, and since we are capable of climbing the ladder of passion with a little help from things that piss us off, we are able to reach equally high rungs of ecstasy induced by the stuff that pleases us, also. Unless we are total morons, that is. Pain and passion do not exclude each other and both can be experienced simultaneously? You bet. If I were wrong, S/M wouldn't exist and the monks would have never discovered it, for your benefit.

Pain triggers a higher intensity of passion. We are more passionate about pain and our mishaps than we are about our openly declared passions and preferences. Plain fun won't bring us as close to ecstasy as does pain. Whatever sucks in our lives has a phenomenal potential to invigorate us. Pain bypasses conscious decision making. You don't think long and hard whether you should get upset over something that hurts you. It happens instantly. SNAP! And you are pissed off, bathed in sweat, and the adrenaline is pumping overtime. Uh, the doorway to ecstasy!

Our admitted passions, like repairing vintage automobiles, quail hunting, or chess, don't get us that animated so quickly. Well, here is an invitation: identify, locate, and evolve the part of you that can be ecstatic and put the damn thing to work, all day, everyday. Impossible? Yeah, right. If you have ever been cheesed off about your superiors and you indulged in bothering your poor spouse with every idiotic detail, you can do it.

Pain is not always an objective fact. Pain and suffering are subject to perception. Increasing your perceived pain level can help produce ecstasy. You know how much you hate and love when you get worked up over a banality. Literally, a fly in love with your bald scalp has sufficient power to get you into a state of mind you don't want to be in all day. Keep your blood pressure up and your physician may advise against it. In other words, a fly on the wall is not worth having a heart attack over--is anything?-- and you have the choice to increase or decrease the perceived level of pain.

Once your passion gets going, you can tune down the perceived pain level a notch or two. Otherwise you'll look silly and you don't want to waste your energy on nothing. I assume your most common pain is not having your guts hanging out of a shrapnel wound but rather work-related grievances, relationship problems, financial worries perhaps, or your teenage daughter's sharply declining grades.

Discover your ecstasy in your painful moments as an option, and once aware of it opt out of the pain gradually if at all possible. No need to stay addicted to pain and hardship as most of our fellow citizens are. Since you don't need to rely on awful things to be passionate, you now have the choice and the freedom to be ecstatic about any experience. Hence fun and enjoyable things become equally as valuable as the realm of pain for your utmost delight.

Hate with joy! I mean, hate with a passion. Realize how much you love to hate whatever it is you may be hating. And when you have bitched yourself into the delirium of hatred, flip the switch. You know by now that behind your lust for disgust lurks the part of you that enjoys your misery tremendously. It's going to continue the excitement without you having to maintain the hatred. Once excited, you are free to move in any direction. To be exact, we are heated up passionately all the time but glaring hatred allows us to see it and to claim that part of ourselves. True excitement is what we want. Now it's time to lose your hatred. It has lost its perverted purpose.

If I'm not too wrong, that kind of excitement, passion, ecstasy or whatever the hell you want to call it is what we are actually after. We say we want a house, a boat, and vacations because we secretly hope to get thrills and ecstasy out of that stuff. The older we get, the more jaded we become and we know all the stuff in the world doesn't come with ecstasy in the bag. Saddening and reason enough to give up the pursuit? On the contrary, with the real source for thrills and passion between your ears, you gain the ability to get the most fun out of house, boat, vacations, snowmobiles, and other toys. You can, at will, but you don't have to. It's what I call freedom.

King Gillette, a traveling salesman, was shaving his stubbly face with a dull straight razor one morning in 1895. It was painful. Mr. Gillette's passion turned that pain into the development of a product. He wrote:

"As I stood there with my razor in my hand, my eyes resting on it as lightly as a bird settling down on its nest--the Gillette razor was born. I saw it all in a moment, and in that moment many unvoiced questions were asked and answered more with the rapidity of a dream than by the slow process of reasoning. It seemed as though I could see the way the blade could be held in a holder; then came the idea of sharpening opposite edges on the thin piece of steel that was uniform in thickness throughout, thus doubling its services; and following in sequence came the clamping plates for the blades and a handle easily disposed between the two edges of the blade. All this came more in pictures than in thought as though the razor were a finished thing and held before my eyes.

Fool that I was, I knew little about razors and practically nothing about steel, and I could not foresee the trials and tribulations that I was to pass through before the razor was a success."

Years of development lay ahead for Mr. Gillette, who formed his company in 1901. He did not put his first razor on the market until 1903, selling a grand total of 51 razors and 168 blades in the first year of production. (source: Smith, Dalzell - *Wisdom from the Robber Barons*) Pain and passion as source for products and wealth is not a novel idea. The ground was broken centuries ago.

Cause and effect are considered lawfully connected. What a hoax! How often have you tried to cause something and the desired effect did not occur? If cause and effect were a law of nature, the same cause would lead to identical effects, again and again and again. That's not so, is it? A bunch of snake oil peddlers would love for you to believe that their proven methods and no-brainer systems perform like clockwork for everybody every time.

Alas, they are indeed no-brainers. Everyone with a brain realizes quickly that a lot of occurrences don't have a discernible cause, and repeatedly applied *cause A* does not always trigger *effect B*. 'If you work hard you'll make plenty of money,' for instance is true for some, sometimes. It is certainly not true for everybody, all the time. Shaken and stunned by especially horrible events, we frantically search for clues and possible causes. Even if we settle for the most plausible one, the officially accepted cause, we'll never have the guarantee of having discovered the real cause.

Vices can be so much more profitable than virtues. You don't believe me? You are saying more money can be made with a school of ethics than with a brothel? Even if you are right, you don't have to motivate people to spend money on their vices. You don't need to spend time explaining the benefits to your target audience. Your customers understand your business. Whatever vices you may indulge in, they are profitable--if not for you, then for somebody else.

Your vices can be stronger as an income source than your strengths. How so? Sell products--and develop products and services--to others who share your vices. Some people are ashamed of their vices--or weaknesses, as they call what's so much fun for them--and they hide their disgraceful sides from family, friends, and from potential customers. Kick your vices out of the closet, put them to work, and you'll see how virtuous they can be.

Losing isn't easy. We are our own harshest critics and we're capable of destroying ourselves emotionally and physically over loss and losing. Responsibility turns into guilt quickly. Shame does the rest to make the last bit of self-respect and confidence disappear. You think success is hard? Try losing! True, some dorks go bananas and destroy themselves over their successes. The droll assembly of Spears, Lohan, Winehouse & Co. present every painful detail to us on a silver platter. Happens, but it's nothing to break out in tears over. Success, no success, almost success, past success, too fast success, too slow success, no hope for success--people find a reason in everything to mutilate or kill themselves, literally or figuratively, if that's what seems to promise the most fun. Anyway, the loser may be more used to torture and self-torture than the perceived winner, but we'll never know for certain. Which camp does Michael Jackson belong to? Regardless of your answer, are you sure? Where you sure 10-15 years ago?

You think you can insult and hurt someone by calling him a loser? Your vile attempt is laughable compared to what a loser puts himself through each day. Not winning is not the typical loser's biggest concern, even though she may think it is. Being content with losing is the greatest challenge at hand. Yep, the loser must train to be a happy loser before she can take the next step. If you can't be a happy loser, you will never be a happy winner--whatever you think winning means.

Isn't every successful person automatically happy? Silly goose! Ask Ted Turner how often he has contemplated suicide. Yeah baby, even the life of a billionaire isn't what it used to be. Ask Jim Morrison, Jimi Hendrix, Janis Joplin, James Dean, Elvis Presley, Kurt Cobain (maybe he wasn't the one who was unhappy with him), Michael Hutchence ... the list is endless. Yes dear, money, fame, and success will make you happy, automatically and guaranteed.

The happy loser, who doesn't give a damn about her mistakes or how often and how badly she has screwed up, will be back on her feet faster to try something new. Well, or she'll be happy without it, but no idiot can hurt her by calling her names. Only sore losers respond to that, the ones scared of losing who believe they should be winners.

Happiness can be a painful experience. Some are afraid what hardship may happen next, while being happy. Naturally, such thoughts sabotage happiness instantly. Others murder wife and children before they blow their own worthless brains out, on the happiest day of their lives. I am not making this up. Happiness can be dangerous. Why else are we so scared of being happy all day?

What is happiness? Losing yourself in an activity.

Entering the trance of a task, any task, and forgetting the rest of the world. You can experience that during sex or while doing your taxes. Doing what you love is, contrary to mass opinion, NOT a prerequisite to being happy. It doesn't matter what you do. Crucial is how deeply and completely you immerse yourself into what you do. To be happy, you have to get lost, completely.

As fervently as we chase it, happiness appears to be so foreign to us that it takes extra effort to live with it in peace. Crap we are accustomed to seems easier for us to integrate as our own than happiness. If you care, make happiness your own and normal self. Hey, it's free.

Dance, when you're broken open.
Dance, if you've torn the bandage off.
Dance, in the middle of the fighting.
Dance in your blood.
Dance, when you're perfectly free.

Rumi

Chapter Twelve
Losing and Confidence

"I've missed more than nine thousand shots in my career. I've lost almost three hundred games. Twenty-six times, I've been trusted to take the game-winning shot and missed. I've failed over and over and over again in my life. And that is why I succeed."

Michael Jordan

Winning boosts your confidence. Success feels good and that's alright. Except, self-confidence based on success is fake. Say what? Yep, success-based confidence is fickle and depends on something outside your sphere of control. I am delighted about you being successful, seriously, but that is subject to change without further notice. If your luck changes and you experience a series of unfortunate events, you don't want to lose your confidence over it. Your confidence is one of your most valuable assets. You need confidence to succeed. If you need success to guarantee your confidence, you are essentially screwed. Self-confidence based on yourself is crucial to survive the volatile times of the markets you are operating in.

To a degree, winning and success are subject to chance, and it doesn't matter how hard you try to control the unfolding of events. Yet without confidence, you won't even begin a new project. Low self-esteem locks people into cubicles, turns them into obedient slaves scared of their own original thoughts. Without confidence you have to be very lucky to win anything anywhere.

When you have zero confidence--either you never had it or you lost it painfully--you are the sphincter of society, and it's a silly idea to work on a career from there before rebuilding a decent confidence level. Not surprisingly, most jobs are dead-end jobs. Getting that sort of employment is the equivalent of retirement. The job retires you from being your promising you, a vibrant life-loving individual with creative potential. Regaining--or gaining--your confidence puts you in a position to have a shot at success and winning, again and again. For a confident person it hardly matters how often you lose before you win the next time.

Losing is not reserved exclusively for a particular group of people, the professional losers. Everybody can lose, but not everybody knows how to be and stay happy during stretches of failure or loss. What does it take to be a happy loser? So many people won't bother to figure that out. They just want to win, be successful, and thus leave the misery of losing behind. Show me the money and I'll be happy automatically. That's right out of the philosophy for chumps, and utter nonsense in the real world of course. Blindly, they're prepared to barrel through the barricades regardless of possible damages. Good luck!

Happiness requires confidence. Not even success can be happily enjoyed without confidence. Lack of confidence can cause you to lose everything you have, and even an occasional winning streak will be bleak and next to worthless. Confidence helps you to win and to enjoy your success. Being happy throughout an unfortunate period of personal famine requires more confidence than anything else. Your entire future depends on it.

Exterior forms of validation often substitute for self-confidence. I keep a distance between me and those people, a dangerous species, who will never be true friends or trustworthy business partners. You are either useful as their backdrop or as a means to their ends. Individuals, craving outside validation will always be users, and the step from being needy to becoming a backstabber is a small one. Draw your confidence from yourself with little or no support from circumstance. You have plenty to feel good about, and you won't escape the need to be confident about yourself precisely the way you are. It is your only option.

Happy winners are not going to remain happy for long if they're happy *because* they won or succeeded. Happiness, dependent upon circumstances, is short-lived and not real. If you are happy only when you win and unhappy when you lose, you are doomed. No one can win all the time, not even you. Things go wrong in anybody's and everybody's life, and success-based happiness is almost a guarantee for a mostly miserable life. Try it out if you must. It sucks, and even when you are successful--and therefore temporarily happy in your little world--success and its enjoyment will be brief and you'll get anxious for your next fix. No leaning back and relaxing permitted. You are just another damned junkie.

Only if you develop the skills to be happy while losing will you be experienced enough to be truly happy in successful times. You are cause and source of your enjoyment and happiness. That stuff doesn't automatically follow certain desired events.

Accomplishments don't provide confidence. Arrogance maybe, but not confidence, and arrogance is an expression of insecurity. If your confidence depends on your accomplishments, you will have to wait for a long time. The results will be the opposite of what you are aiming for. Accomplish all you want, alienate people left and right with your arrogant attitude, and morph into an insecure wretch. However you slice it, you can't develop confidence with accomplishments or success. Confidence can be had free of charge, but you must be free to claim it at any time, for no apparent reason and without conditions.

Bling-bling, eye candy, and exotic cars can be fun, but it's entirely useless for the construction of confidence. You have to be a pathetic loser to think you can impress yourself and others successfully with that kind of accoutrement. I don't mean *you*, of course, because you knew that already.

Solid confidence can get you all that stuff easier if you really care. There is nothing wrong with beautiful and expensive details. Have them and enjoy them, but there is something scarily wrong with those who need such things to show off. Nothing wrong with poor people. Nothing wrong with rich people. But I do feel sorry for poor schmucks with a lot of money. An embarrassing sight.

Sorry, if you have to look like a winner everybody knows

you're most likely a loser with an inferiority complex. A person, desperately trying to be perceived as successful, is painful to watch. Nobody cares whether you are successful or not. Really, we are not that important. What's important for you is to be happy more often than not, during successes AND failures. I don't think impressing bystanding strangers is a valid recipe for happiness, and your friends have known for years what a dork you are. A faked orgasm isn't as exciting as a real one, is it? Well, neither is a fake winner.

The danger of winner's confidence is having to deal with ups and downs--probably more downs than ups--without a chance of being balanced emotionally. You can't win all the time, and when your confidence depends on winning streaks--winning moments, more realistically--you are emotionally in the pits most of the time. That in turn is not a great base from which to start anything new and promising.

Casinos are built on winner's confidence because the average gambler is suffering from it. That's exactly what makes them feel so good after a huge payout. Instead of going home with filled pockets, their fake confidence--and their ridiculous superstition that one nice payout is proof of a loose machine, etc.--convinces the winning gambler into staying until the money won, and more, has gone to money heaven.

Taking credit for winning and blaming others for losing is a clear sign of lack of confidence. Building ourselves and other people up with incidents of winning, and tearing others and ourselves down for losing shows no sense of reality. Both winning and losing occur naturally. Often it is a matter of perspective whether we won or lost. While we are winning at the stock market somebody else loses, and winning and losing happen simultaneously. To be exact, we may think we're winning and the other guy is the loser, but it may turn out that the other guy wins more than we do and thinks we are the loser.

Lines between losing and winning can be blurred. As we have seen recently--during the Tour de France or in Marion Jones' case, for instance--even winning five Olympic medals doesn't mean you are a winner, and it may take months or years to figure out what's what. Larry Ellison, CEO of Oracle, has won or lost a billion dollars or two on a single trading day. I am sure he likes winning better, yet I don't think one or the other affects his self-confidence in the slightest. Of course you want to have an eye on the pulse of the market, but you are doomed if you take emotional credit for winning situations and if you beat yourself or your people into the ground for a loss.

Losing increases the probability of winning? Superstitious gamblers believe the longer, say, the double zero hasn't shown up at the Roulette table, the more probable it will be for the next spin to produce it. Not so: each new spin is subject to the same odds, and the probability of any one number winning remains 2.63%, independent of any series of events. "The biggest gambling myth is that an event that has not happened recently becomes overdue and more likely to occur. Known as the *gambler's fallacy*." (Michael Shackleford, wizardofodds.com)

Similarly, your chance for the market to find your next idea as fantastic and valuable as you do is the same with each new idea you crank out. Three failed business projects in a row do not increase the chance of your fourth idea being a winner. Neither do you *deserve* more to win after numerous losses. That's not how the universe thinks. By the same token, your very first idea can be financially phenomenal, and then you may be challenged by dozens of duds in a row.

Winning motivates you? Success drives you? Too bad. Success is a fickle driving force and when you're in the fiscal doldrums, you need something more uplifting to get you out of bed besides a stack of unpaid bills. Trust me. Motivation to act must come from yourself. Do what you do because you want to do it or better, because you can't hold yourself back. Success, failure, cynical in-laws, lack of money, plenty of money--none of that really matters.

When you work because you can't stop yourself, you can't help but have success eventually. Only if you live long enough, of course. Winning is gravy and you can't take it for granted. You get paid by doing what you want to do. If you happen to win really big, be happy and I am thrilled for you, but I wouldn't bank on such an event to occur. I am so negative? Not at all, but I'd rather see you happy than broke.

You know what is a worse motivating factor than past or current success? Future success! Good Gawd, unless you want to dupe people into your network marketing scheme, don't ever mess yourself up with expectations of future money and successes to motivate today's actions. Future success works like dangling a carrot in front of a donkey. It works, as it keeps the donkey moving, but the ass never obtains its prize. Retirement has elements of this brilliant strategy and personally, I find it depressing.

Winning cannot be controlled, simply because more than one person is involved in any financial transaction. It takes at least two people to exchange money, doesn't it? Hence you'll never have 100% control over the outcome. However, you can control what you do. With the same level of control you have over taking a nap, you can freely engage in your choice of thousands of possibly lucrative projects. Minus two or three unforeseen things, of course. While taking your nap, the phone may ring and the boss of your boss needs to talk to you, NOW. Or your teenage son calls with the great revelation that you will be a grandma soon. Minor distractions are not important enough to prevent you from doing what you want. Trifles may delay your twenty minute walk, but don't let those fools stop you.

You have always decided and you will decide in the future when to pick up the phone, whom to talk to and how long. You even decide who is good enough to be your boss and for how long--unless you get canned first, that is. You better digest that slowly: employees have in-credibly vast options. They have more freedom to choose who they want to work for than employers do about the next person they plan to hire. You don't have to work where you work. That is true even if you own and run a two hundred year-old family business. You control what you do and you control what you don't do. It's almost too simple. You have full control over picking your nose and over the promising beginning of a new business venture.

Failure rates determine your income. Do you have one? A failure rate, I mean? Coming up with a fantastic idea is almost a guaranteed loser. Oh, you've got THE idea of a lifetime? Sure you do. If it doesn't kill you or destroy your family and your friendships, you are in luck. It'll make you rich one day? Right.

Single isolated ideas are almost always doomed. Forget the greatest idea you've ever had and don't listen to other people who beg you to invest in their single most promising idea. A single idea is worth as little as a single sperm. I wouldn't bet a penny on it. Your income is determined roughly by the volume of ideas you turn into actual products, and how--and how frequently--you introduce new products to the market.

But hey, don't listen to me: baby, if you plan to start a business or you have an existing operation--mildly or wildly successful--I urge you to shell out a couple of bucks and get Michael Masterson's book *Ready, Fire, Aim: Zero to $100 Million in No Time Flat*. The subtitle smells of snake oil, I know, but don't let that deter you from discovering a collection of precious gems. I wish Mr. Masterson had written it and dropped this thing into my lap twenty years ago. Bastard!

What were we talking about? Yes, your failure rate. The faster you fail, the better off you'll be. If 5% of your ideas have a chance to be accepted by the market, you've got to be pretty prolific in churning out new stuff. Can you enjoy a royal lifestyle even if 95% of your ideas fail? You bet, but sitting on your keister won't get you there. If that sounds like too much pressure to you, keep working for the post office until you drop. I understand, I am too lazy for such an onslaught of fun as well.

Probability is hard to escape. Hence the most successful people deal with random and perhaps devastating setbacks just like everybody else. There is no guarantee for success and winning, as there is no guarantee for losing and failure. We all lose sometimes, we make unbelievably dumb mistakes fortunately, and damn ... we all die. Not much you can do about that, and up to this day the most experienced medical professionals and backyard healers cannot tell you what to do either. They can't even agree on how much water you should drink.

Survival of the fittest? Nope, not even the fittest survive. Sooner or later everybody loses big time; financially, healthwise, or in the relationship department. So what? No reason to lose any sleep over it or to abandon your comfortable level of confidence. Everybody is a loser eventually. That alone should be incentive enough for you to walk straight and to keep your head high.

Chapter Thirteen
Reward and Punishment

"If people are good only because they fear punishment, and hope for reward, then we are a sorry lot indeed."

Albert Einstein

Reward and punishment are fine motivational tools in the average sucker family. For you and me, reward and punishment are worthless and meaningless. Punishment has hardly any value as deterrent, as research has shown. So, what purpose does it serve besides satisfying an urge for revenge on the side of the punishing party?

If that is the case, the punisher derives pleasure and maybe even lust from the act of punishing. Punishment is good for those who punish. The one who is supposed to change her behavior motivated by punishment most likely doesn't care, unless she also gets pleasure out of pain. Often--and our helpless and hapless justice system shows it--punishment numbs the punished person. Punished people do not correct their behavior as intended by the punisher: they just become increasingly immune to punishment and pain. Or, as we said, some individuals may even begin enjoying the pain and crave higher dosages in the future.

Pain is not punishment, necessarily, and pleasure is not a reward. Oh, pleasure is fine, yet there are pleasures that can kill you, and you may agree with me that most of us hardly consider death a rewarding experience. Then there is pain that works perfectly to intensify one's pleasure, and therefore it's ill-fitted to be used as punishment.

Emotions and feelings take us out of the simplistic world of black and white. Nothing is the same for two people. Neither you nor I enjoy hitting our thumbs with a hammer--I assume--instead of the damn nail. Yet what pain means to you exactly, nobody will ever find out. When does a physical sensation begin to be pain? How far is each of us willing to endure it? Under what circumstances can painful experiences begin to be an experience of pleasure?

Individual experiences and choices separate us and prevent us from understanding each other. It is foolish to assume pain is pain and pleasure is pleasure. One man's pain is another man's pleasure. Using your set of pain/pleasure parameters to punish or reward others may be somewhat meaningful to you, but it is going to fail if you intend to influence somebody else with it.

Pain is a reward. You are questioning my sanity once again? If you think pain works well as punishment, think again. People are proud about their accomplishments when they were hard to achieve. Hard-earned money is more appreciated and treated with greater respect than money won or found. Not just a few messed-up perverts see it that way. No, as a society, we perceive pain as reward.

When the boss busts through the door, unannounced, employees are embarrassed to be caught having fun. Pleasure is connected with feelings of guilt, whether you are talking about your secret eating habits or work. Officially, we hate pleasure and we welcome pain. Some of that we see in a different light during our weekends, and that's when our normal state of emotional confusion gets driven into more tension than some people can handle with a sober mind.

Rewards do not motivate mature people. Children and childlike minds may be inspired by rewards, but such incentives are useless and even counter-productive for entrepreneurs and self-employed individuals. Seeking pleasure and reassuring strokes for an insecure ego is a short-lived kind of motivation. Long term success demands unlimited patience and the ability to weather adversity--outright hostility, even--discomfort, and financial setbacks. Many amazing inventions and enormously successful companies would not exist had their foundation and development been based on someone seeking rewards. *What do I get out of this, what are the benefits?* may be sufficiently motivating for punks and suckers. For you and me it doesn't work that way.

Rewards may help average simpletons to do a bit more of what they hate doing, but even then the benefits fade quickly. Grade school and network marketing may function to a limited degree supported by reward driven ideas. For you, pursuing your dream, reward oriented thinking is like sugar in the tank.

Punishment does not deter people from making poor choices or from doing bad things. Punishment serves hardly any other purpose than to satisfy the mob's cry for revenge and a governor's desire for reelection. A couple of thousand years of Judeo-Christian child rearing haven't been long enough to transcend the unimaginative demand *an eye for an eye* for something of a predominantly constructive nature. And I don't expect Jesus' quite different and rather radical philosophy to become popular amongst Christians anytime soon. No, I am not a religious man. I'm a bloody infidel, in fact.

Religious texts, by the way, are littered with punishing land mines while the promised rewards are disappointingly few, pretty vague, or not to be claimed until you are dead. If religious people took their sacred books literally and acted on the most conservative teachings ("If a man commits adultery with another man's wife--with the wife of his neighbor--both the adulterer and the adulteress must be put to death." *Leviticus 20:10*), many of us would be dead by now and most religious folks would serve long prison sentences. Developing regions insist on gulping down their pain straight up. Developed parts of the world appear to have found a practical balance of pain: dish out and endure enough to serve the godly dictum but don't upset anyone's stomach.

Let's not get carried away with forgiving the wrong enemy or loving our neighbors too much. That could get us into new trouble. Anyway, we love our neighbors already as we love ourselves: not at all. What more can you ask for?! Religious or not, our favored method of choice for the approach of anything remains pain and (self)-punishment, of course, because that's what we know the best and love the most. No need for barbaric punishments like stonings. Our distribution of pain is more sophisticated, evolved, better.

Agreed, murderers and thieves need to be stopped from repeating their crimes. Child molesters and rapists must be locked up. Will they be better members of society after x number of years in prison? Don't be silly. Our forms of punishment are often expressions of utter helplessness. We don't have a clue what to do so we do *something* and keep our fingers crossed. Locking Charles Manson behind bars forever is a fabulous idea. Putting Martha Stewart in jail was a harebrained idea. It was supposed to deter others from doing the same--which doesn't work, as criminal statistics show--and it was aimed to feed the craving of the masses for revenge, to see a big wig's fingers slapped.

The intent of punishment misses its mark in both cases. Manson can't be punished enough for his deeds, and no punishment will ever have an effect on him: he will remain the same Manson. But who cares? He should never see the light of day again. Ms. Stewart most likely got the message long before her correctional ordeal began. Public humiliation was traumatic enough. So, why punish her if not for the satisfaction of the punishing authority?

Monetary punishment--like leaving a smaller tip for a *bad* waitress--works in similar ways. It won't *train* the waitress to be a better waitress next time or change her behavior. She'll be even more pissy for the rest of her shift. Fascinating - there are still dullards who believe they can train waiters and waitresses like dogs. Behaviorism is as dead as B.F. Skinner and besides, it didn't work too well when your parents tried to abuse cash to punish or reward you, did it?

A good waitress having a bad day is fully aware of not being at her best. She is forcing herself to work on a horrible day, trying to make some money anyway. Don't you want to make just as much money on your bad days as you do when you are on top of your game? For your own and for your happiness' sake, DOUBLE your tip for a bad waitress! Important for you, not so much for her--got it? It'll instantly heal your pathological obsession to fix the world according to your image. That would be the last thing we need.

Yeah, but what if she really is that bad? It's her problem to deal with, not yours, and if you don't cough up a decent tip soon, I shall come over there and slap some sense into you. Punishment has the sole questionable purpose to satisfy the punishing party. Besides that it's utterly useless, but I understand this is a futuristic idea whose time won't come for decades.

Emotionally immature people love reward and punishment. It looks like a system simplistic enough to provide solutions for complicated problems. Too many parents try reward and punishment to bypass thoughtful responses to the normal needs of their children. Well, used on 4 - 7 year-olds it may appear to work--deceptively so. But then, the same dull system applied to teenagers may backfire badly. Systems don't work and reward-and-punishment, stick and carrot, is nothing more than another system. Problems of pedagogy or financial problems cannot be solved with systems. Reward and punishment is one of those ideas too good to be true, and it won't become truer with frequent use. Continued use is like beating a dead horse.

We are not cavemen anymore--even though I have days when I'm not so sure--and our children aren't dogs we can teach new tricks. Free people, independent individuals who care to live and work as they choose, have no use for reward/punishment dynamics. Why? Because there is nobody above them to dish it out. And how much more of a reward do you expect from life than doing what you want to do?

R/P is for children. Really? Reward and punishment attacks have an effect on kids, I agree, but is it good for them? If you want your children to turn into little whores, R/P is the way to go. Personally, I have nothing against prostitutes. Most of them have more integrity than their clientele. But teaching your children the ropes of prostitution is a different thing. "If I gave you this, would you do that for me?" "If you refuse to do X, I will hurt you by doing Y."

Wow! Yeah, people who learn to live their lives that way

will be respected members of our society. Eager to live in a society of brown nosers, boot lickers, and back stabbers? No? I am delighted to hear that. The Third Reich is a beautiful example of R/P in action. You bet it works. If a fascist regime is what you want, I recommend reward and punishment as your educational tool of choice.

Reward and punishment is the perfect method to discipline recruits, if you want an army of idiots that is, plain and perfect cannon fodder. If you train special forces, I assume cheap tricks out of the R/P repertoire will fail miserably. Schools and all sorts of corporate or government hierarchies can be managed-- badly--with theories based on reward and punishment. Hardly anybody will notice that R/P directed organizations function in spite of that system and not because of it. But who cares?

Reward and punishment oriented environments are the morass of modern day slavery. People are expected to be unhappy, and they stay for an additional couple of years for the benefits. The most absurd fact in those organizations is perhaps that the worse they treat their employees, the more loyal they'll be. Cut the bonuses and increase the threat of getting sacked, and your employees hang on to their jobs for dear life. The more miserable they are, the more precious the perception of their job. There are limits, of course, but they don't mean all that much.

Behaviorists have bored us for decades with wholesome news of the Pavlovian pooch and rat crap straight out of the Skinner Box. Mr. Skinner didn't believe so much in the merits of punishment. Yet he inspired hordes of school teachers and management types to experiment with *positive and negative reinforcement* to increase *adaptive behavior* and to kill *maladaptive behavior*. School children and employees were--and still are--the guinea pigs.

On the positive side, Freud's frauds have been more damaging than Mr. Burrhus Frederic Skinner's claptrap. Speaks for Freddy, kind of. I am convinced the slave owners of previous centuries would have loved the man at least as much as desperate employers do today. Care for individuality and freedom anyone?

Then please leave B.F Skinner in his rotting box.

Prostitutes are raised like this: 'If you get an A for your upcoming math test, Grandma will give you 5 dollars.' 'If you sign up 5 new sales representatives for our MLM scheme, we raise your status to Diamond Dork.' Rewards, real as in cash, or perceived as in status, subdue the intrinsic motivation each of us was born with. Individuals have something to offer, valuable enough to be turned into serious income on the market. But when we permit others to sucker us into their well-oiled reward/punishment system, we butcher the inspiration to use and develop what we have.

People don't need outside motivation to live. We are alive already and when we exploit our lives a bit, we have a great chance to discover the gems in our characters. We don't need slave drivers and the inspiration of whips on our backs to produce something useful and to turn it into cash.

Reward systems may increase adaptive behavior in corporate rats, but they inhibit the individual and choke an individual's chances of ever making it outside of that system. Oh, you find my language demeaning and inappropriate? I was not the one who called it a rat race first, was I? As long as corporate pimping is not only accepted, but rather demanded in quiet desperation, it'll be fine--for the pimps.

Punishment trains people to live with punishment. That's it. Punished individuals get used to it, they become numb or immune, and they begin to crave higher dosages. You have seen statistics of kids being institutionalized throughout their entire lives. Plenty of stories began in foster homes and ended in prison. Brief periods spent outside were just sufficiently long to cause more severe punishments.

Permanently infantile creatures are made by way of punishing people. Punishment can be as addictive as any other thing. No pain - no gain taken to the extreme finds its expression in the average prison population. Some personalities thrive there. "Punish him with the rod and save his soul from death." (Proverbs 23:14) Yeah, some creeps were born to be punished. Why not beat up everybody?

Helplessness is all I can see in this reward/punishment cycle. MLMers giving new network marketers a litany of incentives to run faster in their hamster wheel is a pathetic show to witness. Nobody wants to be there. Nobody wants to do what they do. The off-chance of future rewards is the only thing that matters.

People who have nothing to offer but rewards are helpless. Those who have nothing to gain but rewards are empty. What greater punishment can you endure than living for rewards? A real punishment? Punishing parents are helpless. They don't know what else to do and in desperation they punish their disobedient brats.

Remember an instance of your parents being angry with you when you were a kid? Are you sure they were angry at you? Or were they angry about themselves because they were at their wit's end? Shaking, pissed-off that they didn't know how else to respond to your misdeeds, they punished you with something laughably stupid. Rewards and punishments are pitiful. If you really consider yourself more sophisticated than a donkey running after a carrot, you better come up with something smarter.

Freedom is free. The world of causality is not. Addicted to cause and effect, we search for causes like maniacs. There is another school shooting somewhere, and we are obsessed to find the reason to prevent the next mass murder in a classroom. We know there was a cause and if we control that cause, nobody will get hurt in the future. As David Harsanyi puts it in *Nanny State*, 'the five most frightening words in the English language: something needs to be done.' The ultimate fascist mommy won't be happy until the last student is shackled to his chair. Uh, safety at last! Except, one of the next shootings will probably be committed by a disgruntled ex-teacher, and the futile cycle to feverishly hunt for a cause starts anew.

We settle for causes we *believe* have led to undesired effects, but the causes we believe in are not necessarily the true causes. Otherwise the identical cause would have to propel the same effect each and every time, yet we know two children with similar troubled backgrounds will NOT both turn into cold-blooded murderers as the behaviorists would have you believe. In fact, if dysfunctional families, hours spent playing violent video games, poor supervision, and depression are indicators for creating dangerous teenagers--I am surprised anybody is still alive. Seriously. Some fifty school shootings have happened world wide in the past ten years, and the theories I have heard about the possible causes were factually as solid as UFO sightings.

Reward and punishment is based on thinking in the limited realm of causality, an obstacle in the way to free thinking and acting. Not all causes have measurable effects. Not all occurrences have a clearly identifiable cause. Your happiness, for instance, exists without outer cause: you are happy being you, doing what you are doing right now, or you will never be happy. No cause, no reward, no other person, no circumstance will ever do the trick. Happy we are because we decide to be happy, for no reason, with no plausible chain of events leading up to it. That's how some people decide to be something else and to do other things, faster than a behaviorist can finish lunch. Reasons? Causes? C'mon, let's not embarrass ourselves.

Money as a reward will be limited. Firstly, because someone else decides how much you can have. No matter how great the monetary reward, its size is capped by either a person or by a committee. You will always have to report to that superior authority as long as you are after reward money.

In the open and anonymous market, there is hardly a limit to how many people you can approach, expose your products to, how many may buy from you, and how you experiment with prices. The market is a playing field for free-thinking individuals. The reward oriented person still craves the parent-child relationship, complete with fixed allowance and designated paydays.

Rewards are nice--please don't reject them when you can get them--but it is infinitely nicer to grow beyond the stuffy reward mentality. Pleasing mommy and daddy is not what I have in mind when I think of freedom and financial independence. As if 300 years of industrial serfdom weren't enough, bemoaning job outsourcing is as embarrassing and shortsighted as it was when the typical job hating employee aired her angst in the 1970s that computers would steal her miserable typewriter job, including carpal tunnel syndrome. You are afraid to lose something? So was the elevator man when those things got buttons any idiot could push. Ah, the good old times ... everything was better then. Today's IT specialist is tomorrow's elevator man. Obsolete and out-dorked.

Many of us believe in jackass theories because they help to make the world look understandable. The reward/punishment theory appears deceptively useful to manage dependents and employees, and we take to such nonsense faster than DMV workers drop pencils at 5:00 pm. The emotionally immature derive comfort and structure from reward and punishment. Both sides, the *giving* and the *receiving* parties, understand R/P transactions and and may even develop a dependency for such rituals. Hence the popularity of the Old Testament, the Qur'an, and their root--the Torah--throughout the millennia. Or is it the other way around? Sometimes I am so confused.

The majority of people thinks in black and white schemata, and wants to see evil bad guys get crushed and good people to triumph victoriously. Human beings may be a bit simplistic, but people in general are not stupid. We can learn. Within a short century and after paying the reasonable price of 100 million dead bodies, history has taught us that we can't solve problems by separating the good from the bad. Hitler tried that to the delight of his serfs. So did Stalin, Mao, and Saddam. The idea alone that *I am good and you are not*, is of fascist nature.

Non-smokers believe they are better than stinking smokers. Educated people think of themselves as higher than high school dropouts. Poor individuals are convinced they are morally superior to the rich. I assure you there will never be a shortage of Nazis, and they'll continue to cry for reward and punishment as loudly as they can. It's childish stuff, and those of us who care about quality of life don't have a newer car in mind. Rewards, punishment, revenge, and the measurement of one group against the other have no place in our lives.

Pet theories are just that: theories of a pet. R/P is ideal for domesticated entities, and if you want to be a pooch you'll feel right at home. But I am not writing this for the dwindling number of the unfortunate who demand to have social bones thrown their way. We have been enlightened for hundreds of years, or so *they* say. Intelligent and educated men and women have been around for ages, but enlightenment didn't do it. Neither did literacy. As a species, we are still toddlers in a sandlot. We draw a line in the dirt and threaten each other with ridiculous consequences if and when the other steps over that line.

The morons of former Yugoslavia had to form half a dozen new countries to stop bloodshed. Maybe they'll complete a baker's dozen by next Christmas. I guess that's one type of peace when everybody gets their own playpen, protected by barbed wire and land mines. Intelligent people have been discussing the division of Iraq into multiple countries to end their gory idiocy. Are we as a species that dumb? Then we should be kept in individual boxes of God's barn for his favorite pets. On some days I am close to denouncing evolution.

You disagree? Me too. Idealist that I am, I believe we can leave reward and punishment behind with those who insist on staying in the dark ages--humanity's kindergarten--for another 500 years. Individuals, who choose to think and live freely, thrive with the consequences and benefits of free markets and free trade. The free can't handle the borders of the old order, rules of employment, rewards for the poor, and punishment for the rich.

And it chanced that the Lord of the Universe, the Divine Creator Himself, did come to send a Message to mankind, a Message which would liberate men from the heavy burden they had come to encumber themselves with. And He sent the Message to earth and it was spoken and it was written and men did not hear and men did not see.

"How can this be?" asked the Lord of the Universe. "I have sent the Message that will liberate all men from the burdens they needlessly carry and yet they do not hear it, do not see it."

All the angels stood in embarrassed silence at the Lord's question except one, Our Beloved Whim, who dared to speak.

"Mighty Lord," said Whim. "In your Infinite Wisdom and Love you have sent men the Message, but they have neither ears to hear it nor eyes to see it."

"I know," said the Divine Creator. "But how can this be?"

"It's simple, Lord," Whim replied. "Human beings don't want Messages, they want burdens."

"But they suffer from their burdens," said the Lord.

"True, Lord," replied Our Beloved Whim. "But not as much as they suffer from Messages."

Luke Rhinehart, 'The Book of the Die'

Chapter Fourteen
Excellence and Performance

"Over-seriousness is a warning sign for mediocrity and bureaucratic thinking. People who are seriously committed to mastery and high performance are secure enough to lighten up."

Michael J. Gelb

Excellence is not a means to an end. If you don't strive to be excellent at what you do for the pure enjoyment of it, you are still Mama's boy. Excellence is its own reward. When doing anything it is simply more fun to do it well. It is harder, more difficult, to bungle along. Flying a plane poorly with the constant fear of crashing is more stressful than flying the damn thing right and with ease. Windsurfing well doesn't wear you out as much as constantly getting thrown off the board and climbing back on. Excellence is pleasing to the eye of bystanders and smoother to live through for the acting person. Being paid or not for what you do is not as important as it is to be fabulous for its own sake, instead of being a greenhorn.

Getting paid for an excellent job is great--don't try so hard to misunderstand me--but you have to be a moron to be excellent in order to get paid. Besides, in the market there is no measurable correlation between excellence and pay. More money is being exchanged for mediocrity than for excellence, with Microsoft exemplifying the rule and Toyota an excellent exception.

Performance is a yardstick for people's monetary compensation? Dream on. Do you know somebody who doesn't perform as well as you do and yet he gets paid better? Do you know anybody who is so much better than you are and she gets paid less? So there you have it: as of this minute, it is scientifically proven people are not paid according to their performance level. Payment in correlation to performance is a myth. Companies push performance as an incentive to get the best out of their working units, their employees, without the obligation of paying a penny more.

At a conveyor belt, performance can be measured somewhat. In a cubicle, the stuff done by the obsolete caste of middle management is difficult to quantify. In higher executive regions you will find folks who get paid royally for gargantuan screw ups and, believe it or not, some people get paid handsomely for not doing anything at all. If they lifted as much as their pinky or opened their mouth, they would forfeit their lavish compensation. No person on Earth gets paid according to her performance. Don't kid yourself. Sometimes it just looks that way.

Crap manufacturers like Microsoft and Starbucks, network marketing schemes and scams, and everybody in-between try to dupe their job hating employees into the concept of excellence as a corporate value by promising all sorts of things. Yep, even a company relying on a crappy product still demands at least a hint of excellence somewhere. Real excellence doesn't have to make it into the hand of the customer, God forbid, nor does it have to show up in the pocket of the shareholder, but the perception of excellence must be evoked before it gets explained away.

Excellence has its place, I agree. That does not mean the most excellent performers are making the most money, but a scent of excellence serves any operation as a welcome fig leaf. *Perceived* excellence is key. VWs and Audis have been garbage for decades, but their perceived value as products of fine German craftsmanship gives them the air of something worth paying for. Arrogance and obnoxious German management is no substitute for true excellence, however. Hey, I am obnoxious and German enough to say that.

Excellence is not necessary to make money. As in Microsoft's case, an excellent product may even be in your way and reduce your profits. Partially, Microsoft's success depends on selling an inferior product. Its flaws make you eager to spend money on the newer, better upgrade coming on the market soon.

The advanced replacement, of course, will be delivered with a brand new set of flaws built into it, installing the need in each customer for future and amazingly superior editions.

You can overdo it, as we have witnessed with Vista, but that strategy has worked quite successfully for a long time. Combined with techniques to almost force your clientele into your newest deception, you can strike the mother lode indeed. Implementation of that business model, however, must be executed flawlessly and with the highest level of excellence you can employ.

When excellence is not an option or too much of a bother, addictive products and services may work in your favor as well. The wireless world has managed to sell you air by the minute. Read customer feedback on any cellphone or PDA and you know they all are far from being excellent. MP3 players and similar scrap work so well as cash cows because of their addictive nature. You aren't trying to tell me that several billion dollars of annual sales in the ring tone industry are based on excellence, are you?

Employees survive in spite of the companies they work for, and employers survive in spite of their employees. Let's face it, people who hate what they do aren't at their best. Despise what you do and you will be a poor performer. Companies don't need or want creme de la creme employees to produce their mediocre gizmos. Mediocre ones will do. A company's obsession to look out for top people stems from their experience that the best candidates are mediocre performers, while the mediocre candidate is likely to hate her performance into the nether regions of unacceptable.

Companies aren't proud of their people. They just put up with their units. Showing up is usually sufficient to get paid. Displaying a flicker of excellence now and then won't win you a lot of friends amongst your colleagues--especially not if they happen to be union members--but it may get you noticed for future promotions, besides for your excellent scheming and backstabbing skills that is.

Too much excellence and continued outstanding

performance, possibly combined with confidence that you are better qualified than your superiors, can get you fired rather quickly. Excellence is a double-edged sword and not without danger. Employees, truly excelling at what they do, are oxymorons. If you are near perfect, incomparably magnificent, why the hell are you still a damned employee? You are excellent or you are employed but you can't be both.

Sweet severance packages of a garden variety of executive losers in recent years--Carly Fiorina (Hewlett Packard - $42 million), Robert Nardelli (Home Depot - $210 million), Jill Barad (Mattel - $40 million plus), Stan O'Neal (Merrill Lynch - $161.5 million)--made me realize that the financial success of a CEO depends on the ability to find an equilibrium between excellence and bungledom. You've got to excel in messing up. Plain excellent performance won't do. These clowns with their platinum ass kick into early retirement were already awful when they were interviewed for their jobs, and I bet my family jewels some esteemed members of the hiring squad were keenly aware of these people's shortcomings and the possible consequences.

Take Krispy Kreme's former Chairman, Scott Livengood. I am convinced this boy intentionally destroyed a fine company. Pick anybody in your neighborhood high school parking lot, choose the first guy you find sleeping under a bridge, and they could not have done worse. Troubling to me is that somebody responsible for hiring such douchebags may have sensed the outcome in advance and secretly hoped for it.

Being awful at what you do can make you so much more money than simply hating your job. Becoming the worst CEO of the year is better than a lottery jackpot. It's pure gold. I wonder if any execustiff is still wasting a thought on trying to be good. And imagine a regular Home Despot employee being told by his half-wit supervisor that excellent performance counts. Not if you plan to get sacked with 200 million chips to jingle.

Excellence is unlikely to lift you into exalted positions, and if you're lucky enough to make it there anyway, your excellence may very well be your downfall. Excellence can be as much a hindrance to a high flying career as it is to be a bum.

You, as a customer, are required to provide excellence to companies you consider doing business with. Your paperwork needs to be in perfect order, and your payments must not be late, or else. But when was the last time you experienced excellent performance at a car dealership? Can you name an excellent insurance company? Another oxymoron. Some strange companies seem to prefer to treat their customers like governments treat their subjects. Condescending, deceiving, like dirt. "We are here to help you!" I am sorry, I don't mean to generalize. Not all corporations operate that way, but those with monopoly status sure do. Not all governments treat their people badly either but, since my knowledge is extremely limited, please do inform me of the good examples.

Demanding excellence, perfectionism even, from your customers is the ultimate demonstration of confidence. And confidence, in turn, creates the perception of excellence in your target audience--unless they know better, that is. Lack of confidence has to be compensated with real excellence. Hence the requirement for new companies and for insecure employees to show some excellence. However, excellence is not what gets you paid so much. Your insecurities determine that you get paid so little.

Markets don't favor products or services based on their quality. Quality helps but it's not always necessary. Any beer soaked family daddy can produce better burgers than McDonalds, but that's not the real argument here. The behavior of markets depends on you and me voting with our pocketbooks. We the people are quite erratic and nearly unpredictable. That's why products need testing. That's why even a superior and temporarily successful product won't make money indefinitely.

Excellent stuff sells sometimes but not always. We the market are a fickle bunch, and excellence, quality, or high levels of performance are not the formula to ongoing success. Simply because there is no formula--no system--to figure out the market. No truth to be discovered. You have figured out what people need to do to be successful (*write down your goals, be consistent, follow the Law of Attraction*)? That's fabulous baby, but you are full of it.

You disagree? Fine then, get in line with myriads of individuals longing to *break the code*. Somehow, the system believers and seekers--it matters not whether these crack heads waste their time on deciphering the patterns of slot machines, the market, lottery, or spiritual formulae handed down by channeled cheats--remind me of those diehards who hang on to their silly conspiracy theories. They're brethren, and I prefer to stay out of their path of raging love.

Money is not a reward, at least not when it shows up in greater sums. In your early years, grandma may have promised you 5 bucks if you could improve your grades in math. Dear granny and the other people brandishing reward money right before your nose don't have the kind of dough you are actually after. You need excellent performances to benefit from reward related pittances or to avoid monetary punishment, but such peanuts don't count in your quest to generate real money.

Parents love to show off excelling brats and they gloat with their brood's straight A's. Yet the most successful entrepreneurs were rarely students parents brag about. Flunking tests and dropping out of school is not a formula but still a relatively common denominator of some super successful people.

Billionaire Kirk Kerkorian didn't make it through high school. Becoming an amateur boxer was more important for him. Ralph Lifschitz, college dropout, went to the army before selling neckties. You may know him better as Ralph Lauren. Here's a hacker who built blue boxes that allowed people to place free and illegal long distance phone calls which he used to prank call the Pope. One semester in college was all he could take before backpacking through India, shaving his head, seeking enlightenment, and pestering us with his stupid iPhone: Mr. Steve Jobs.

Taiwanese billionaire YC Wang has a complete elementary school education. Francois Pinault (Gucci, auction house

Christie's, Samsonite) didn't finish high school. Spain's richest man, Armancio Ortega: high school dropout. "He'll never go anywhere in life," said one of Michael Dell's teachers and who would question a teacher's opinion? Richest Chinese and Asia's richest man, Li Ka-Shing ($18.8 billion or so; don't you just love his name?) in Hong Kong was forced to drop out of school at age 15. (pennylicious.com)

The list is endless. Bored yet? What excites me is to see the remarkable concentration of wealthy individuals who were either unable or unwilling to follow society's established success formula--the venerable school system--that sells hundreds of thousands of children into slavery each year. Each one of the aforementioned people had to invent their ways and their lives from scratch. And now they're being asked all day, "What was your formula?" "How can I do the same?" Silly. Research the history of outstanding, accomplished individuals and you'll discover a significant proportion of misfits and black sheep. You know what else many of them have in common? Parental or society's approval is not that important to these guys. They don't care if they're liked.

Excellence and performance oriented thinking may limit your income. You know the pitfalls of perfectionism. So there! Striving for top quality is powerful enough to prevent you from making money with your products. You may have something you could sell today, but your pathological obsession to meet your impossible standards of quality guarantees that your valuable something will never turn out a single penny. Wasted brilliance.

In fact, a plethora of businesses do NOT get started because people believe they are not good enough. Erroneously, they think their education is not good enough, their idea is not good enough, or their bank balance is not good enough. Close to 100% of employees fit into that category: they *know* something about them is not good enough. They live their entire lives under the spell of the damaging excellence myth.

Almost every employee represents a wasted opportunity for some crazy ass product that would have a chance to make a shitload of money while turning your and my world into a more interesting and playful place. If you can still afford to hate your job, you don't hate it enough yet.

Reward and punishment thinking combined with excellence and performance oriented strategies is perfect for the business of pimps and whores. If you are in a similar profession, yes, I can see how that furthers your interests. If not, it doesn't mean you shouldn't implement excellence but you may gain from rethinking its value and its place in your operation.

I have said it before, pimps and prostitutes can be respectable members of our society, often more so than their deranged customers. I don't think they are in any way less truthful than the average politician. On the contrary, representatives of *dark side professions*--preferably hidden or denied by so-called respectable members of society--are usually refreshingly honest about their intentions. Anyway, I'm not peddling morality and you must evaluate for yourself how important key elements of pimping are in your business environment, like reward and punishment, excellence and performance.

Performance and excellence are fine. Relax! If you do the same thing continuously you can't help but become better at it. If you enjoy a large chunk of your work, good for you. It'll increase the quality of your output tremendously. I am not promoting intentional screw ups. That would be insane and equally as dumb as it is to develop fake excellence for the business' sake.

I am confident you are excellent at being yourself. If not, you have larger problems that I refuse to address here. If you are good at being you, products resulting from your ideas and character will have excellence built into them. Naturally. Your neck hair would stand on end if you forced yourself to perform poorly.

Embarrassing theory, this excellence and performance stuff. I don't know whether school teachers continue to pester their kids with such nonsense. It has always been and will be subject to ridicule, like teaching ethics. If someone has to teach you, it's too late.

Money is never the measurement for performance. I must tell you once more, performance related pay is one of the nastiest myths pertaining to money. Money and performance have no correlation whatsoever, anywhere, anytime. That theory has only been used to turn school children into employees, and employees into lifelong dependents.

People know the performance myth is not true, yet they don't stop deceiving their own children with it, as if it *should be true*. Performance related theories exude the musty smell of fairness. That's what makes it so difficult to root it out as the weed that it is. Instead of cleaning it out of their backyards, people smoke it. Life should be fair, and if it were fair money would be paid according to people's excellence and performance. Endearing, but a loser theory, nevertheless.

Freedom is a nice word and waving it like a flag always has an effect. But hardly is there another term or value as void of meaning. People want freedom but do you have it? Reminds me of the sticker *Safety is our goal*, on work trucks. Ridiculous. I don't care for safety as a goal. It scares me. I want safety right now, please! Same with freedom. Unless you claim it this minute, nobody is going to give you permission to be free anytime soon. Laboring and longing for financial independence suggests the proper size of your portfolio will give you permission *some day* to be free. I hate to break it to you but that won't happen.

People tend to misunderstand me. My use of the term freedom does not imply you can drop the money making process today and go on a permanent cruise around the world or buy yourself a dozen mansions in exalted locations.

You have the freedom to do what you want to do means here: take one of the 479 ideas that have crossed your mind in the last ten years and do something practical with it, with the intention of making an extra buck. Choose the most simple idea you can implement and execute with the change in your pocket. Do it PARALLEL to what you are doing anyway or the pressure to succeed will kill your new freedom in its infancy. Really, you are free to get off your ass. Everybody is.

Chapter Fifteen
Regrets and Motivation

"If you wind up with a boring, miserable life because you listened to your mom, your dad, your teacher, your priest, or some guy on television telling you how to do your shit, then you deserve it."

Frank Zappa

Regrets are painful. Are they? You have made mistakes in your life, plenty of them I hope. Perhaps you have done things that were not only painful for you but for other individuals. How can you live with that? Hardly anything in life is as important as our mistakes. The cutting edge turning our actions into roaring success or into miserable disaster brings us to an intensity we cannot experience playing it safe. Regrets can be milestones. Tell me, are your extraordinary successes sticking out in your memory as noticeably as your worst screw ups? If I'm not too mistaken, you are aware of your greatest mistakes every day, day and night. I am, and by Gustav, my closet is choke-full of skeletons.

People you have met may think of you as the greatest loser and jerk they have ever come across. For you, the same incident they remember so well woke you up perhaps, enlightened you, and beat a real taste of integrity into your hide that you believed you already had, long before you messed up so badly. Regrets are precious commodities, cornerstones of your character. You would not be you without them. I know--as much as plenty of people will disagree with me--you are a finer person because of every single thing you regret. Well, possibly.

Regret what you have not done. You will never find out what would have happened had you taken that trip on the Trans Siberian Express. No regret is more horrible than the 'I wish I had done that,' type. 'I wish I had eloped with that girl 23 years ago.' Awful!

As brilliant as our noodle may be, we cannot figure out intellectually what we can find out practically. We can't predict the future of markets, relationships, or anything else. We cannot predict the response of a stranger we are interested in talking with. Mind over matter? Yeah, right. We can't even predict the next move of a damn cricket we're struggling to get out of the house. In most cases, we must DO things to discover what works. Doing allows us also to access the enjoyable. You can't *do it* in your mind. You ought to practically do what you are interested in to see if you like doing it or not. Sure, with action things get messy and that's what we prefer to prevent by playing it safe. As human beings we will never be safe. If it's legal, go do what you have in mind or you are in hell already--literally--in the hell of *I wish I had tried that*.

Doing something new and different is easier said than done, obviously. Otherwise you would have done it. You gained something from not doing those things. At least, you believe you benefited from not doing it. You didn't risk losing your inheritance or the family jewels, for instance. You could have attracted HIV or knocked up more moms than your budget permits. Yet you don't know. Those terrible things may not have happened had you followed your dreams. Maybe and maybe not. You will never know. The benefits of not acting are baseless beliefs for the most part, justifications to compensate for missing out. And you are right: hideous things could have happened in the wake of your unlived life's activities.

Consider this: in a lot of instances we don't know what's crowned with the better outcome until we act. We must choose if we prefer to die in bed, eventually, or on the battlefield of our dreams. Once that is settled your regrets will stop. If you chose the *bed* option, you don't have to worry about not doing anything. Doing stuff and risking your toupee to shift positions is just not for you. If you picked *battlefield*, you won't have time to contemplate doing or not doing, to regret or not to regret. You'll burn in the middle of it.

Regretting mistakes you have made in the past is a waste

of time. Nothing can be changed. You did what you did and no regret can undo it. I suspect our regrets are internalized actions of self-punishment. Mom told us to feel bad after messing up, and regret is the adult equivalent of her asking us to stand in the corner for awhile, to think about what heinous crimes we committed. Perhaps we were grounded for our mistakes, and regrets do just that: self-grounding immobilizes us and we become inactive. Think about the three most grave screw ups in your life and chances are you'll be paralyzed and useless for the remainder of the day.

Adults may indulge in self-punishment by way of regrets, but mature it is not. Procrastination has its beneficial side--and I am the first to defend procrastination--but denying ourselves the joy of life because we are so busy feeling bad is pretty dumb. You regret mistakes you made in the past? You are wasting precious time. Grow up, and make more mistakes.

Relationships are messy, including our relationships with our own mistakes. Mistakes are results of actions with a different turnout than the one we anticipated and aimed for. When the result is better than what we had planned, we don't call it a mistake. Some of us thank God for that stuff, we call it luck, or-- depending on the development of our narcissism--we take full credit.

Well, it also kinda depends to whom we are telling the story. When results are worse than the achievement we had in mind, we feel either solely responsible for the outcome, guilty even, or we angrily point out somebody we can blame for this malaise. We don't thank God for it, neither do we blame God. Why? Since I don't peddle religion nor its opposite, I shall leave the answer up to you.

As poor as our judgment has been historically, it's not probable that a high percentage of our actions yields exactly the results we had in mind. My wild guess, in most cases we were wrong. Honestly, results deviating in any way from our plans are mistakes, and it matters not if they are better or worse than what we wanted. In both cases our judgment is off, and we are responsible for the surprising outcome. Wrigley's chewing gum was a mistake: they did not plan to make money selling chewing gum. The gum was a freebie in their packages of baking soda.

Moral: be happy and grateful for both kinds of mistakes. Or, if your world contains one or more gods, thank these guys for all deviations, for your lucky breaks and for your most embarrassing screw ups. That would be strange, wouldn't it? Even the most religious of us hesitate to thank their gods for decent heroin addictions and car crashes. I don't understand it but then, there are a lot of things beyond my comprehension. Love thy mistakes as thy love an ugly child.

Mistakes are the bread and butter of our lives. Chances are most things we do will reveal themselves as mistakes because we're not likely to judge life correctly much more often than 50% of the time. If you are better, play roulette and you should do well for yourself. It is not that easy to predict the future.

Of course, if you don't start anything new, you can't do much wrong. Holding down the same job for 30 years doesn't leave you much of a chance to make grave mistakes. Well, unless getting that job 30 years ago was the dumbest thing you ever did. Let's assume more than half of our business ventures and decisions are wrong, and before we act we can't figure out which one will tank. We decide to:

a) never make a decision again and refrain from any and all action; we even ask the kids to fetch the potato chips;

b) hope to get lucky with our next move. If that fails, we never do anything new again and feel like losers for the rest of our miserable days; or

c) increase our failure rate: we increase our output of ideas and action, and we radically increase the frequency of possible mistakes.

As the bible says, "Love thy failure as thyself and make more mistakes more often, damned--or hang yourself young." (Profits 13:17) Mistakes are crucial elements of life in freedom, if not the most important ones. How free would you be if everything you did, I mean everything, had to bring no less than perfect results? Twenty years from now, even in hindsight, planning, execution, and outcome would have to look immaculate from your perspective and from everybody else's point of view.

You would not be able to live another day. You'd be afraid to pull up your pants in the morning. If the making of mistakes were out of the question, all of us would be inhibited little creeps, too scared to mumble a single word. And damn, in some ways we are like that, scared of life and of the pathetic opinion of people we don't care about. There is no freedom for you without the freedom to make mistakes. Freedom requires mistakes. Freedom can thrive only in an environment where you can do things incorrectly. It's not pretty, nice, or pleasant. Freedom is a painful thing and you'd better enjoy it, baby.

Trial and error is often described as the path to success. The more we try, the better our chances to discover what works for us. As with the throw of dice, each new trial does not have a better chance to succeed than any of our other attempts. It's just that a high frequency of trials increases the probability of digging up a winner.

That's nothing new. People try stuff. If it works, great. If not, it's disappointing and the signal to try the next idea. We are success junkies. With one eye on a favorable outcome, we are never really content with what we do. Moments of success can be rare and short, and dry periods of trying things that don't work out may take up long parts of our lives. That doesn't promise much happiness, does it?

We have the ability to focus on the process of trying and tinkering and putting the elements of a new idea together. When we try a lot, regardless of failure or success, judgments from other people or from ourselves, we will be more productive and most likely more successful. The pain of failure is self-chosen. You can enjoy trial and error from scratch and have a grand time through both.

Mistakes have a bad reputation in our society. We see our mistakes as problems, something to get away from. We are *solution oriented*--cliches like that yank my gag reflex into gear-- and problems pollute the air in our artificial world of idolized success. Failure is a problem, success is the solution. Simple and moronic. True, mistakes can be problematic and nasty, but looking frantically for a solution, for the straight way out of the morass, has not worked too well in the past, has it? In many instances we cannot find what we are looking for, simply because we are looking for it so grimly. We are not playful enough.

Here is a suggestion: solutions for your past mistakes may be found in your future mistakes. Instead of struggling for a solution with grinding teeth, relax and sail happily into a fresh pile of new mistakes. Chances to inadvertently discover solutions for past problems are greater anywhere than in an environment of panic and pressure. Permitting yourself to make mistakes equals a vacation from notorious and futile performance anxiety.

Regrettable as some of our mistakes may be, we can't go backwards in life. We can't change the past, and if we want to live we must do regrettable things. We must make new mistakes. You have the choice to make two or three more mistakes you can regret for the rest of your days. Tell your grandchildren what a failing dumbass you were, over and over again until they snicker behind your back. Or you decide to engage in a flurry of mistakes, making it impossible to follow up with regrets and stories.

With only a handful of regrettable mistakes in your life you are a loser and a failure. With so many mistakes under your belt that you can't remember all of last month's failures, you cannot lose. Well, you can but it'll be difficult. A high frequency of mistakes makes regrets fall by the wayside. Allow your mistakes to motivate you to make more mistakes. Good-bye to your inhibitions.

Learn from your mistakes, is well meant advice every one of us has heard repeatedly while growing up. And? Have you learned from your mistakes? I doubt it. We make a mistake and then we don't do it again. Like getting married to the wrong person--and figuring that out took us ten years--and going down in the all consuming flames of humiliating divorce procedures. We will never, I mean NEVER, do that again. Until next time, that is.

Some mistakes we make once and it's over. We really don't do it again. You found out the hard way you are allergic to strawberries, and I am confident you won't go near those nasty things again. Other types of mistakes will be repeated indefinitely, no matter what you think you learn from them. Ask Larry King how often he has been married and divorced. He is running out of fingers to count.

Larry is not alone: all of us have favorites, mistakes we have repeated for the umpteenth time and we still don't know for certain if we have learned the lesson. Learning from mistakes is nonsense. It's a myth that we can do that. Some mistakes--like soiling our diapers--are repeated thousands of times, and then we suddenly stop. Human beings make mistakes until they stop. Once, twice, a hundred times and then we just stop. Mistakes are a major part of your life and you can't opt out of it.

Learning to make less mistakes in life, or none, hasn't been too successful a strategy, historically. During your and my lifetime, we won't learn enough from making war throughout centuries and millennia so that we can enjoy peace everywhere all the time. In areas of our lives that matter the most, we are the least capable of learning from past mistakes. Asking people to learn from their mistakes is pathetic. Sounds like an idea school teachers came up with first.

No reason to get depressed. If learning is so important to you, here's what you can improve through training. Learn to make more mistakes more frequently. First of all, that strategy moves you quicker to the point of stopping. The more you repeat a particular mistake, the faster you wear out your fascination with it. While you are at it, happily multiplying mistakes and failures, you will learn a lot more than while you're sitting in a corner, too inhibited to screw something up and too embarrassed to make the same mistake twice. Oh, now you do learn? Yes, you can learn from making mistakes but not the way mom told you to do it. You learn from mistakes by way of *making* them again, not from mistake prevention.

The average school teacher wants you to stop in your tracks, to analyze your last mistake, and to learn enough from your shameful deed through introspection that you can't make the same mistake a second time. But school teachers also prepare you for a life in job slavery. They want you locked up and under control, incapable of surpassing their miserable lifestyle. Hence I wouldn't trust their brilliant ideas. Making mistakes is not shameful at all. The shame and pain part stems from other people's unsolicited disapproval. Forget public opinion and discover the beneficial properties of your mistakes and their repetition. You will learn significantly more from making mistakes and from duplicating previous ones, than from wrecking your fragile little mind over the last mishap.

Motivation is commonly founded on crutches. Goals, possible future results, are supposed to motivate us. Wow, all the money we could make, all the glitzy stuff we could buy. Yawn! When you need to come up with next month's rent or mortgage payment, money motivates somewhat, I agree. You plan to buy your first house? Sure, money and your goal will be motivating to get there. But that kind of thinking does not motivate Lakshmi Mittal--the richest man in Europe and fourth wealthiest person in the world--or Warren Buffett.

Money motivated thoughts and action will NOT produce financial surplus. Money based motivation works like a walker, helping you to shuffle from the TV set to your bathroom and back. Goals are prosthetic motivators, as if you didn't have it in you to work on something productively without being led by the nose.

Since we know the motivational factor of goals and money is extremely limited, we need more tools in our arsenal. How about challenges? Some of us perform better in competitive environments. Greyhounds do, too. The motivational industry assumes people are as dumb as a bale of straw. Hell, maybe they are right and we are so stupid that we deserve to work in slavery for another century. Politicians will love us for it because they can continue to ingratiate themselves with the promise to never let us run out of carrots and sticks. Simultaneously, they'll wiggle themselves with their greasy elbows into control positions, making sure we will never experience a market we'd call *free*. God, we are cheap.

What's the ultimate motivational crutch? Meaning. Oh yeah, people's eyes glaze over and they lose themselves in hymns of philosophical masturbation over meaningful work. The deeper the better. C'mon. Knowing that my work serves a good, even a sacred cause makes scraping crusty toilet bowls so much more meaningful. Meaning is the slimiest kind of extrinsic motivation and the most reprehensible. You and whatever the hell you do is not that important. And, if you think you are important, you will learn sooner rather than later how dispensable you really are. But we are desperately looking for this little pathetic something that gives us a tiny feel-good-advantage over the next guy. Think $1,000 rims, is all I can say about that. Are yours still spinning?

Yeah, yeah, I know all those crutches do work, including the *meaning* thing. So what? I don't say anything against the use of a walker either. If it helps, by all means use one. Yet it's not as much fun as walking free and upright on your own two feet. Your resources for intrinsic motivation are unlimited. Your regrets of what you have not done, for example, can throw you into new and valuable adventures for years to come. You don't need motivational clowns to kick you into action. The supreme motivation, with its modus operandi built into you: playful curiosity. Works perfectly for every damned child. Why not for you?

Playfulness fosters activity. Allow yourself to inject the idea of play into every single compartment of your life, and your activity is likely to increase. You will automatically be motivated to try new things, and you won't have time to brood over old regrets. You need more willpower first, more discipline, to start a new venture or to stop smoking or to ... Rubbish! If you wait for sufficient willpower before you act, you will wait for a long time. It's not going to happen.

It works the other way around. You have listened too much to new-age priests babbling about *power of the mind* and *mind over matter*. Act first, take a small step--a smaller one even--and boom, your willpower expands and increases, enabling you to make the next step larger. Our noodles are as stupid as they are brilliant. Forget your mind for now and act, playfully.

Regrets are not productive and neither is motivation. Someone tries to motivate you, and you know he wants you to do something you really do not want to do. Yeah, but the benefits!? Right, I forgot. Millions of employees drag their sorry asses all day around the Bermuda triangle, defined by cubicle, outhouse, and water cooler, hoping for the next 40 years to mysteriously disappear. They have husbands, houses, kids, cars, pooches, and BENEFITS, motivated to do anything that furthers retirement. Sleeper cells! Living for the questionable benefits of a mediocre job, it's not probable you will do anything stupid you'll have to regret. Well, except that your entire life is a regrettable faux pas. The only exciting thing a benefit junkie can look forward to is becoming a grandpa and dying.

I promote a different addiction: collect actions you are likely to regret some day. Chances are, most of them you'll never regret. The benefits of that lifestyle aren't exactly guaranteed but I promise you won't complain about boredom. Do things you may have to regret and early retirement loses its appeal. Leave retirement to the rotting mummies and zombies who retired a day after their last job interview.

Chapter Sixteen
Money and Meaning

"There is a theory which states that if anyone discovers exactly what the universe is for and why it is here, it will instantly disappear and be replaced by something even more bizarre and inexplicable. There is another theory which states this has already happened."

Douglas Adams

Money, cold hard cash, won't do it for us. When we don't get anything but a paycheck out of our jobs, we feel empty after awhile, no matter how handsome the pay may be. Nothing against money, but if it's all there is we start looking around for more. Some think more money would fill the void. It won't. Again, there is absolutely nothing wrong with more money. Yet the hollow, stale feeling you are trying to *fill* or to get rid of will stay. We want something else, or more, and we can't really put a finger on what it is. In this situation, people grab and hold on to any straw promising relief from the tension of feeling flat and exhausted.

We have tried alcohol and a garden variety of substances, unsuccessfully. Volunteering. Doing pro bono work on the side makes us feel good, but even volunteering can't deceive us about our real bread and butter job. We continue to feel drained and insignificant enduring our daily grind. Uh, maybe the insignificance is why we need to do something that provides our lives with deeper meaning? We want to serve people, make the world a better place, give back to the community, discover our purpose, fight for a greater cause--we are on a quest to discover our sacred mission. Yes, we want to be on a mission from God.

Importance becomes a necessity for insecure individuals. What on Earth makes you think you are not important enough and you need an upgrade? People judge others as greedy who make more and more money, but they don't find anything fishy in the desire for more and more importance, significance, or meaning. Those who make rather large amounts of money know it's meaningless. More money makes no difference to their importance. It's just another number with more zeros, and the game is what really counts. Folks who are obsessed with meaning--*why am I here?*-- are having a huge pathological issue with their lack of self-worth, just like the sickos who need more money in order to feel good about themselves.

You are not that important. Nobody is. A lot of people, who believe themselves to be irreplaceable today, will be dead or out of office next week. Guess what, the world will continue to run its course, and even these people's families and businesses will survive, possibly do better without them. Indeed, the world is a better place without Eliot Spitzer being in charge of anything that counts. Trying to read importance artificially into the things we do is bizarre and insane. I can't see how the work of Tiger Woods is so much more important than the job of a janitor. Pay is slightly different, but other than that who does more for humanity? There is no answer to it. Forget asking such questions. The pious search for meaning is a socially accepted way of craving MORE, without actually becoming or producing more than you are.

You! Yes, I am talking to you! Don't you think you are enough and just fine as you are? Do you have to become more, do more, represent more? People seem to be having a hard time being themselves. Then, they somehow gain pride by becoming a sales representative of some dipshit company. Why would you want to represent something else? What's so wrong with being you exactly as you are? Our species, the crown of creation, is the only one capable of suffering from low self-esteem. In general, the average human beats any amoeba as far as lack of self-esteem is concerned.

Wanna know how sickly human beings are when they think of themselves? *The world is drowning in over-population.*

There are way too many people being born as we speak. But, *I can't wait to see my first grandchild.* What? That is insanity. There are too many Chinese babies being born, but of me and my kind there aren't enough around yet? That type of arrogance is a clear expression of insecurity. Individuals, seeking ultimate value in their children all the while being scared that people in Africa may not use enough condoms, disgust me.

Here is the kicker: the more you want to be--systematically upgraded with education, meaningful work, g-brats, your pathetic shopping list of values, all the goody-goody stuff you try to foist on humankind--the less you'll think you are. You will feel like a ridiculous, worthless lump. Perhaps the first time you grasp a piece of reality.

You are enough. You have *what it takes*. You are all there is. No reason to be insecure about yourself. Once you begin catering to your insecurities, there is no end to it. Taken to the extreme, you'll end up like Cher or Michael Jackson, pitiful caricatures of their former selves, barely capable of food intake without a straw. The most gorgeous, assless world class fashion model thinks she is an ugly owl or a fat pig, in desperate need to throw up again soon.

You are fine just as you are, and you have all the importance you will ever have while napping on your sofa. Do whatever is enjoyable for you to do. Save the damned world if you must, but do it for the fun of it, not because you feel the sick need to make a name for yourself. Even your children are better off without you trying to leave a legacy behind for them. Most kids of pathologically important parents are pathological lifelong wretches. You are plenty today. No need for improvements. If and when you feel the urge to disregard my advice--and I can't really blame you--do yourself a favor and give Michael Jackson a call first. Ask him how the seams are holding up and how happy he is today, the king of self-improvement.

Greatness originates where? You are the one thinking up after-market modifications for yourself, like added meaning or the option of serving the greater good. Guess what? You are the source of that stuff and naturally your products have elements of your greatness, yet they can't be greater than you are. Got that? Nothing you can invent, think up, or employ makes you more than you already are. The funny thing is, newborn babies are the center of attention. Everybody thinks little screaming, giggling, uncontrollable bundles are the most precious things on Earth. The more years we pack on, the more experienced we become, the less we think of each other and of ourselves. Nuts, don't you agree?

Meaning and missions have only one purpose; to be impressive. They are meant to pacify our insatiable greed for being more than we are. We explain our addiction to importance as the necessity to transcend our ego and to live for something greater than just being the individuals we are. What a perverted theory from the new age numb nuts. Whether you work at an assembly line in Detroit, you are a Pilates instructor in Beverly Hills, or you run a non-profit organization protecting children from swallowing Chinese lead, who the hell cares? If you think one is better than the other, you've got problems and professional help may come too late.

Play around with meaning like a child in the sandlot. It's fun and entertaining, but there is no higher purpose or deeper meaning in your calling besides the value you possessed before you got kinky with that motivational crap. Children play and droves of adults stand around in admiration and excitement. None of the kids has the slightest awareness of meaning or purpose while immersed in their play. We don't deny children and their activities any deeper meaning. It's absurd to think children would be better off if their presence in the sandlot had a purpose. How then do grownups fare better looking for the deeper, higher, greater, and more sacred in the ways they pick their moves?

With meaning and missions we can pretend our lives make more sense. Just living and having simple fun--as our brats do--is too basic for us. It needs to make sense and since life doesn't make any sense we pretend, religiously and defensively so. Man's search for meaning--as much as I admire Viktor Frankl and his book with the same title--is one hell of a waste of time. There are a lot of great things you can do once you quit the idiocy of trying to make sense of everything.

Trust yourself: if you want to do something, anything, it has plenty of meaning. We don't have to make life more complicated to make it interesting and valuable. Since you are still alive it's obviously valuable to you. Otherwise you would've hung yourself a long time ago. We eat, we sleep, we do things. If you don't like it, do something else, eat something else, sleep with somebody else. Pretty simple, too simple for most. Unhappy? Be happy, damn it! Won't take a penny and it won't take longer than a minute to be happy. But WOW, NO, there must be something more sophisticated and hopefully impossible to being happy.

Wrong. Simplicity pisses people off. So does happiness. They prefer to be moody and miserable, drowning in their quest for depth and meaning. No, it can't possibly be that easy. The notorious truth seeker shuns happiness. She longs to feel the weight of the entire world on her narrow shoulders to feed her egotistical greed for meaning. This type of person is usually convinced she has no ego, and her militant defense to prove her position reveals more ego than Donald Trump will ever call his own in 100 lifetimes. Simple things, like goofing off, having a beer and a burger, or--God forbid--making money are obscenely shallow to her. Screw her!

Playing is serious and it is *play*. Next to watching two-year-olds with delight, we are fascinated with sports. The deeper meaning of football? Geez, it's a game. It's dead serious. And it is still play. It's not warm and fuzzy. There is not much love and peace to be observed on the football field. It's not gentle nor pleasant. People get hurt, seriously hurt, and they don't sue each other over it. People play football because they *want* to play football, pain and all. People who want to make money by doing what they love, and they have only fun and nice things in mind, are freaking morons.

Uh, we are feeling a tad offended, I surmise, and indignant over my use of improper language? Good! All that stuff you want to yell into my innocent visage to prove me wrong should be powerful motivational material for you. Instead of getting worked up and upset, just get rich on what you love. I invite you: prove me wrong. Deal? If it works out well for you, I shall be delighted. Think football and hockey when you consider doing what you want to do. Instantly, that will give you the sense of intensity you must expect. The taste of blood in your mouth from a knocked out tooth, and the sound of splintering bones. Takes unconditional love for your cause. You said it, I did not bring that up. Get real, get serious, enjoy the pain and the parts you hate, too. Screw the meaning. At all times be aware you are playing. It is a game, seriously.

Theoretical constructions to make sense of life are popular and always will be. As brief as life is, we crave a structure to hold on to, something of lasting value. As if that would change anything about diarrhea. Anxiously trying to make something out of life other than the obvious tells me the meaning junkies aren't happy with their lives. They hate it. They are pissed off how banal it is.

People who want *more* from life scare me more than those who want more money. Materialistic greed is harmless compared to spiritual greed. I don't trust the spiritual crowd who doesn't appreciate matter and materialism. Shit, that's what we're made of: matter. No fancy thought possible outside (our) matter. Mind over matter? How do you get the mind away from matter so you can watch the two compete? Like it or don't, money is an integral part of all that matters. To say 'money doesn't matter,' is a clear sign of someone who despises life itself. Hell, that's not the type of person I want to see busy changing the world.

We think individuals who have more sex than we do must be perverted--or we secretly envy them--and people who rake in more dough can't be anything but greedy. Shameless sinners. Unethical characters at least. Common sense tends to degrade what works. Maybe the solution for monetary disparity in the world is not to fight greed but to promote it heavily.

Could it be that the self-declared poor do not appreciate

matter and life itself? It's too basic, and therefore they feel inclined to denounce materialism? It doesn't help them or the state of the world to make sure that you'll never have more than they approve of. The fact that Ivan Boesky went to jail for things he shouldn't have done does not debunk his thought "I think greed is healthy." Doing illegal things is illegal, duh. Greed is not illegal per se. Nor is it evil or wrong. Lust is underrated, and so is lust for money.

What if there were no meaning to anything? There's just you, other people, and the things you do. Everything else; emotions, feelings, thoughts, etc., are nothing but a mix of chemical and electrical processes. Thoughts plus bodily sensations equal feelings/emotions. Good or bad doesn't matter much. As you have seen in the hockey example, we can get excited and thrive on both, desired outcomes and painful situations are potentially exhilarating events.

We give too much credit to sacred cows like feelings. Yours or mine, I don't respect feelings or people who are dumb enough to act on that stuff. Truth and absolute for some, it's outlandish from my perspective. People kill each other over feelings. Anything convincing you of such self-righteousness and infallibility, has to be contrived and entirely ridiculous.

Doom is upon you if you're upgrading your feelings with meaning. I prefer the void of meaning. You always wanted freedom, or did you not? So, there you have it. Freedom and meaning don't co-exist well. Do as you damn well please. Play some ball.

The meaning of the things you do is not what makes money for you. The market responds to what you do and how you do it. And if the markets don't react favorably to your offers, you have to do something differently. Changing the meaning your work has for you is nothing your clientele cares about. I know, for the spiritual industries like religions and new age-- which is just another religion--peddling gods and channeling entities is a multi-billion dollar market. Don't they sell meaning? Nope. Like any other retailer, they sell hope.

You hope to feel better after your purchase, and that's what everybody is selling. People don't buy a pair of jeans because they need pants to cover their legs. Jeans are purchased because somebody hopes they'll make their ass look good. Same with church stuff. People want to feel good about themselves. What better way of achieving that goal is there than by giving money to charity? The actual content, the specific meaning, is negligible and next to meaningless. The money is made with the cheapest part, the stuff that pacifies your emotional cravings, even if you are in the meaning-selling business.

The purpose of meaning is to eliminate time. Say what? We don't think much about the meaning of life while playing soccer or while skiing down a steep slope. There are times when contemplating the meaning of life can end it, your life that is. I suggest you concentrate on opening your parachute when you're sky diving, and not on the meaning of life. Perhaps your life is at all times more important than its meaning. Thoughts, pregnant with meaning, can kick in when we don't do anything actively, when we have time to think and when we realize how limited time--our life--actually is.

First of all, while we are pondering the meaning of life, we are not having fun. While we think about the meaning of life, life is losing meaning rapidly. We have arrived where the exalted truth seeker meets the average job hater. The job hater wants to be kept busy so that the day goes by faster. Those who despise their work also hate time. Time (work) is too long and it moves like molasses. Leisure time is too short and it disappears faster than quicksilver.

Our perception of time is not as linear as watches make us believe. Time can be stretched or shortened. The seeker, violently wringing meaning out of his useless existence, tries to make time irrelevant. Short life, long life, it doesn't matter. He craves to grasp the grand scheme of things. The long time after he's dead counts for him. Several billion people think their afterlife is more important than the time they spend with you. They don't give a crap about your stories, and they hate real time even more than the most hateful employee: time keeps them separated from freedom and from life.

Some of us hunt down meaning at every street corner and we seek the community of a church *to find relief*. Relief from what? People down a drink or two, *to take the edge off*. The edge of what? Individuals have sex to have fun? No way, they do it to get rid of a feeling they have. Hence the brevity. We don't deal well with tension. We seek to kill it whenever it appears. What if tension was the most fun you could possibly have?

Having sex, you can build tension for as long as you like and not get rid of it at all, if you so desire. Nothing against quickies, but there is something else with which to enjoy long winter nights in Alaska. Same with alcohol. I have nothing against savoring an ice cold beer or a fine glass of wine, but when you are trying to use it as a handyman's tool to take the edge off, you are probably murdering exactly what you are after: tension, enjoyment, and the adventure your life has built into itself.

Relief may be good for someone who does not like being herself. People don't hate their jobs. They hate being themselves on that job. You know what? Meaning would just screw it all up. Not even meaning can offer you relief from yourself. A well-placed bullet can do what meaning can't, or your deliberate decision to live with the tension you generate. No meaning necessary.

And since we are at it: there is hardly any truth worth its name. Truth is a whore and you may enjoy her as you please--as long as you pay the price, of course. I have seen anything and everything being told and sold as truth. Most importantly, the exact opposite meaning of any truth is sold as truth also. In fact, successful religions are selling both agonizing antagonistic truths simultaneously and every truthy looking thing in between. When that practice raises eyebrows, a church worth her salt replies with, "Credo quia absurdum est." I believe because it's absurd.

Supreme criterion of certitude is authority--says the Catholic Encyclopedia--not reason. Churches can sell as many truths as their subjects are willing to swallow. Here is the trick:

say you offer truth and that truth shall set the seeker-sucker free. Now you go ahead and dump a couple of thousand truths into your congregation's laps. Identical truths, radically opposing truths, and some partially overlapping in their meaning. Sorting it out will keep them busy for the remainder of their mortal existence.

If there was an absolute truth, the one and only, we would have discovered the damn thing by now, don't you think? Alas, we are after myriads of truths. One won't do. As many truths as there are on the market--and I'd happily add a few dozen for your convenience, if you insist--none of them are true. You know what the bible says about meaning?

Ecclesiastes 9:7-9, *"Go eat your food with gladness, and drink your wine with a joyful heart, for it is now that God favors what you do. Always be clothed in white, and always anoint your head with oil. Enjoy life with your wife, whom you love, all the days of this MEANINGLESS LIFE that God has given you under the sun--all your meaningless days."* Well, if the bible says there is no meaning, it must mean something, and it means truth is bitterly scarce.

Hassan Ibn Sabbah said, "Nothing is true. Everything is per-mitted." Take your pick. Naturally, whatever you do has consequences, but you are free to do what you want, to the chagrin of the professional truth merchants. You are the one who chooses the meaning you want to give to life and anything else. No meaning, any meaning, a particular meaning--it'll always be up to you what you want to believe.

Life is but a walking shadow, a poor player
That struts and frets his hour upon the stage
And then is heard no more. It is a tale
Told by an idiot, full of sound and fury,
Signifying nothing.

William Shakespeare, Macbeth

Chapter Seventeen
Common and Not-so-common Sense

"The English have better sense than any other nation--and they are fools."

   Metternich (Klemens Wenzel Nepomuk Lothar Fürst von Metternich)

Repetition of brainless phrases does not make them more intelligent. 'Nothing is more important than a good education.' For what purpose? To become an obedient and educated slave? If education could solve life's most pressing problems, members with the highest levels of education in our society wouldn't have problems. Higher education doesn't mean it's more likely you have your life together. Educated people are not the richest, the happiest, or the most morally stable--whatever that means. Education is alright, if that is what you want, but most important it is only if you want to join the teacher's union.

   Apartheid governments in South Africa, from 1948-1994, produced perhaps the finest education on that torn and troubled continent ever:

   "Apartheid placed great emphasis on "self-determination" and "cultural autonomy" for different ethnic groups. For this reason, "mother-tongue" education was strongly emphasized. Thus, in addition to pouring resources into developing Afrikaans educational material, resources were also poured into developing school textbooks in black languages like Zulu, Xhosa, Sotho, Tswana, and Pedi. As a result, one of the consequences of apartheid was a South African population literate in black-African languages (a rare thing in Africa where schooling is normally carried out in colonial languages like English and French). (Wikipedia)" What? You expect me to applaud?

   'We must learn to be tolerant.' Why the hell is that? We tolerate a mosquito sucking blood from our leg because we can't swat it while holding a baby. We tolerate the noise of drunks in the street at night. We tolerate a toothache over the weekend, with the help of Jack Daniel's, until we can see the dentist on Monday. I do not want to be tolerated, and I don't want to treat anybody else that poorly! Tolerating people is the ultimate impertinence, a threat even, "I hate you but I'll let you live for now." Tolerance is the last thing we need between each other, and tolerance is not what your job needs from you.

Value is one of these commonly accepted and respected platitudes. No two people agree on the definition of such value. What's valuable to one person is worthless to another, and an atrocity for a third. Honor is such a monstrosity. It was a special honor to be chosen as a Kamikaze pilot in Japan. Returning from a mission alive meant shame for decades to come.

By the way, the majority of Kamikaze pilots were exquisitely educated young men. Proof that education is good for something, I guess, if you intend to die young with honors. Butchering sister or wife is honorable for a lot of religious zealots; for me honor killings are the hideous crimes of worthless creeps.

Love, family, ethical behavior--we throw that stuff around assuming everybody else's definition of these things is congruent with ours. Common sense for one individual is a roadside bomb for the next. Common sense, expressed with sanity and confidence, often crosses the line to common nonsense. The more nodding heads I see in agreement of anything, the more skeptical I become. Quick and easy agreement is almost proof to me that imminent danger is in the air, the bristling danger of misunderstanding, deceptive unity of latent violence.

'More money, if I just had more money, life would be easier.' Immediately convincing, yet utter nonsense. More money is fine per se, but the expectation that more money equals less problems is as commonly accepted as it is dumb. Those who have the kind of money you think would mean instant salvation for you, struggle with at least as many problems as you do. Worse, these idiots believe the same myth: 'If I only had more dough right now, life would be easier.'

Whatever you think about money today, in general and in

particular, will be exactly what you'll be thinking if and when you have more money. If that stuff is hard to come by today--in your perception--you'll also believe in the future that it's hard to make a buck. I have serious doubts your tripling income is powerful enough to change your mind.

If money issues cause arguments and strife between you and your spouse these days, don't kid yourself, increasing assets won't quell your favorite source of entertainment. Stress, worry, and sleepless nights are typical for your current relationship with your money? Surprise, surprise, more money will not buy you out of that. Money makes the greatest fools out of educated, intelligent people. Well, it's not money's fault. Money only shows us what fools we are or can be. In expectation of and hope for money, we make fools of ourselves and money--as hard to grasp as that may be--cannot change us. Greater sums do not turn us into smaller fools.

Financial independence is a legend. If you don't consider yourself independent right now, I'm afraid you aren't going to gain independence in the future. Amassing sufficient financial power to guarantee independence, please note, is impossible. There is no such sum that could do it for you.

Several years back, Ted Turner was as close to losing all he had as the average poor guy. The pile of dough you're sitting on, even if it amounts to literally billions of dollars, cannot save you from any nasty fate. Mr. Turner made proper turns at the right time to prevent disaster. Ted Turner saved his money from disappearing. It was not his pile of money saving Mr. Turner's behind.

You will have to work with your finances independently of their current size and purchasing power, or there won't be much independence. And, since finances don't buy independence, I prefer to understand the term financial independence as independence *from* finances. You may also choose to claim that today. Without doing that you will never experience financial freedom.

It is this freedom--anybody can have it at any time--that

permits you to play with new options and possibilities. Money can be a result of your freedom and independence, but not its cause. All the paper in the world cannot give you freedom. "Paper is poverty, ... it is only the ghost of money, and not money itself." (Thomas Jefferson) That's why.

'If I had more money I could do what I want.' Really? Those who have more money know this common myth is backwards. If you bother to meet a few people with decent reserves--and they happen to be honest with you--you will hear that the opposite is true. When I choose more often what I want to do, it is more likely I'll make more money. *What you want to do* is NOT identical with *doing what you love*. Love in regards to business and work is so overrated.

The emphasis is not on doing what you love instead of doing what you despise. Self-determination is key. And so is a series of continued choices and course adjustments versus vegetating along the rusty tracks of a decision you made years ago. Are you hesitant to even admit you made the fateful decision of applying for that job before retiring altogether from your freedom of choice?

Money will not support you in making better choices. Goodness! On the contrary, it can help you to get in touch with your worst imaginable choice making abilities. Trust me. Just this once. Making a lot of choices is likely to lead you to making better choices, with some of them possibly leading to more money.

Money is ill-chosen as a means to an end. It can be the result of what we do. Of course, if doing what you want is exhaustively covered by hanging out at the mall and shopping, or watching TV, that's not magically going to generate tremendous income. Doing what you want must be translated into marketable products or services, otherwise you don't get profitable results from it apart from an entertaining afternoon. 'If I had more money,' means in reality: 'I am a lazy dumbass, and I don't even want to do what I pretend I want to do.'

Nostalgia with past pain--and this is something I am personally guilty of--can successfully keep us from enjoying and exploiting the current moment. Some people exist in a trance of reliving the most traumatic time of their lives. Many veterans are doing that. And in certain ways a lot of us are veterans of personal wars and tragedies. We know those grueling times are over, yet we can't seem to get over it. Uniquely horrifying experiences may have shaped our lives, but they are not what determines our living.

We need to shape our next day. Your decision from 35 years ago to work for the post office was fine back then, or stupid, or whatever you want to think. Today you'll do well to make new choices. Same with emotionally or even physically crippling experiences in our past. It was whatever the hell it was, but it can't give meaning to our lives today. My parents were born in the early 20th century: their lives were defined by two world wars, and I have seen how difficult it can be to escape the pain--or the joys, for that matter--of our past.

For some people it's a volatile relationship. For others monetary disaster, a horrible accident, or active duty as a soldier somewhere in the dirt. If you believe in therapy and you feel the need to support a theraquack financially, by all means, do it. They'd like to buy the newest computer games for their kids, also. But with or without therapy, you have to take new steps, risking new mistakes and new pain.

Since we are so obsessed with pain--with our old pain, at least--there's no reason to be scared. Old pain, new pain--what's the damn difference what pain you obsess over? That's why therapy and working on your old wounds doesn't make too much sense. If you live a lot, there will be more pain and wounds than you'll have time to chat about with your shrink. Be grateful there's new pain to look forward to. You have been bored to tears by the re-runs of the old dusty, musty thing anyway.

Imaginary lines separate us from where we want to be or what we may allow ourselves to do in the future. 'First, then ...' First, we have to take care of problem A, then we can do what we actually want to do. Our parents taught us to think that way. *Work first, then play. When you are as old as your sister, you can do that, too. On your 18th birthday, ...* Lines we were required to pass may have been defined by age, time, sums of money, or tests in school. They became tools for self-censorship of our freedom. Pretty soon, we hardly permit ourselves to have any fun because there will always be the barriers of new lines ahead of us.

Try to tear down such a barrier once in awhile. Do something you normally don't allow yourself to do before X happens. Do the after-X-thing first and you may be surprised. Perhaps the imaginary line vanishes and the oh so important task X loses its snake eye powers over you. It can't hypnotize and immobilize you anymore.

Maybe with less weight and expectations attached to event X--the thing that must happen before we're allowed to really live-- we can even attack task X easier, from the other side of the barricade. Playfully we can cross the lines we have drawn in the sand now, or cross them later with tears. Diligently working on our chores won't help us.

'You need a lot of money before you can start a business,' is a common lie people employ to indefinitely stay in job slavery. It doesn't become more intelligent no matter how often some dork repeats it. This week, I read about a 17-year-old girl who borrowed $8 from her mother when she was 14. She started a website (whateverlife.com) and offered free background design for MySpace web pages.

Today, she generates revenue of $1,000,000 annually from advertisers, and employs mom and a couple of friends. Content? Value? Meaning? Nonsense. She generates massive web traffic and reliably so. That's all that counts. Meanwhile, she bought a house and she and her mother have moved out of their one-bedroom apartment they lived in three years ago when she began her business. You can start a million dollar business venture with eight bucks. Ask your mom. She may be nice enough to help you out.

Anecdotal evidence only, I know, yet sufficiently powerful to shame and shut up armies of mumbling idiots. $8 out of mom's cookie jar and a teenage girl offering pink hearts online for free.

Beats thousands of serious people calculating for years and decades how much funding they may need first before moving rapidly to step one. Embarrassing. Money you don't have yet can't stop you from doing anything. It's not there, remember? Being a victim of money you don't have is like allowing imaginary friends to run your life. I feel for people like that.

Hard-earned money, once again. What does that mean? If gained with pain, money is more precious and worthwhile to hold onto than money you have made easily with relatively little effort? That scares me. Suckers for hard-earned money are doomed because they have no sense of the real value of their money. Such dullards respect their pain but not money itself. If they did, they would treat all money the same, hard-earned or easy-won. I have made expensive mistakes in this regard. Learn from me if you can, and never go into business with a partner who has hard-earned-money issues.

Most people earn their money the hard way. True. The largest sums of money, however, are not at all made with pain. When we don't treat relatively large amounts with the same care as small and painfully acquired sums, we can lose the large amounts just as easily as we made them. That's why lottery dollars and inherited money often disappear quickly. Beware of choosing hard-earned money as your sole income and of respecting yourself and the hard part too much. The hard-earned money syndrome can destroy your options of ever having it easy in life.

'Safety first.' Duh. What can you gain without it? *Safety is our goal*, is even worse. How safe am I if you don't reach your goal while I am standing next to you? Slogans are supposed to teach and train us to move in the right direction, but they're plain awful and useless. All of them. Bullshitting people lull us to sleep with common nonsense. Every slogan is a lie--this one included. Common cliches do not heighten awareness. That stuff numbs us, prevents individual thought and mindfulness, and reminds me of idiotic attempts Eastern European communist governments used to make before the 1990s to communicate with their enslaved societies.

When I use someone's guest bathroom and I see more or less subtle territorial markings the lady of the house left behind (cutsey signs 'put the seat down,' etc.), I know the lady of the house is not a lady. Utter lack of class, 'Arbeit macht frei,' comes to mind--Labor shall set you free--signs adorning entrances of German concentration camps. Oh my God, I know I'm so wrong ... but that's what I like about me. Slap people in the face, kick their shins, ridicule them--do anything offensive instead of nodding your damned noodle in quiet agreement with every worn-out phrase imbeciles bombard you with.

'I need to learn more first.' In other words, you are not enough in your perception. With that line in your head you will never be ready regardless of how much you learn. Truth is, you are probably good enough today. *Read Rich Dad, Poor Dad* by Robert Kiyosaki if you must and you will see his poor dad was far better educated than his rich dad. Education is not a bad thing in and of itself, but when you put it between yourself and what you want to do, education is a deal breaker and a nightmare.

There will always be things you have to learn and understand, but that will go along with you doing what you want to do. Recently I had the demented idea to ride a unicycle. Of course, I had to learn how to do it. For several months the damn thing threw me off until I managed to ride it shakily for a few yards. I'm aware I have told you this before, but my point here is that learning must increase your activities and not delay your taking action.

Change is overrated. Corporations are eager to change behavior and increase the performance of their employees. Teachers want to change their students. Wives intend to change their husbands, parents try to change their kids, and children engage in the futile attempt of changing their parents. Some folks mean to change governments, entire countries or even better, the world. Worst of all, people want to change themselves, improve themselves, better themselves. It is so cute and endearingly idealistic, but it won't work I'm afraid.

Yeah, oodles of money can be made--and precious prizes can be won--with people's silly hope for change, but most efforts are wasted. If you don't like your fiancee's alcohol consumption, you are an idiot if you think you can change her behavior after you get married. You disapprove of some of your boyfriend's ways and you think your miracle-working love will change him over time? He ain't going to change--at least not for you, you dork--and you better consider upgrading instead of marrying that bastard.

Trying to improve yourself is not only a waste of time and money, but you are also telling yourself constantly you are inadequate. You have always been good enough, but your self-improvement trip will guarantee that you won't ever muster the confidence to put your damn improved self to practical work. 'Today I am worse than I will be tomorrow,' is the tenet of self-improvement addicts.

Waiting for the right time can kill you. You are an inventor 'ahead of your time'? Nonsense. We have mentioned powerful methods to belittle yourself so that you feel worse off than you actually are. People ahead of their time think they are better than their contemporary human environment, condemned to wait until the idiots catch up with their brilliant inventorial minds. Awful.

You can't do what you want to do right now, means your reasoning is as crappy as the rest of your life. No, you can't buy the $2,000,000 hacienda in Mexico you fell in love with. But that's nothing you want to DO anyway--it's something you want to HAVE. I didn't say you can have anything you want, but there is hardly a reason for you to wait when you are set to DO what you want. It's the right time, and there are literally millions of things you can do, immediately. We don't because we love waiting for doomsday.

Money will solve all your problems. Then you will be able to live as you please. Do me and yourself a favor, will you? Shoot yourself today and we have that problem taken care of with a lot less anxiety than you are about to endure over the next years. If money--some money, loads of money, absence of money--separates you today from the YOU you wish to be, convert and change your religion. Join the French foreign legion, emigrate to Korea (North), but do something that gets you out of sight of your loved ones because they don't deserve to watch your insanity unfold. No one deserves to listen to you through another dinner. Money can't solve your problems. Money can't solve anybody's money problems. Hence there won't be a hereafter you could hope for.

Common nonsense is an excuse not to live. Most of us are scared of life, with good reason. That's why the government is the largest employer here in the U.S., and perhaps everywhere else. People want to be taken care of. I would never attempt to talk you out of that. Too dangerous to kick you into your luck. I don't want to be responsible for your happiness. Go vegetate until you keel over. At least you have benefits. Just know, it is fine to spend your days in the treacherous security of mama's lap and bosom. Really, it's alright, but you can't have both, maintaining the perks of infancy and leading an adventurous life filled with options.

If it's common, it doesn't make sense. Common ideas describe how the crowd thinks and lives. Groups don't provide freedom, as open minded as they may think they are. People who think alike will do anything to prevent each other's individuality from developing too freely. Freedom can be yours to be explored and exploited, sure, but chances are you will be alone and misunderstood in many ways. Nobody will understand you completely, and common folks may not like you. If you need to belong, you better kiss your freedom good-bye. Freedom is not a group event, and it is certainly not common.

Chapter Eighteen
Love and Hate

"Do what thou wilt shall be the whole of the Law." "Love is the law, love under will."

Aleister Crowley

Love and hatred--what's the big difference? Aren't they often the same? Your no good piece-of-shit ex-husband is loved by another girl so much that she can't wait to marry him and to get this jewel of a stepfather for her brood. Which one of these two figures is he really? The garbage heap you learned to know too well, or the fabulous loving and caring hubby material she can't be without? Both perhaps? None of the above?

We are brilliant in making things up about people, and even what they *do to us* can be seen from a variety of angles. The most hurtful things our parents did to us, the stuff right under our skin, is what we hate them for AND what we deeply love them for. It may be difficult or impossible for you to see it that way currently, but in a quiet moment think about things you utterly despise about your mom.

Then think of all she has done for you, things you are thankful for, and everything you love her for. I'd be surprised if you didn't have a couple of the same points popping into your mind both times. Shock of shocks, as freaky and radical as it may sound, we love our parents for some of the same experiences we hate them for: emotionally intense moments.

Guess what? Same with other people, except it's not that obvious. We don't stay or keep them around long enough to see the overlapping areas, and it's too explosive an issue to think through this minute. Traumatic events that can make parents and their children inseparable may drive acquaintances apart. And then there is your job, your work. You bet, you love it for the same reasons you hate it.

Money does not care whether it is made with love or by way of hatred. Perhaps most money is earned by people who hate what they do. At least, most people work for their money by doing something they don't love. Hatred feeds more people than love. A large percentage of our planet's population pays for rent and mortgage with money they received in exchange for hatred.

Hate is a safe concept almost guaranteed to work. You can hate all the way to the bank. We don't trust love as much as a money generating factor. Love is on the suspicious side, but that's not the issue at hand. I'm not suggesting you drop your awful job, replacing it with work you love.

It's a no-brainer: you try making money with something you love and the pressure to make mortgage payments, feed the brats, and pay bills runs so high that you will quickly hate your desperate attempt to make money with work you love. Within days, weeks maybe, you are likely to hate what you now love to do.

Go the other route. Realize how much you love what you hate doing today. If you don't love it, why are you so damn proud of doing it? If you aren't proud and happy with your misery, why have you done it for decades? Why are you still at it? <u>Because loving to hate it beats hating to love something else.</u>

The public display of affection can be corny. Nobody stands on the street corner expressing eternal and unconditional love for Exxon Mobil. You may very well love owning a couple of their shares but you won't take your love to the streets as picketers do with their hate. Hatred is somewhat more accepted and kosher. We hate freely and our expressions of love are a bit more on the inhibited side. You can hit someone over the head with a bat in a kid's movie but you cannot allow the same two people to kiss each other. It would deform our children's characters. If we didn't have closets, we probably wouldn't love at all.

Hatred makes the world go 'round. Hatred puts bread and butter on the table. Hatred buys cars. We depend on hatred. It stabilizes our economy and provides jobs for millions of people.

Jobs that unions fight for and politicians promise are understood as sources of, and subject to, hatred. It's not just that hatred is an important foundation of people's income. Hatred is practically synonymous with income and with the making of money.

You can make money with love, hatred, or both. As long as you are making money, you shouldn't worry with what underlying emotion you are earning your income. Money certainly doesn't care about the love life or hate life of its makers. Here is what you should care about as far as love and hatred are concerned: don't be a victim of love or hatred. When we say, 'Oh I hate that,' it sounds as if we played an active role. That's a lie! The average person does not actively choose to hate something. Our hating of jobs, for example, is more like an involuntary reflex. The job *makes* us hate it, because the coworkers did this, the boss said that, and I can't do blah blah blah. We fall into hatred as we fall into love. Nothin' we can do about it, right?

Wrong. You can make a crucial change without having to do much. When you realize how much you love hating your job, your role converts from being passive to active. You become the one who hates and the one who loves. You are assuming a control position. From here onward, love and hate become your tools of the trade and you can apply them appropriately. Your awareness of loving what you hate allows you to keep your cool. You can hate better than your colleagues ever will. The same erratic superiors who used to get you riled lose power over your emotions and their intensity. You may even smile at things that used to have you by the throat before.

Victims of love are not in control either. You can't start or stop at will. You can't slow down or accelerate. A pretty sad thing to watch. You almost wish for the ones involved that it'll be over soon--and it will be--so that these people are free again to do what they want. Involuntary love not only robs you of your control over love relationships, passive love often overrides people's brain functions and they happily destroy their lives in other areas as well. Victims of love are incapacitated. At least their judgment is impaired. Imminent danger looms in the air surrounding them. Money must be locked away--theirs--and they should not be permitted to buy and sell stocks or anything else as long as the illness persists.

As we have seen with hatred, if you don't detach yourself enough to assume a control position--control, not over other persons but over your mind altering emotions--there will be nothing cute or sweet about that love. It can be devastating. When you become aware that you love to hate, you have regained your power and you can take your foot off the hate accelerator. Same with love: when you love to play with it, you can accelerate and slow this thing down at will also. If you *let love happen* to you and you stay passive, you'll get run over eventually. You can't afford to relinquish your power over your feelings.

You want to do what you love and make money with it? What a joke. People in love generally lose money, they don't make any. Before you make money doing what you love, you must gain total control over the love part or I see cumulations of dark clouds on your cash horizon. Do you love what you do because you *chose* to love it, after initial sparks of lust? If you can't help but love it, I suggest you tread carefully. Better yet, do what you hate doing. Most of us have learned it's safer for everyone involved when we don't act on our hatred. Hence we can do what we hate for a lifetime and still function in a somewhat reasonable fashion. Your money will thank you for it.

Victims of hatred--their own--are perhaps the largest group among the employed. Involuntary hatred is triggered by something outside the hater. His 45-minute commute, something in the voice of a harmless coworker, or a monotone workday shifts that emotion into gear. Again, no control in sight. Somebody or something appears to be doing it to the poor hating soul. The hater feels powerless. She is not in charge of her hating. Too bad, because hating can be so much fun when you actively choose to do so. Hey, as long as you don't act on your hatred, it's safer to hate than to pretend not to.

I am amazed how well an economy works in spite of so many employees who hate away all day. What appears to be sabotage on first sight turns out to be a smoothly functioning machine when you take a closer look. Let us recall: a person in love loses marbles by the dozen. So does someone who hates uncontrollably. Whose gain is it? Your subject of love or hatred gets the prize. The guy you hate, the girl you love, or the company you despise gains power over you. They ultimately control what you can't. Between hatred and love, hatred is the stronger emotion and you can engage men and women in it with no holds barred.

Bless the gods for making hatred! How many hours people work or their level of performance is not as important as their ability to hate. That's where they hand over their ownership to the employer, similarly to guys offering their balls on a silver platter to the girl of their dreams. Give employees an opportunity to enter a hate trance and they will hate productively for your benefit. Naturally, job hating people of both genders lose control over their faculties in the same ways as people in love do. The party in control of the collective hatred gains: the employer. Companies do well BECAUSE people hate their jobs. Correct that: because the average employee is a victim of his or her emotions. Can you see why it is important for you to hate your job intentionally and, yes, with a whole lot of love?

The power of love can bring you to your knees. Power in connection with love that's useful to you is your power over your love. Any dumbass can fall in love and be overwhelmed by it. Can you walk straight and employ love for your purposes? If you can't, love is counterproductive for you. In that case, nothing better has ever happened to you than finding yourself on a job you despise. A true blessing.

How can that be? Let's assume you hate your job. It's awful, in short FUBAR. You are not in charge of hating your work. The conditions of your job situation are in control, pulling the strings of your emotional make-up. Next step. You become active. You consciously decide to hate passionately what you were hating involuntarily before. You with me?

Now you DO the hating. You can intensify it or mellow it

down at will. You will get the hang of it fairly quickly and what happens? You are enjoying the hating part. You are now close to loving your job hating, with a twist. You gained power over your love to hate. You love at will and you hate at will. The ugliest job on the nastiest day has lost its sting and its emotional powers over you. You have become detached. The difference between actively loving what you love and loving what you hate is marginal, because you are at the center. No thing, like work, can get a hold of you and grab you by the lapels.

Hate crime sounds like a tautology, but it isn't. If you hate someone while stabbing him to death, it is worse than stabbing him to death without hating him. Say what? If you happen to be the one getting the stabbing treatment it won't matter much to you, but apparently there are people with a keen interest in the distinction between the correct definition of one and the other. I always thought violent crime was a heinous act in itself, but I guess it can be understood as *just business, nothing personal*. And once it is personal and not business related, it is worse than business motivated murder and therefore a hate crime. Be that as it may, we will concern ourselves with love crime.

No one talks about love crimes yet and we need to change that. Not every sleeping preacher gets shot in the back by his loving wife. But if one gets murdered and the victim is not a criminal--because criminals have the tendency to get killed by other criminals--it's likely someone who loves the victim dearly, or used to love him/her a lot, committed this crime of love.

If your grandkids or your ex-husbands haven't made an attempt on your life yet, maybe they will soon. Just kidding. No, I meant you are probably pretty safe and you won't fall victim to a love crime if all the knives are still in the kitchen drawer. Arrgh, don't listen to me. I really don't want to scare you. You are fine and everybody loves you. I, however, believe love itself is a crime if it impairs your judgment and narrows your freedom to make decisions. Falling in love is a crime where you are both victim and perpetrator, robbing yourself of freedom, money, and possibly years of your life.

Hate is a window of opportunity for monetary gain. Especially since all the suckers are preoccupied with love and what they love to do. Hate is such a perfect field to till and to exploit because it's untouched. People are afraid to think along those lines. Think of hate as a gold mine. We love this today and something else tomorrow. We fall in and out of that fickle thing called love, but we are adamant about the stuff we hate. No need to remind people to be persistent in that area. Damn, it's serious and quite personal. If we do anything religiously, it's hating. Watch our fellow nutcases in traffic and elsewhere. There is intent behind hatred and a measurable charge. No comparison to wishy-washy love clouds. No giggling here.

As you control what you love to love and what you love to hate, it becomes meaningless which course of action you choose. You can work with any emotion when you are able to lean back and enjoy them all from a detached point of reference. Make money with the things and themes you hate. The market of those who understand you and agree with you is so much larger. With the things you hate you can even start a movement--think of MADD or PETA--and get tons of support and droves of volunteers for your cause. Hate is the way to go. Love is for pussies. Oops! Uh, well ...

Happiness is overrated and misunderstood. Generally, we divide feelings and emotions into ones on the positive side and others on the more painful or negative side. We prefer to increase happiness, joy, excitement, love and we'd like to experience less sadness, anger, frustration, worry, etc. Bad idea. That strategy leaves us with long, dry stretches in pursuit of happiness, but happiness itself pops up sporadically only, for brief moments.

Real life is chockful of every emotion. They are all bad if you allow them to get the better of you. You have noticed this, I'm sure. Life doesn't care about your preferences and dislikes. Here's the trick: abandon control over what specific type of emotion you need as a background to be happy. Give yourself permission to experience the entire bandwidth of possible emotions.

That's how you gain control to do as you please with any and all of them--including, but not limited to, deciding to be happy with every damn step of the spectrum. Being a little happy here and devastated the next moment is for emotional teenagers. C'mon, be happy all the time with all you've got or not at all, but please make up your mind. It's silly and a waste of time for adults to seek and pursue that stuff. We have better things to do.

Lusting to work. Can you imagine? You love what you do or you hate it, and you LUST after doing more of it all day. Lust has a bad reputation, which makes it all the more attractive. Similar to the bad-boy syndrome. They are rarely loved, but so much more attractive and irresistible than a lovable nice guy you may settle with and for, choosing him as a dependably boring provider. What better thing is there than lust? Everybody experiences it. Most deny enjoying it. Window of opportunity? Too narrow. Lust is the right size doorway for you. Greed is too tame and love won't do. Can you handle lust for work and money, for fun and profit?

Extreme sports are for dorks incapable of pulling their pants up over their asses. Extreme lust for your work is a prerequisite if you are interested in more than average income. I know, I know, some extreme dorks on skateboards are top earners, but most of them just break bones like the rest of the grinding majority. The point is to leave the majority, and lust for work is guaranteed to turn you into a lonely freak, abandoned by the masses.

Evolution is too slow for you to wait for, and self-improvement will never satisfy you. Never. Self-improvement keeps you on the brink of something good, but you will never be good enough. When you get close, you'll feel the urge to improve yourself some more. This insanity won't end until you stop it. Teaching and understanding are too slow, also. Leave that stuff to the dark and musty school environment. For you today, it is worthless. You will never understand how money works. Very, very few people really do. No universal law or truth to comprehend. There isn't any. But what about the Law of

Attraction? Give me a break!

Your self, or better your array of selves, can't be improved. Put the ones you have to work and they will improve or they won't. Who cares? Wanna speed up your personal evolution? Speed up trial and error. It's all a numbers game. Explode in activities for fun and profit. Bust your bubble of comfort and safety. Love makes you blind? Often, and usually against our will.

Lust, however, is putting a blindfold over your eyes intentionally to intensify the fun of the game: jump into all sorts of activities blindly. You're into fly fishing? Take a yoga class. You've done yoga for twenty three years? Goodness, go to the race track and bet on some horses. Handicapping horses is like second nature? Try water skiing. Something new and different every week. Leave the damn family at home. This is work. Inspire that ugly noodle of yours until it explodes with ideas.

Meet people who are NOT on your wavelength. Who cares what you are interested in? Go meet individuals who do something else. Meetup.com is a vast source, for instance. Meet collectors of Japanese swords, crazies who practice chaos magick, spend a couple of hours with individuals you would never ever meet in your regular circles. Why? For the sake of exploring. For the hell of it. Something will happen, if you do it continually, that you cannot possibly anticipate in its material value and its fun-inducing properties.

Love draws its victims close to the object of their love. Hatred draws people just as close and it drives them equally mad. Well, only as long as you are an involuntary hater. Love or hatred, whatever it is: move close but not close enough to get slapped. Investigate and scrutinize your object of interest like an artifact.

To exploit your hatred, stay cool and collected. Don't allow other people's emotional outbursts to raise your body temperature or increase your heart rate. Neither instigate an escalation. Be in the face of unpleasant things and individuals to study them well. Usually we run away from tension too willingly.

Or we feel the need to end it. Your opportunity lies in dedicating yourself to studying tension and its details.

More money won't make you love your hated job more. I know, I said it before but can you see how ridiculous such expectation is? *Pay me more money so that I will begin to love what I hate?* Absurd ... and childish. Give me more and I will do X. Give me much more and I'll even feel better. *Reward think* makes people believe they could love by the buck--work, women, men. We are whores.

But you are different. You wouldn't love for money, endure more for cash, or raise your level of tolerance for monetary gain and benefits. Not you. Love your blasted job more, and more money may come out of it. Hate your job or love to hate it increasingly, and more dough may fall into your lap. Or tell your superiors to go screw themselves and choose a new line of crap to hate or love for mammon's sake. But do not insult your intelligence, demanding better pay in order to love what you hate a bit better and more patiently.

Chapter Nineteen
To Do or Not To Do

"There is no pleasure in having nothing to do; the fun is having lots to do and not doing it."

Mary Wilson Little

You are doing all day what you want to do. Nobody can make you do things, can they? You know very well what you want and what you don't want. All your bitching about your terrible day is a facade, masking your free will to live the way you want.

You chose your profession. If you are working for somebody else, they did not send recruiters after you who threw a potato sack over your head, extracting you forcefully from paradise. You picked the company, filled out an application, and scheduled an interview. You were after that awful job, weren't you?

If it's your own company or business, you made it what it is. You can quit any day. You are doing already what you want to do, all day, every day. If it wasn't your idea, you would have stopped the madness a long time ago. Your complaints are the ultimate luxury and they are expressing this: I have a fabulous life, but I tell you it's crappy from morning to evening and I love every minute of it. Congratulations!

You hate what you do? Most people do, but I don't want to talk you into it if you are not one of them. So, let's not talk about you, just about job haters anonymous in general. Job haters are not slaves, at least not involuntary slaves. These guys have choices, and freely they have made a minimum of three decisions. They chose to do what they dislike. They chose to dislike what they do. They chose to continue doing what they hate, probably for as long as they continue hating it.

That's what freedom is for. "[They] got a right to be as

miserable as everybody else," said Chris Rock about gays who fight to get married. Well, it's true also for the average emslavee. Oops, I forgot that *average employee* is redundant: either term covers the other.

We are masters of bad choices. True, but maybe what we picked for ourselves is not that bad after all. Perhaps it is the lesser of two or more evils. Could it be that your current work position with all its problems is indeed the best option you can see for yourself? Hey, no reason to blush or to be embarrassed. I mean it. If you can handle taking a five minute break from your kvetching, you may want to acknowledge yourself for the great choice you made by landing this job you're clinging to and hating so masterfully.

Freedom is tough and not necessarily friendly. We are free to do as we wish, and even when we are not aware of our freedom to choose, the choice is ours. We are not enslaved by evil corporations. Corporations can do nothing, NOTHING, without the army of suckers eager to acquire and to keep their positions. Employees run 'big oil' and 'big tobacco.'

Secretaries, nerds, and doormen own big oil and big tobacco with their 401(k) plans. Finger pointing and Us vs. Them rhetoric help political dorks to blow off steam publicly and proves how much they too love to hate--their pet theories for instance. Neutered cats going through the moves are equally efficient and cause similar merriment but hell, journalists have got to be good for something. 22,000 Enron employees--and shareholders--turned into poor victims at the drop of a hat.

Several hundred thousand loving German family daddies and murderers--according to official numbers several million daddies is closer to the facts--turned into innocent victims of one evil dictator, practically overnight. The innocent ain't innocent, for they are the true magicians with their depraved alibis: I didn't do anything, I didn't know what was going on, I wasn't even there.

Lucy and Walt, the genuinely friendly seniors greeting you at the door of your neighborhood Walmart Superstore, they ARE

Walmart. Innocent? Perhaps not, but what did you say you want to accuse them of? Now you are trying to make a case of me comparing Hitler and his henchmen with Walmart and today's corporate world. I did NOT: I compared those who faked innocence then with people who are faking innocence today! What exactly you are innocent of, I shall leave up to you to decide and live with.

Circumstance does not dictate a particular route for us to take. Your parents may have tried to nudge you in a professional direction they favored, but even if you followed their suggestion, the ultimate choice was yours. Nobody is to blame for your current spot in life, not your gallery of ex-wives, not the fifteen-and-a-half children you are supporting, and not even you are at fault. You may blame yourself for that hideous tattoo on your ass, but fault? There was a time when you didn't think of it as a fault. It was a goal perhaps.

See, that's how precious goals are. What motivational quacks promote as the sacredness of goal setting creeps me out. Wrong as I may be, I believe there is an ambivalence to goals like piercings and rims and God knows what else. Once more I have to prevent you from deliberately misunderstanding me: enjoy your rim jobs and as many holes in your head as you see necessary. The Cult of the Goal I find so trifling.

Granted, you have done stupid things but you chose all of them, whatever type of influence you were under. You don't like what you're doing today? You are not sentenced to do it tomorrow. It's not your fate to continue until the end of your days. The largest portion of our emotional charge about our jobs has nothing to do with that job. It has everything to do with the-- artificial--finality of our decision to do it. You could laugh about it every day. Allow yourself to quit any time and then don't quit. Giving yourself permission to leave whenever you want, like a college student on a summer job, may be sufficient to stop your yellow teeth from grinding in your sleep. Who knows? If you could leave any day, you may enjoy working there for another ten years.

Control can be hard. Most people have total control over their sphincters most of the time. We had to learn that and it didn't come easy. Daily practice and thousands of unpleasant mistakes were necessary to gain that control. Funny? No. We conveniently forget how hard we worked--especially our parents--for basic accomplishments we are now taking for granted.

We can enjoy immense control over things we do. To a large extent, we cannot control the results of what we do. People are obsessed with results and frustrated with their inability to do much about them. Preoccupation with specific results and their control steals our time to do what we CAN do. Besides, the things we can do provide 99% of the fun we have in life. Enjoyment of the things you want to HAVE--the stuff you are so eager to control--is usually short-lived and nearly meaningless for your happiness. You can do what you want to do, all day, every day. Any child can do it, limited only by imagination and parental approval ratings.

Mind-over-Matter faithfuls are arrogant enough to take a shot at predicting the future. To them it's not wishful thinking. They believe their minds actually control matter and therefore also the material results of their minds' activity. Impressive! Dullard that I am, I have discovered my mind can't even reliably predict future states of my own mind, especially not if I do something physically between now and then. I knew you'd ask me for an example. Be that way.

My mind cannot predict what my mind will be thinking after I confront my ordinary taste buds with a sample of cheese of a kind so far unknown to me. I may be thinking hard for days but the damn matter, this tiny sliver of cheese, will beat my mind every time. You see, my mind is not much to brag about. It ranks below the stinkiest of matters.

Unless I do something first physically, I won't be able to figure out intellectually whether I'll like or dislike engaging in that particular activity. I may be an arrogant son-of-a-bitch, but I am quite humble when it comes to my predictions and prophecies. I do not know how it feels and what I may be thinking about it until I actively do a thing. I'm afraid I am such a bloody materialist that my mind is occupied and controlled in its entirety by evil lowly matter. And then, I'm thinking, without matter and a human body we wouldn't have a mind to lose.

What do you like to do? Besides activities you have tried, you don't know the answer. Small wonder most people don't have a clue what they want and they will never figure it out in their heads. Never. Neither will they be happier by peeking over their neighbor's fence, trying to copy what he is wasting his life with.

I don't know how else to break it to you: if you want to know what you want to do, you gotta try a lot of different things. A LOT. Sounds almost like work, *you have to do a lot to find what you want to do*. And work it is ... or is it freedom? Both? It takes discipline to find what you want and to stick to it. Doing what you really want is free, but it takes so much effort that the majority of individuals give up on the search. They settle for some money, for a so-so job, and the so-so crap they can buy with their allotted pittances. Doing what you want is harder work, better pain, and closer to freedom than anything else I know of.

People don't hate what they do because what they do is so bad or hard. They hate what they do because they feel deprived of what they could have done instead. People hate their lives and their work and their retirement thereafter because all of it represents the death of their happiness, in their flawed belief. Once you are looking forward to retirement you know as much as I do that your life sucks. If your life sucks, the quality of your work sucks. That's why those who pay you would be insane to pay you a penny more.

Aim to fail in everything you do. You think I am joking? Didn't I say a few pages back it would be insane to fail intentionally? Yeah, what's your point? The stress we put ourselves under by expecting to win with our projects is not causing us to lose. Nothing wrong with a good helping of stress. When we are operating at breaking point, any number of small things could throw us off course. But usually they make us more resilient.

Our worst obstacle to overcome is the desperation of having to win every time at all cost. That's what makes it hard to truly enjoy ourselves even if we win. The anxiety to win can make it outright impossible for us to love what we do, even when we started out with something we originally liked doing. If you <u>must</u> succeed, you probably won't.

Against all odds you may achieve the results you are after, but you are pretty much screwed for the entire time it takes you to get there. The following project will turn out the same way, of course, because you will have learned the pattern by then: if I put myself under constant unbearable pressure, thus killing every thing that used to be fun, I may have a real chance of succeeding in the end. Poor schmuck! Sure, this may work for a while for some people. But making a life and a living out of that? You gotta be whacked in the head to continue on that path.

Aiming to fail provides immediate relaxation. Your carefree and playful attitude is likely to produce a wealth of additional ideas and contacts you wouldn't have had the time to pursue and to exploit. So many of us plan to win and then we often fail. Who knows: the more you plan to fail, the more often you may win and succeed against your negative expectations.

Do it if you are in doubt. A handicapped person in a wheelchair is not as immobile as someone who is indecisive about what to do. If the idea has crossed your mind and you have felt the slightest itch or twitch that you would like to do it--DO IT (only if it is legal and you don't trample on anyone or anything in the process). Ideas sneak into our minds and excite us until little voices in our heads pipe up with more whens, ifs and butts than we are willing to handle. Each of us has thousands of fantastic ideas constantly, and our brilliant minds kill them like spermicide, constantly. Our mushy brains predict most of our ideas can't work, but the same brains are too limited to predict the taste of Black Pepper & Garlic Chablis Jelly.

If I were you, I wouldn't trust the infallible idiot who claims to be your mind. When you have an idea attractive enough to get your attention for a moment or two, go put it into action and let the market decide whether it was a dumb idea or not. No matter how long you think about it, you can't figure it out. The longer you think, the more ideas you will talk yourself and your friends out of.

Form follows function. The method you are using, or how you approach your next project, is not as important as the fact that you do something at all. Methods can be adjusted as needed. Your methods and the how-to may have to be changed several times, constantly perhaps, during the life-cycle of your project. BEGIN and everything else is likely to follow.

We use how-to as an excuse not to become active too soon. Learning how to approach the execution of an idea often and easily prevents us from getting things done. We may learn a lot but we won't do much. Contemplating methods first will keep you safely from realizing your ideas practically. Highly educated standstill remains a standstill. That's why I refuse to teach you a damn thing.

Result-oriented individuals are in high demand. No kidding. We want to be part of the solution. Get used to the fact you will always be part of the human problem. More so when you pretend to predict the future, trying to shape it to your will. Smoke machines of I-get-things-done personalities have impressive effects. In awe, we forget to ask about the price a result addict--or their human environments--pays. Interviews with Richard Branson are cool. An interview with his secretary or her therapist may not be so cool and a bit more bumpy. Interviewing Mr. Branson's former friends and business partners is probably not a pleasant and inspiring event at all.

Do you really want results? At any cost? Can you afford to become the prophet of your actions? It doesn't require clairvoyance to predict the future, you know. Recklessness will suffice. Ask Kenneth Lay. Oops, I forgot you can't. Apropos forgetting: why don't you forget the pathological need to produce specific results altogether? Have fun doing what you can do. No, I didn't give you permission to call me Sunshine and to paint a rainbow on your Lexus.

A.C.F. What's that? Active, Challenging, and Fun. When I hear talk about quality of life, it's B.S. to a large extent. Do you want real quality? You can afford to have it today. In fact, everybody can have it on a daily basis. You have to look for only three basic elements. Do something *Actively*. Watching reality TV ain't it. Make sure you face a *Challenge* doing it. And lastly, it has to be *Fun* for you. Choosing your bicycle over your car to bring a letter to the post office is fraught with too much reason to fit into this category. Too difficult to do? Don't make me come over there and slap you out of your well deserved lethargy! Money, *the millions*, is never going to solve that puzzle for you. If you can't entertain yourself today to the fullest extent of happiness, nothing and nobody else will.

Altruism is built into us. Being selfish must be practiced. Do something for yourself. Don't take the kids with you. No, don't go on a feel-good-shopping mission, girls. Don't buy anything! Do something with yourself, by yourself, for yourself. Christ, no manicure, no movies, no consumption of any kind! A premeditated act of utter selfishness. If you are working out regularly anyway, taking your buttocks to the gym won't count here. Gotta discover something new, an uncharted path to train and strengthen your egotistical nerve. Oh, no: NO rewards! Like, *I have accomplished X, and now I can reward myself*. And please, no I-deserve-it nonsense either. You deserve nothing. The I-get-what-I-deserve myth emerged straight out of the new age religions. It was a waste to begin with, but now we all know how outdated it is. In real life, nobody gets what she deserves.

Don't be afraid though. Altruism is the most egotistical scam out there. Whatever selfless thing you do for others makes you feel real good about yourself, doesn't it? Yeah, the Mother Teresa kickback. On the flipside, living for yourself automatically benefits more people in more ways than any pious altruist will ever admit. Screw altruism. Your own children will prefer you doing more for yourself over you living only for your brats, shamelessly neglecting yourself. By the way, if they see throughout the first two decades of their lives that you have no respect for yourself, don't be surprised about you not getting any respect from them.

This would be a good moment to read Shel Silverstein's The Giving Tree with your brats--and then BURN it (good God, those Germans and their book burnings ...). Sure, you can talk about it too, but first burn it. Crazy? Of course it is, but not as crazy as raising your innocent offspring in the spirit of *The Giving Tree*. Have you made a fire yet?

Doing it beats not doing it. Once you have a particular action in your mind, your greasy gray matter may run wild and simulate a number of plausible directions and outcomes, but none of it is real. Do something physically with your idea and reality changes. Your perspective changes, the position of the players involved is different, and even the options your mind comes up with will be altered and expanded instantly. The minute after you take action, you will be a different person in a new location. Better? How do I know? But within one minute of being active you will experience and know things your shiftless mind cannot tell you anything about in a hundred years by sitting on its soft arse thinking hard.

Thinking will not provide you with solutions for all your personal problems. Thinking has not solved the world's problems either, as history proves so painfully. Of course, action and hyper activity won't solve our most pressing problems. Rest assured-- and later on in peace--some of the things that cheese us off the most will not be solved during your and my lifetime, and I wouldn't be too worried about that stuff between breakfast and lunch.

For instance, you don't believe the *war on terror* will end sooner or later, do you? With a nice peace treaty written in calligraphy perhaps? As long as we drive cars there'll be car theft. The Club, or a police force twice its current number won't change that fact. It's alright, and since lost causes appear to be our dearest pets, we will find ways to live with unsolved problems. Taking action--doing it--is the only way I'm aware of to separate the impossible from the possible, but don't get too obsessed with problem solving or the pretense thereof. Who cares about your problems?

The invention of the Frisbee or Barbie were not answers to intensely problematic issues. They are proof that human beings are capable of learning from otters--the most playful species on this planet--and that we can use our precious noodles for the sheer fun of it. The evolution of the bicycle has been more rapid and radical in the last decade or so than in the century of dreadful cycling before. Since bicycles are not meant to be solutions for transportation problems anymore--not in most geographical regions at least--these things have been subject to incredible improvements. Nobody who needs a bicycle for transportation is willing to spend $8,000 for such a device. $60 will cover your need for a good two-wheel mule at Walmart, the evil one. If you don't need it, however, you are free to spend ten times as much, and some of us do so happily.

So-called rich people work more hours than the so-called poor. Retired folks work harder on average than those who have to show up for work. We are busier when we don't *need* to work. We are making more money, more easily, when we don't work for basic needs like bills, debt service, and shelter. We are more creative when we aren't desperately trying to find answers to a dull transportation problem and BAM! the improvement of a thing as useless and as simple as a bicycle can break through 80-year-old engineering walls with lightning speed.

Do you see the correlation? We are able to solve some problems, but by far we are not as good at it as we are at having fun. Trying to solve our problems first, before we permit ourselves to have some fun, stifles creativity and perhaps prevents a multiplied income. We are more active, more creative, more productive, more in charge of our intelligence, and in the position to make more money WHEN WE DON'T HAVE TO. Oh yeah, and action might take care of your chronic boredom, too.

Money is not related to the hard part of work. The occurrence of money correlates with doing though, and it's customary for most of us to label an activity 'work' when it is used to generate income. The part of work we call hard is what we think we have to do to get paid. Large or small, it is precisely the element that does not help improve income. The grind, the hardship of our workday, can be mind numbing and robbing us of creative freedom. We need playful activity to thrive way above the level of problems and solutions. Nothing is wrong with work, with productive activity 16 hours a day or more. But the stuff we call hard, repetitive mechanical work, turns us into plump uninspired idiots within five minutes, robots who get paid by the hour or with a flat fee.

By instigating you to be active I am not suggesting your mind is useless. On the contrary, like a playful brat--had I said *child* you would have wondered off to the lala-land of inner child crapola but we aren't going there, boomer baby--our mind craves to be inspired by trying out new things. You have to do physical stuff to feed your mind. Ideas for untapped income sources can be triggered by your activities and, indeed, also by mistakes you are making.

Goal setting and planning is not what it is cracked up to be. But if you insist, sure there is a place for it. Having goals is no substitute for deliberate action, as some individuals choose to believe. Goals can focus your activities, yeah, yeah, and for the moment I don't care to fight with you over your stupid goals. However, one of the worst pastimes to waste your mind and time with is hope. Hope is the flipside of worry and both are vicious time thieves, like television, which destroy your options. Don't tell me you can worry and be productive at the same time. While hoping (or worrying), individuals are not creative, productive, or having any fun.

"We are free even when we think we are not." Viktor Frankl promoted his unshakable conviction of human freedom in the most unlikely place: a German concentration camp! When everything has been taken from you but your bare life, you are still free to choose your attitude. You are free to choose humor and happiness in the darkest of hours. The most dire circumstances cannot force you to wallow forever in pain, self-destructive thoughts, or in hatred unless you choose to enjoy that.

Take money for instance. I have seen individuals losing their mental faculties over the loss of money. For some of us, losing money equals inevitable loss of freedom and happiness. It appears to be pretty real when that happens and no, it's actually not that pretty. For awhile self-pity can be perversely enjoyable and you may receive a minimum of attention from people who will eventually prove useless for your further development.

If disaster strikes and you experience such monetary trauma, you'll have a grand chance to discover that the loss of every blasted thing you thought of as an equivalent of freedom and happiness means the definite loss of material assets only. Period. Your idea of freedom and happiness--and lastly, your idea of yourself--is too damn limited if you believe it went down the drain with your precious dough. If losing your money deprives you of being happy all day and of the freedom to do what you want to do, you are a poor tormented soul indeed and you have lost your marbles.

It's not circumstance or other people robbing individuals of freedom and happiness. It's smallness that does that.

Chapter Twenty
Getting and Giving

"We do not quite forgive the giver. The hand that feeds us is in some danger of being bitten."

Ralph Waldo Emerson

Getting is painful! Getting what? Anything: things, support, money. We do not easily ask others to give us something because we know getting those things--or just friendly help--spells pain. Nobody may have told you, but there are growing pains attached to getting rich. Money is not as much of a problem as all that comes with it.

Allow me to digress. Normally we think getting stuff, like a million bucks, is exciting. On the other hand, giving money to others is no fun at all, especially when it comes as a surprise. Your car's radiator leaks suddenly and you have to replace it, today. Such giving of our money is not popular. You get the idea, getting is fun and giving hurts. Right?

Wrong. Under the surface we know different. Thinking of timing belts we had to replace, forced purchases of new refrigerators, or nasty bills we had to face in the most uncomfortable moments, we believe paying money--giving--hurts us. By the same token, whenever we are in a situation where someone else gives money to us, we believe it must hurt THEM to do so. Hence, in connection with getting or receiving money people feel all sorts of stuff, from shame and embarrassment to fear and guilt. Some individuals believe it to be bad, committing a sin, to accept money from another person.

We don't want to cause others pain. We don't enjoy feeling this confused mess of guilt and shame and a bunch of other things we can't put a finger on. We don't care to experience the pain of receiving. Therefore we minimize the occurrence of this dreadful event by making sure not to get too much too often. No wonder get-rich-quick schemes sucker in only the brain dead and numb nuts.

The joy of giving is the flipside of our experience. We love showering our grandkids with truckloads of gifts and we enjoy the feeling of supporting our favorite charitable causes. Giving money can be fun. But--and this is a big butt--between joyful generosity and the blood-letting we perform with grinding teeth, we are drawing a line. It is this very line that's more costly than anything you could possibly spend your money on. If you don't understand this, you are doomed to work a lot harder in life than necessary. So, I need your full attention. Thank you.

What is it now? Is giving fun or does it hurt? Both? Factually it is the same whether you pay your utility bill or you buy your son his first bicycle: there will be less money in your bank account and somebody else will have that much more. The difference between pain and joy lies between your ears. You are making it up every single time. It's an esoteric problem.

Cutting a check to the Department of Treasury sucks? Why? You are threatened by force to pay, it is involuntary. Not for comedians like Senator Harry Reid, though. Senate Majority Leader Harry Reid on March 31st, 2008: "Our system of government is a voluntary tax system." Cute, but for you and me paying taxes is bloody involuntary. Of course we don't like it and we could use the money for less wasteful purposes. You could reinvest it into your business and expand your operations, or you could take your family on a vacation. Legitimate reasons--not that original, but acceptable--why paying taxes may be less pleasant than a Caribbean cruise.

Your reasons why giving money to particular recipients is less cheerful an event than giving your buckaroos to others don't make a scrap of difference in your bank balance. You have paid the damn wireless bill already. So shut up! The only thing your sophisticated reasoning manages to accomplish is butchering your happiness. If you have ever experienced the joy of giving--it's still money we're talking about--what would it take for you to expand that idea into your business dealings?

If giving is fun in the gifting department, maybe it can be fun everywhere. If you make up the difference in your mind anyway, why don't you make it up the same way all the time, with happiness as your aim? Selfish bastard that I hope you are, you can be happy even while stuffing your moolah up the government's wide and roomy monetary channels.

The enjoyment of giving has limits. Gifts for friends and family members--a select few only, of course--tithing to your church, support for Red Cross or Greenpeace etc., maybe a cheap Thanksgiving turkey from Costco for a family in need. That's about it, and it's a relatively small portion of monies we spend on a regular basis. The mother lode of our income is spent with a *I don't want to, but I have to* kind of mind set. We don't like dedicating the better part of our lifetime to the unpleasant acquisition of money for the purpose of painful distribution to a mob of recipients we don't care about.

There, we spotted another reason work sucks for so many of us. Making money for landlords, mortgage banksters, Mastercard, and the tax man is not considered amusement no matter how we're earning it. People hate their jobs whether they are good or bad. After someone has spat in your soup it doesn't matter how delicious the soup was.

It gets worse. When we experience spending as mostly painful, we believe in turn that most money that's given to us is given involuntarily and in a painful context. Since we don't enjoy inflicting pain on somebody else, there is only so much money we are willing to accept with a clean conscience.

We invented the hard-work theory to show we endure a certain pain level and are therefore entitled to monetary compensation. We get all worked up and talk ourselves and each other into theories about how terrible and mean our employers are--the evil corporations--and we join unions to help us demonize the hands that feed us so that we can bite them remorselessly. Oh sorry, you don't have an employer you can hate? You only have a child support spitting ex-husband? All the same: the more bad and guilty we can make somebody look, the more willing we are to take as much money from him as we possibly can without losing our good conscience. Yes dear, it's not only that we bite the hand that feeds us. Hatred for our jobs contains a good chunk of intention to make a hand appear worthy to be bitten a lot. Our hatred permits us to take money relatively free of guilt.

We don't take money from friends easily. We are tempted to sell our products to friends for wholesale value because we are not willing to cause friends as much pain as we do strangers by making a hefty profit. Some folks believe profit itself is evil because it is inevitably linked to causing pain.

Each individual has a limit on how much money she is willing to take, determined by how much pain she is willing to inflict on the human source of that money. We have less inhibitions when accepting money from a corporate entity—or when cheating an insurance company out of an extra buck--than we feel when we take cash from the hand of a breathing human being. Our frequent abuse of the word 'need' helps us to stretch that limit of pain distribution somewhat. As long as we can make ourselves believe we *need* something, we aren't in conflict with our conscience about asking for and accepting the funding. *I need this new dress: I have nothing to wear*, justifies the expense and the necessity to get the money for it. Hey, I really do need it and I am sorry if that causes you any discomfort.

When the absurdity of our artificial needs is maxed out, some of us reach the limitation of voluntarily causing pain to others. That's when income increases can hit a soft plateau. The spiral of pain appears to have come to an end. Is there a way out? For most people: no. For you there are indeed other options, and they are simple but not easy. Can you get used to the idea that spending money is always enjoyable, no matter who receives it and for what outlandish purpose?

Money for nothing is what I call *the third level of giving*. Level One: Presenting cash gifts to loved ones, friends and family--voluntarily, I hope--and donations large and small to church, charity, and other beggars. Level Two: Paying bills and taxes, purchasing life's necessities and luxuries--pizza, beer, and Hummer H2 included. Level Three: Giving cash to persons who are *not* in need and who are *not* close to you, emotionally or otherwise, without the expectation of getting anything in exchange. In short, giving for the fun of it.

Average people enjoy level one. Dutifully and at times with grinding teeth they'll perform level two, pushed by responsibility and pulled by the credit rating system. Level Three is definitely not part of our practical world of financial affairs. Handing money to someone who will not return either value or favor in form of products and services? Even worse, distributing cash gifts to individuals who are obviously not in need? Giving my money away to strangers? Meshugge!

Yet I described what most people want and hope for throughout their miserable lives. They dream of receiving large amounts of money from strangers, without any obligations attached to give something in exchange. You know, like Stan O'Neal screwing up as CEO of Merrill Lynch and getting a $161.5 million severance package, about twice as much as Jack Welch pocketed for doing a fine job at General Electric. People long for money, for loads of it, for their performance good or poor, for disastrous snafus, for bad hair days, for the hell of it. Quite frankly, they don't want to be bothered with exchange issues, value systems, or other petty measurements.

That's perfectly alright and the fact is, a bunch of individuals are making mucho moolah that way. We admire them for it. Billions of dollars are paid to sports figures for contracts and endorsements. Nobody works hard for that money. C'mon, how hard does one work for wearing a Nike cap? Exchange value, performance? Exchange of what? People are paid staggering sums for showing up in movies. Quality of acting? Not required. If your fame or your scandals draw crowds to the box office, you'll do. Level Three income: not hard-earned but given *just because*.

These people have something in common; the willingness

and the ability to take something for nothing, and you'll do well not to underestimate that ability. Without this ability to receive money and to remain relaxed, your desire to get a lot, fast, just shows your incredible ignorance. You, too, have ideas how to get money for nothing. No? State lotteries, the poor people's tax, function well as something-for-nothing income generators. Las Vegas has been built on people's hope to get money for nothing-- but you are squeamish about GIVING money without receiving anything in exchange. Do you think that is sane?

I don't believe in the obscure laws of the universe that if you want to *manifest* or *materialize* money, you must first give money to the universe. Then somehow, mysteriously, the green, large-eared, hawk nosed goddess of dollar bills connects the dots, deems you worthy, and makes the universe shit oodles of cash into your lap. The Dollar Goddess may seem a bit of a stretch, but if you leave her out of the picture, plenty of people believe this connection between giving and receiving to be reality. They talk of *seed money*, the *Law of Attraction*. They concoct affirmations: 'Every dollar I circulate supports the economy and comes back to me multiplied (Rev. Ike),' and so on. Cute, but nonsensical nevertheless.

The universe is pretty dumb. Stare at a piece of the universe, the next available brick wall for example, and tell me its IQ. It knows nothing, it has no memory, and it doesn't keep track of your digestion or of your monetary transactions. The universe won't record your personal balances of giving and getting. You, however, do know what you are doing. If you remain in a dream world that includes the possibility of you getting free money, but you're making sure you will never give money to others unattached to obligations, your crappy dreams are unlikely to pan out. Write down your monetary goals all you want. The dumbest wall is laughing at you.

You believe it takes a stupid person to part with his money for no reason, and you don't want to be the retarded sucker transforming this valued belief of yours into painful reality. No smart individual would do that. You for sure won't. So, the odds are stacked against you because one way or the other exchange of money for nothing does not happen a lot in your presence. You don't do it. It wouldn't be prudent to do. It's not realistic. It is not normal. It doesn't exist, and because no sane person will give you nothin' you may just blow your brains out. As great an idea as that may be for the rest of us, please do know you can change probabilities swiftly. You can easily kick a phenomenon into existence that is hardly noticeable so far. Ready?

Manipulate the quality of how cash flows. Pay your bills and taxes when you are in a playful or even giggly mood. Whistle a tune while writing checks. Joke around while paying for your groceries at the cash register, instead of frowning. Goodness, I watch people acting dead-serious during their $14 transactions. Some look like they're signing their will when they punch in their sacred PIN. I doubt they are radically happier before and after.

Escape the grip of your demon of the day! Laughter will do that. Help people lighten up. Hold on to your dollar bills for a second longer than you normally would, perhaps pull your hand back slightly after the cashier grabbed the money from the other side. That alone can disrupt someone's gray day and cause her to bust up laughing. Give larger tips than you are expected to give. Double-tip a bad waiter. Give tips to people who don't expect it. Experiment with the fun of giving strangers money for no reason. A dollar here, a few bucks there. If you don't enjoy giving money without an exchange on your mind, why should anybody else give cash to you for the fun of doing it? Free lunch? If I were you, I'd expect more than that in the future. Forget your serious self: make free lunch normal here and now.

Condition your giving to ways you like to receive money, and then leave your dumb expectations at home. I am going all out on a limb here, assuming you prefer receiving your money as painlessly as possible. You are free to disagree with me, of course. Further, I surmise you'd love to get money that is not penny for penny measured as exchange for work hours or for products and services you are expected to deliver. You would appreciate a healthy profit over and above hours and sweat equity you invest in your business or on your job? You don't care about feeling guilty for accepting profit. Last but not least, you don't want other people to experience hardship or pain in connection with giving money to you. Am I vaguely on the right course?

Naturally, there is no guarantee that you'll ever GET all or any of that, no matter what you do. But, you can start a trend, leading yourself and your environment into exactly the kind of direction you wish to go. You can make this experience a reality in your presence, and automatically it will become a normal event for you. You can witness the fun of it today by GIVING it to someone else. Too expensive? Rubbish: it costs you a buck at a time.

So that means you give to get? Don't make me throw up again. If you spend money in order to eventually get some--or to get it back somehow--you didn't give it for the pure fun of it, did you? No, I instigate you to give cash to people regularly without expecting to get anything in return, from anybody, ever! You don't do it for something to happen later. It's for your enjoyment right this minute.

Detach pain from your spending. Disconnect ideas of hurt and loss from paying money to individuals and to companies. If necessary, lie a lot ... to yourself. We both know you can do it, so why not for a good cause? If you hate mailing off another chunky check to the IRS, talk yourself into liking it. Have a helluva grand time paying your phone bill. Since you are an addict like the distinguished rest of us, you will get the hang of it quickly and habitually; you are going to cut the most offensive checks cheerfully soon.

Next, you know already you have never been paid according to your performance and you never will be paid *what you are worth*, *what you deserve*, or whatever the hell you think you *should* get. It's not happening. So? Stop measuring the stuff you do--hours, hardship, and so on--against your income. You are not doing time. Quit acting as if you are. You aren't paid by the hour even if your employer says so. A slap in the face would be more valuable than the pittance they are giving you per hour. You don't get money in exchange for hours, you get it for the lack of confidence you are displaying for everyone to see.

Without comparing money with the work you do, the following happens: you work AND you are getting money. You don't get paid BECAUSE you work or in exchange for your damned work. You are receiving money PARALLEL to your work. Are you with me? Disconnect your activities from the money someone or some corporate entity pays you. Work a lot, expect a lot, but don't expect a lot *because* you toil much and hard. Giving a dollar randomly to others supports precisely this mental process of circulating cash parallel to people's activities, detached from anything measurable.

You want profits and bonuses, expectedly and unexpectedly? Slip a dollar bill or two to the bored girl in the toll booth. Pay a dollar bonus. Permit someone to profit. Allow your imagination to run amok! Give a little extra to everybody. Yeah, why not everybody? Then you don't waste time thinking who should or who shouldn't get your dough. Your immediate environment will become more enjoyable overnight.

By the end of this week giving money is likely to have a different meaning for you, and you won't have to lie about it. In a variety of ways giving money to people--strangers--will literally and practically be a source of fun for you, causing the pain level you once connected with involuntary spending to drop rapidly.

Something else will happen. <u>With the collapse of your old belief in the pain of spending, your fear will gradually disappear that you might hurt others by accepting their money.</u> Don't underestimate this detail! It is key, THE key, enabling you to accept unlimited amounts of money, free of guilt. You will more easily accept money from others. You will permit others to pay for your lunch, without going through this embarrassing fuss ritual every single annoying time you eat in public.

You won't need to display the hard part of your labor as an argument to crank more cash out of someone's tight ass. You won't have to hate your employer or your customers to justify taking their money. You will be ready, willing, and able to take more profits without the compulsive need to hate and bite the feeding hand of the paying party. Guess what? Cheerful giving pulls the plug on your limitations to receive. You don't feel the pain of giving, and the pain you thought you might inflict on others by receiving vanishes. What should stop you from happily accepting more? You will make a lot of people happy by accepting their money! I am not kidding.

Free money is upsetting for many. What if everybody did that? Nobody would want to work anymore (factually wrong: the more money people make, the more they like working; they like working more even on projects they aren't too fond of). 'I have to work hard for every dollar I make and so should everybody else.' Blahblahblah. Getting what we want is most unsettling. The threat of freedom comes with it. Albertson's, the grocery chain, ran a radio commercial a few years ago, "We are making your life easier." And then, after a brief pause: "Easier is better!" Bingo. Albertson's advertising agency was well aware of the fact that the majority of people do NOT know, believe in, or trust the idea that *easier is better*. Our society believes harder is better. Those who surf through life smoothly are suspicious characters and not to be trusted, or envied to the point of being hated.

Accepting easier options and decisions requires conscious effort from us on a constant basis. You cannot take for granted that other people prefer easy over difficult. The average person welcomes a difficult life and you can bet your hairy arse they want your life to be difficult also. Take away what burdens them and they will feel deprived. You desire an easy life? I am on your side, but do not expect your social or professional environment to like you or to support such a crazy and far out idea. You are on your own.

Beggars. How do you respond to them? Do they upset you, make you feel guilty, insecure, compassionate? Are you reacting in their presence or are you acting? Can a street person residing on the sidewalk control your feelings? Does it make you feel better to give them a couple of coins? Are you feeling somewhat uneasy whether you dropped money in his hat or not? Do you have habits around beggars, identical behavior each instance you encounter one--like giving change only--or do you look into his eyes, talk to him, and then make up your mind if and how much you want to donate? Do you believe there shouldn't be any beggars polluting your pretty world? Cities should be cleaned up? Nobody should live that way and you certainly don't care to face anyone who does?

You know, when you see a beggar in the street and his very existence plays your emotions like a musical instrument with the virtuosity of a concert pianist, the beggar is NOT what's causing you to be troubled: you are. It's nonsense to wish him away, as it is futile to wish away the bank building at the next corner.

Beggars are fine and just like lawyers, secretaries, and architects--they won't go away any time soon. Take advantage of their presence and scrutinize your messed-up relationship with money. Apparently, a harmless beggar can manipulate things under your skin from ten feet away. And by Jupiter, give these people real money, a five dollar bill, a twenty maybe. Even cheap booze is not as cheap as it used to be. Don't embarrass yourself making nickel contributions to somebody's cause.

Philanthropy is cheaper than you think. Got to be a billionaire to give money to charity? I don't believe in the distinction between the poor and the rich, as you know. It's utter nonsense, especially if you consider yourself are a member of the civilized world. At the very least, drawing an imaginary line between rich and poor is as outdated and demeaning a term as third world country. The rich-poor idea provides short term rhetorical mileage, but it doesn't serve anyone, especially not those who are considered poor.

Before I get too distracted, let me point out one major problem of those who insist on being poor. They are terrible at math. In fact they are worse than I am. Professionally poor people believe 10% for one person is not the same as ten percent for another. With all due lack of respect, I argue that giving away

10% for a cause of your choice is equally difficult for someone who makes $35,000 annually as it is for an individual who makes $35 million a year. Yeah but ... yeah, butt, what?!

The difference is not in the number. It's in your noodle. The person who appears to be better off financially has discovered the benefits of giving away money. Philanthropy deeply satisfies the giver, provides meaning--if that's what you are after--even if your cursed job itself isn't that meaningful to you. Trust me, the one giving money derives more short-term fun and long-term satisfaction from this than the receiving party.

Too many of the self-proclaimed poor won't learn the joy of giving cash away, because they believe they don't have enough yet. Stingy bastards have a chance to experience that depriving themselves of the joy of distributing money equals a common form of perceived poverty. Adding money won't end that type of poverty: giving as little as a single dollar can end it before this day is over.

Giving pleases the giver more than anybody else. Numbers do not matter. Doing it regularly counts. Another thing the mind can't figure out intellectually; moving a single dollar from your pocket into someone else's will perform this magical trick.

Did I say numbers don't matter? Well, abundance does have a number. How much cash do you need to pile up before you can live in abundance? Yeah? What? I'm waiting for your answer ... how much? What's the number permitting you to cross the chasm from where you are--you don't want to call your current situation *poverty*, unless you are completely out of your mind--to the monetary state of abundance?

None of us will come up with a number that matches anyone else's. There is no objective abundance barrier stopping us, you see? Your number is not real and you made it up, just as we collectively made up this idea of abundance lurking somewhere in our future. Abundance equals the freedom to give. If you don't claim your freedom to give money away today, it's not likely to happen in the future when you may have more money. You are not subject to either of them, freedom or abundance. There is no abundance without you, and no, you cannot produce it in your square head. You can experience abundance in three minutes, by taking a dollar bill out of your wallet and handing it over to a stranger. A STRANGER, I said.

Need is often the cause for an individual to give away money without getting anything in exchange. Someone close to you desperately needs a cash injection and you jump in. If you can do it, beautiful! I have done it and I have been on the receiving end, also. But watch out, if your friendship is not the real thing, the cash-help action can destroy it.

Apropos 'help.' Giving money to someone who needs it badly won't solve the problem of that someone. Your help delays the solution. That alone can be a welcome breather, but it won't get your relative or friend out of the mess he is in. Credit cards usually enlarge people's credit problems, remember? Money doesn't solve money problems. Still, it's a generous gesture, and possibly a lifesaver, to help individuals that way once in awhile.

Abundance, however, cannot be fostered by giving cash to a person in need. To express abundance and to train yourself to enjoy it, give money to people who do NOT need it and who did NOT ask for money. Hand cash to individuals who don't expect it. Often, and then again.

Giving back to the community is guilt-ridden drivel. Works well as a publicity stunt or to make one's slaves feel good about 'their' company, but you and I know it's B.S. Do what you want to do for your community. Fine. The giving back part is suspect. Haven't you given something to somebody in exchange for the money you took? Not even fun and entertainment? You mean there was no exchange of goods or services for the dough you earned?

The giving-back speech often comes from those who insist on hard work, performance based pay, exchange instead of free lunch, and similar corporate tripe. The giving-back cliche unmasks the ridiculous guilt trip of someone who lies in every one of her sales pitches about the benefits her customers should

221

expect. The confused stammering of an uninhibited exploiter, or of an apologetic dumbass, looking for meaning in the wrong places, that's what giving back means. Well, it could also come from a detestable politician, who evokes that stuff to gain mileage with those he hopes feel sufficiently underprivileged.

Good God, develop a decent spine and figure out fast that you and what you choose to do IS what's best for your community, taking hard currency for it included. Value in the stuff you offer has a chance to be known and appreciated by the greatest number of people the more you are at peace making a healthy profit selling it. If you don't make a profit, your incentive and your ability to spread your gizmos to the corners of the Earth will be limited. And if you deprive people of knowing about your stuff and of the opportunity to purchase it, you limit the benefits they may enjoy otherwise. The ultimate way to give back to the community is by taking money *from* your community, by making a healthy profit.

The difference between volunteering and work is that we love doing something we are told to do for free, while we hate doing something we're told to do for money. Come again? Oh yeah, because the meaning of what we do in our volunteer job, its purpose, is so damn sacred. That's how much people hate money! Cash is considered dirty compared with the tremendous accumulation of incompetence we spot so easily in every volunteer activity.

Granted, there is a spark of inspiration in the volunteer world. Instead of starting a business, you may fare better planning a non-profit operation wrapped around a cause, like MADD or PETA. Exploiting the somewhat deranged volunteer character, you can discover the *Power of the Lost Cause*. You can't change the world but you can generate oodles of cash with the help of volunteers who refuse to work for so dirty a thing as money. It's alright, let them work on their beatification while you collect and count the dough.

Again, hatred is a key engine propelling such movements, practically guaranteeing scores of free employees. Hatred against people--who drink and drive (MADD) or who treat animals unethically (PETA), for instance--and hatred against money made by greedy individuals and evil chicken torturers. See, hating people is not a crime as long as you want to change them into a human version you approve of. Hatred of money and other people's greed appears to mutate into something else when the process of taking money and your greed is purified by the perceived depth and purpose of an organization: yours. Individuals getting money is bad. Individuals taking lots of money equals greed and that is considered very bad. Your favorite cause raking in money is a good thing. Your idealized not-for-profit charity getting greedy and taking all it can, however, places those eager to be affiliated with your organization precariously close to sainthood.

Never underestimate the beneficial power of hatred. It's good business to build for-profit or non-profit organizations on people's hatred. So-called negative emotions are notoriously underrated in their importance for economic growth.

Volunteer driven organizations make and take plenty of money. The volunteer does not, but the people she is working for, do. If you enjoy lying to yourself about the greatness of meaning and about the filthy lucre that money seems to be in the eyes of the damn meek, go on and volunteer by all means. But if you are really passionate about a particular mission and about expanding it, invent a new cause, start a non-profit thingy, enrich a bunch of vapid volunteers' lives with meaning and purpose, and take money for it. The more the better.

Giving $100 to the Red Cross is easy. Giving $100 to a guy on the street corner can be difficult. Individuals scare us. While driving, listen to your self talk about other people with whom you share the road. You tell me, do you like people in general or do you despise them? *Other people* don't drive properly, they can't think right and hey, they don't even vote right, eh? God, people are awful! And giving my hard-earned money to them is supposed to be good?

Some of us experience terror at the thought of giving cash

to our own children. DANGER warning lights are flashing. We are afraid money could hurt our children. Strangers we attempt to give money to may feel threatened some dark and unknown secret is attached to the cash offered. And as sane as we believe we are, we won't even think about wasting our money on a stranger because strangers represent a threat almost by definition, and we would never empower such a thing voluntarily. After all, strangers are the people who steal our children with candy bars.

Individuals are tempted to refuse cash gifts from unknown persons because they can't see the reason behind it and they assume the worst. They can't take it because they have not worked for it, or they talk themselves into the belief it must be a counterfeited note. People--family members included--refuse money because they expect they may be asked to do something unpleasant in exchange, at a later date. And on and on and on.

Indeed, there is money in the world and people willing to disperse it. Few individuals can take it for no reason and without making the giver feel uncomfortable. Hence it's easier to feed organizations with cash until it comes out of their ears than it is to give a single buck to a stranger.

Tip EVERYBODY. Every day, always. I know, you cannot do it. You think it's silly, you're going to make an ass of yourself, and you'll make up other lame excuses. Truth is, tipping every person is just too easy to do. If you have the balls to do it, though, you will find out the real inner workings of giving and receiving. Books can't teach you that. Human beings, individuals, will tell you new details about getting and giving, each time you try it. Listen to the scarce words being uttered when you drop a dollar bill inappropriately. People will crack open their closet doors briefly and reveal the weirdest truths about their relationship with money. That three second revelation is worth a multiple of your shabby tip.

By the way, tip anonymously also. When the receiving party has no idea you left a tip, you will learn more about your relationship with money than you care to know. Do you want to be seen when you do a good deed? Sick sucker that you are, do you crave to hear a hearty "Thank You?" Corruption reaches deeper into our own messed up little souls than we like to think, doesn't it?

Shock the world! No, no, don't hurt people! Playing within the rules of your society--keeping your actions legal and somewhat tasteful at all costs--guarantees you and everyone else involved will have fun for a long time to come. Shocking people for the shock's sake? Don't be silly! Shock people with your individuality. It may come as a surprise to you, but there is no individuality in the act of receiving. The plunder your house is filled with doesn't certify you as an individual. Craving more of that clutter is one cause for us to bitch about the things we have to do to get it.

Whining and complaining works for babies. That's how they attract their parents' attention. Look cute, smell like dirty diapers, and scream at the top of your lungs: the law of attraction in action for the typical newborn. Tiny people's communication tools are limited and being crappy is their most effective way to get stuff. You may have noticed it doesn't work too well for you and me. Sure, millions of job serfs still get stuff by being crappy from high school to retirement. It works, except they have to live with their crappy selves all day. Babies at least switch to giggling between their brief periods of purposeful kvetching. Grown-ups, who are still trying to get attention the way infants do, usually end up on the fast track to self-destruction. They don't giggle. You have seen some of them locked into a hate-pain continuum. Not an enjoyable option, nor pleasant to watch.

Employment and self-employment often contain every detail of an addictive cycle, from paycheck high to the low of anger and the despair of self-hatred. Hatred for work has nothing to do with work. It has everything to with the job hater who refuses to grow up and integrate, or own, the dissatisfaction her parents supposedly caused by not being there at all, by not being there in the *right way*, or by never doing what they *should* have done. Parents are human beings and our greed is insatiable. Your parents never could have given you what you really wanted and they never will. Your employer will <u>never</u> ever grant you what you really want. Get over it!

Individuals hate other people's greed to the degree they hate themselves and their own desires. For decades I have listened to hate speeches against greed, but honestly I can't find anything wrong with your greed. Except, there is not a single source outside you that will satisfy it. So what?! You can only get what you really want--and by Zeus, I'm not talking about stuff you want to buy or otherwise acquire--by giving it to the world, to other people.

Your freedom to unfold your individuality is more fun than anything else I know of. Developed, or better developing the individuality of children and adults alike easily gathers the interest of other individuals. You, being different without acting crazy, is what people are looking for. If attention is what you want, there you have it. Cash in on it at your leisure, or don't.

So, what's the shock? Nobody cares about what you want. That makes you a member of the herd, but what are you bringing into this world besides a bunch of brats, another pooch and your kids' cat? Do I care about your contribution to humankind? Nope. For you, however, it can mean the difference between boredom and happiness.

You won't change the world. Disagree all you want, but I have my doubts you will change yourself very much. You can have fun being yourself, though, every hour of the day, including your bad hair days. Here we are: trying to love in the future what we've hated in the past is nonsense. Trying to change what we have hated in the past, so that it turns out to be more enjoyable in the future, won't work either.

Realizing that things you hate have your full attention is an easy first step. Step two is admitting that you probably wouldn't give these things much attention if you didn't enjoy hating them on some level. Step three: it could be that you love hating these things. Has tons of overt and hidden benefits, as you now know. Makes you feel alive. Prevents you from getting bored out of your mind with another twelve-step hoax. If you have a boss, she loves it when you hate both your job and her. She's a bit into S/M too, you know? Her income depends on your hatred and so does yours. Of course, she won't ever voice such a crazy thought in your presence.

If you are self-employed, an entrepreneur, and you tell me you love everything you do, you like all your employees and all your customers, you are full of it. You hate paying taxes, some of your clients drive you up the wall, you have employees with terribly bad breath, and then there is something else you hate ... right, exactly, you do know what I'm talking about, don't you baby? Then there are people in your professional environment who don't like you, in fact they hate your guts, but you love them from the bottom of your heart? Don't be creepy. It scares me when you pretend to be the noble one.

Truth is, you can't stand some of these bastards and being hated is not without merit, is it? Being hated for the person you are, for the stuff you say, and for the things you do, can be utterly delightful. I know you: on Sunday evenings--just like any job-hating slave--you too can't wait to get back into your familiar realm of beloved pain. Admit it, you do not want to change the world into something you love. Yuck, just think of the germs that thrive in such warm and fuzzy habitats! Gross.

Perhaps you will playfully develop new ways to make money with this idea of exploiting your and other individuals' precious hatred. You hate things, and therefore you have what it takes to make yourself individually useful. Happiness and its pursuit is overrated. All you need to be happy is admitting that you are indeed already happy. A five second pursuit or, depending on your Kvetch Quotient, it may stretch over a couple of lifetimes. In an insipid way, happiness may be somewhat important, but freedom is better. Problem is that since hardly anyone knows what freedom looks like, we don't seize the opportunity to live freely.

You do know, however, the fabric of the stuff you passionately hate. Crap you hate is kind of your star of Bethlehem, shedding light on your quest for freedom. Your individuality is bursting out of the cracking seams. Do something productive and profitable with it. People will thank you profusely, and you'll get as close as humanly possible to what I casually call ecstasy.

The world is deep.
Deeper than day had been aware.
Deep is its woe;
Joy--deeper yet than agony:
Woe implores: go!
But all joy wants eternity--
Wants deep, wants deep eternity.

                Friedrich Wilhelm Nietzsche, Thus Spoke Zarathustra

Appendix

More stuff to clutter your mind with:

Francois Marie Arouet "Voltaire," Candide or The Optimist

Elizabeth M. Butler, The Fortunes of Faust: Magic in History

Julia Cameron, The Artist's Way: A Spiritual Path to Higher Creativity

Albert Camus, The Rebel: An Essay on Man in Revolt

Peter J. Carroll, Liber Null & Psychonaut: An Introd. to Chaos Magic

Crystal Dawn and Stephen Flowers, Carnal Alchemy: A Sado-Magical Exploration of Pleasure, Pain and Self-Transformation

Ramsey Dukes, Blast Your Way to MEGABUCK$, with my Secret Sex-Power Formula

Lanny Ebenstein, Milton Friedman: A Biography

Sondra Horton Fraleigh, Dance And The Lived Body: A Descriptive Aesthetics

Frater U:.D:., Secrets Of Western Sex Magic: Magical Energy and Gnostic Trance

Michael Gerber, The E-Myth Mastery

Michael Gerber, The E-Myth Revisited: Why Most Small Businesses Don't Work and What To Do About It

Jerry Gillies, Money-Love: How to Get The Money You Deserve for Whatever You Want

Jay Y. Gonen, Yahweh versus Yahweh: The Enigma of Jewish History

Jennifer Michael Hecht, Doubt: A History: The Great Doubters and their Legacy of Innovation

Eric Hoffer, The True Believer: Thoughts on the Nature of Mass Movements

Christopher S. Hyatt, The Psychopath's Bible: For the Extreme Individual

Timothy Ferriss, The 4-Hour Workweek: Escape 9-5, Live Anywhere, ...

Michel Foucault, Discipline & Punish: The Birth of the Prison

Viktor E. Frankl, Man's Search For Meaning

Carl Frederick, EST: Playing the Game the New Way

Christopher S. Hyatt, The Psychopath's Bible: For the Extreme Individual

Walter Kaufmann, Critique of Religion and Philosophy

Walter Kaufmann, Nietzsche: Philosopher, Psychologist, Antichrist

Michael Masterson, Ready, Fire, Aim: Zero to $100 Million in No Time Flat

Friedrich Nietzsche, Daybreak: Thoughts on the Prejudices of Morality

Paul Ormerod, Why Most Things Fail: Evolution, Extinction & Economics

Dave Ramsey, The Total Money Makeover

Ayn Rand, The Fountainhead

Luke Rhinehart, The Dice Man

Diana Richardson, The Heart of Tantric Sex

Jalal al-Din Rumi, The Essential Rumi

Jean-Paul Sartre, Essays in Existentialism

Richard Schacht, Nietsche

Robert Scheinfeld, Busting Loose from the Money Game

George Ryley Scott, Flagellation: The Story of Corporeal Punishment

Jon Spoelstra, Marketing Outrageously: How to Increase Your Revenue

Nassim Nicholas Taleb, Fooled by Randomness: The Hidden Role of Chance in Life and in the Markets

Lewis Wolpert, Six Impossible Things Before Breakfast: The Evolutionary Origins of Belief

Muhammad Yunus, Banker To The Poor: Micro-Lending and the Battle Against World Poverty

www.reason.com

Author's Biography

Egbert Sukop was born and raised in Germany and has since traveled extensively. Farmer, trucker, insurance salesman, cab driver, gasoline station attendant, he also founded a construction company that he managed for a decade. Egbert knows the perspective of employer, as well as that of an employee, firsthand. He has worked with a charitable organization for the benefit of children and the elderly as well. His studies include Psychology, Pedagogy, and Lutheran Protestant Theology.

Egbert has 20 years of experience as a public speaker. His views are controversial and provocative. In the seminar business he is *L'enfant terrible*. He currently lives in Arizona.

www.ingramcontent.com/pod-product-compliance
Lightning Source LLC
Chambersburg PA
CBHW022005160426
43197CB00007B/282